SANKOFA UNIVERSITY

SANKOFA UNIVERSITY

STUDYING AFRICAN-CENTERED HISTORY AND CULTURE

BURNETT GALLMAN

Imhotep -The Drum

The Sankofa University
Studying Afrikan-Centered History and Culture

Published 2021 by Imhotep-The Drum

ISBN: 978-1-63901-977-9

Contact the author at kwadwo816@icloud.com

Ordering Information: www.epitome-llc.com

Printed in the United States of America

Praise for *The Sankofa University*

Catherine L. Adams (Claflin University):

The Sankofa University is most certainly an intergenerational gift from an elder to those of the ages to follow. Part memoir, part bibliography, part almanac, part collection of essays, Dr. Gallman provides strong advocacy for study groups and reclaiming classic, nationalist texts. This book embraces the past, diagnoses the present, and envisions a future of liberation for Afrikan people.

Joe Benton (Past President, National Association of Black Social Workers, SC State University):

The Sankofa University is a phenomenal accomplishment and deserves to be on the bookshelves of those seeking a great source of African Centered thought, philosophy, ancient history and action. The free flowing, refreshing style presents information in an understandable and non-pretentious way. Until now, a person had to attend multiple conferences, workshops, seminars, read countless books and articles, and view countless historical and documentary videos to glean information regarding African Centeredness.

The book is a one-stop shop for a beginning researcher (and those more advanced) to grasp the basics, while directing that same researcher to vital source materials. I was pleased to find information and critical source materials to consider and supplement presentations to students and workshop attendees, and for instructing our children and grands. It is pleasing to see clearly and concisely organized information to fit the needs of scholars, casual readers and those seeking to know more about African Centeredness.

Baba Derrick Jackson, Pastor of KRST Universal Temple:

Dr. Asa Hilliard once said that people of Afrikan ancestry have reached a crossroads, that only our "purposeful actions will determine if we will choose the right road." He concludes: "[B]efore we can successfully choose a road, we must solve our problems of spiritual and identity confusion." Burnett Kwadwo Gallman has made a significant and valuable contribution to solving that problem with the publication, The Sankofa University: Studying Afrikan-Centered History and Culture. It is a major contribution to our liberation struggle, a struggle people of Afrikan ancestry have been in since the first Afrikan was taken from his/her family and loved ones on the continent.

Many people of Afrikan ancestry are looking for books to read and study to satisfy the "Who" in Frantz Fanon's great question "Who am I." Now a new generation of young people and others who love reading and/or who seek knowledge have a resource for knowing what to read and study to become familiar with our Afrikan thinkers, history and culture. What Brother Gallman has done with this magnificent addition is to challenge those who would say that people of Afrikan ancestry do not have an intellectual history and help to dispel that notion. The Sankofa University will inform readers of the many contributions people of Afrikan Ancestry gave and continue to give the world.

A great compilation of information, I highly recommend this book as a resource to every library. To the beginner and lifelong student of history and culture, I encourage you to read, study and follow Brother Gallman's recommendations for material identified as beneficial to beginners and material designated as a must read. Thank you, "Kwadwo," we needed that!

Dedication

I have been blessed to have had many teachers and inspirations. To these people, I owe much.

I would like to dedicate this book to my parents, Burnette William Gallman, Sr. and A. Lenora Doyle Gallman Hunter. I tried to run away from my father's love of history, his dedication to our people, and his accomplishments in education; but, as they say, blood is thicker than water and the apple of my life didn't fall far from the comforting shade of his tree. His genes and the DNA of my Ancestors who were educators won out in my life. I love history and am dedicated to improving the lot of Afrikan people all over the world using the ancient Afrikan dictum, *Know Thyself.* My mother's quiet brilliance and her ability to envelop my environment with positivity, love and pride and to look for the good in everyone is the major key to any success that I have experienced in my life.

Then, my twin hearts, my very air, my lifeblood, the loves of my life, Khali and Jodi. You are the reason I work so hard. Your love and confidence inspire me. Your presence in my life stimulates me to strive even harder. You have had patience with my imperfections and have put up with my foolishness so many times. I love you so very, very much!!!

Much of the work in this book was inspired by the work of scholars, friends, teachers, and Jegnoch with whom I have been blessed to develop relationships and for whom I have tremendous respect. Included in this number are Marimba Ani, James Small, Charles Finch, Wade Nobles, Tony Browder, Leonard Jeffries, Rosalind Jeffries, Adelaide Sanford, Theophile Obenga, and Runoko Rashidi.

I am also profoundly thankful for the work of Na'im Akbar, whom I have been blessed to meet, briefly, several times.

There are people around me every day who inspire me, who stimulate ideas and who reinforce a comfort zone in which I can not only relax but bask. This is not a small feat when one considers the two wars that Afrikan people are engaged in simultaneously: the world war and the civil war. The paranoia required for survival can be disorienting but many thanks to Derrick and Yvonne Jackson, Joe and Almateen Benton, Sterling and Lisa McKinney, Jerome and Cynthia Boykin, Ron and Barbara Johnson, Brandi Pinkston, Bill Gunn, Seitu Amenwahsu, Bennie and Sherry Thomas, Tanya Brice, Gloria Boutte and George Johnson, Marvin Brown and Kwame Osei-wusu for helping me navigate those treacherous waters. Shout out to all the current and past members of the study groups in Columbia that I've been involved with. Thank you, my brothers and sisters! Also appreciated is the love and support that I've received from my beloved cousins Glendora Williams and Norma Donaldson-Jenkins.

I am inspired by the energy and efforts of my energetic elder, Marjorie Hammock.

I would also like to acknowledge and thank Don Frierson, the host of the radio program *The Urban Scene* that has aired on multiple stations. Each Thursday, for more than twenty years, he put up with hearing me talk unapologetically about an Afrikan-centered interpretation of our reality and our history and culture.

The Priests, Elders, Members and Drummers of Krst Universal Temple have been steady friends and have inspired me greatly.

The Association for the Study of Classical African Civilizations, its International officers (Drs. Mario Beatty, Greg Kimathi Carr, Valethia Watkins-Beatty, Joye Hardiman, Ife Carruthers, Yaa Asantewa Blake), its Council of Elders, Executive and National Board and membership have been and continue to be a tremendously positive influence on me.

The National Association of Black Social Workers, The Association of Black Psychologists and M.A.A.T. have taught me lessons that I will never forget.

I must mention the young people that I have been blessed to be around including my other "daughters" Charlice Hurst, Michelle Lanier, Marta Notai Washington, Mina Addison, and Jennifer Daniel. Carlos Grant and Ahmad Washington have kept me grounded and cognizant of the current realities that we all face daily.

I love you all.

Perhaps I truly am a missionary to the Negroes as my Brother-Ancestor Listervelt often accused me of being.

Acknowledgments

Giving thanks to the Uncreated Creator who has been known by many names, by many people, throughout time;

Giving thanks to our ancient Afrikan Ancestors who left us beacons that we need to recognize, study, understand and act upon appropriately so that we can rescue and reconstruct the just society that they were creating before they were rudely interrupted;

Giving thanks to our more recent Ancestors who gave us life and who still watch over us;

Giving thanks to our youth, our future, who gave us reason to continue to fight the frequently absurd battles in which we find ourselves embroiled.

I am tremendously indebted to the esteemed Ancestors whom I have been blessed to know personally and be influenced by: John Henrik Clarke, Asa G. Hilliard, III, Frances Cress Welsing, Nzinga Ratabisha Heru, Baba Hannibal Afrik, Larry Obadele Williams, Charshee McIntyre, Jacob Carruthers, Richard King, Kobi K.K. Kambon, Ankh Mi Ra, Anderson Thompson, and my brothers Listervelt Middleton, H. Randolph Scott, II, James Harriot, Jr., and Nicholas Cooper Lewter.

Ancestors I have not known personally but whose works deeply influenced me include Ivan Van Sertima, Amos Wilson, Chancellor Williams, John G. Jackson, Bobby Wright, and the Great Pharaoh, Cheikh Anta Diop.

I want and need to express my thanks, gratitude and appreciation for my editor, Ms Lynn Suruma and my graphic artist, Ms Natalie Stokes-Peters. Not only was your attention to detail and excellence appreciated, your patience with me was remarkable. Thank you!!

Last but not least, I would like to thank profoundly Professor Anthony Browder, Dr. Catherine Adams, Dr. Gloria Boutte, Dr. Tanya Smith Brice, Dr. Greg Kimathi Carr, and Dr. Bobby Donaldson — six-excellent scholars whose work I greatly admire — for their help in reviewing this document.

CONTENTS

FOREWORD

Through Their Own Eyes: Dr. Burnett Kwadwo Gallman's Intellectual Journey

Bobby Donaldson, Ph.D.

As a professor of African American history, I am very pleased to write an introductory essay for *The Sankofa University*, a volume penned by my friend and brother Dr. Burnett Kwadwo Gallman. Fortunately, our paths intersected several years ago in Columbia, South Carolina. On our first meeting, I was immediately taken by his immense knowledge of history, his indefatigable energies, and his exuberant (indeed contagious) passion for teaching and sharing. Nearly three decades ago, Dr. Gallman penned a front-page column in Columbia's newspaper, *The State.* The informative essay called for a deeper and more rigorous exploration of African and African American history. He observed: "It is important that African people all over the world learn again to look at themselves through their own eyes and not through other, frequently hostile, eyes. This would help clear our vision of the present."

For decades, Dr. Gallman kept the faith and remained committed to helping his sisters and brothers to view "themselves through their own eyes." He published essays, led study groups and tours, attended conferences, delivered lectures, and conducted workshops. *The Sankofa University*, an important, impactful, and instructive project, is yet one more gift that Dr. Gallman has bequeathed to us and generations to come.

As I read the early drafts of this work and spent time speaking with Dr. Gallman about his manuscript, I kept thinking about that ONE book that opened my young eyes to the wonder and power of African American history. I read Dr. Vincent Harding's *There is a River*, and something got a hold of me! In the introduction, Harding pens these arresting words:

> This work is an experiment in history, solidarity, and hope. It is part of a continuing attempt to discover and develop the sources of creative tension among my responsibilities as a historian, my commitment to human liberation, and my urgent determination to keep faith with that magnificent company of witnesses—my mothers and fathers—whose lives form the wellsprings of the black struggle for freedom in America.

Similarly, *The Sankofa University* "is an experiment in history, solidarity, and hope." In this project, a lifelong student and master teacher pulls books from his library, shares his reading lists, reveals his extensive notes and offers insights gleaned from researching, traveling, and conversing with some of the world's leading minds, scholars, and griots. With this work, we gain greater clarity—one that debunks myths, uproots mischaracterizations, and one that TRUMPS deliberate confusion, obfuscation, and contrived deceit and deception.

Here, in the tradition of Maria Stewart, David Walker, and Bishop Henry McNeal Turner, Gallman renders a sermon and an appeal. He summons us to dig more deeply, to read more broadly, to think more critically and to converse more insistently in the full hope that we will be transformed and empowered by the "renewing of our minds." Here Gallman explains how history is a vital component of our identity, our orientation, and our outlook on the world. With this project, he evokes a central theme that was echoed in the November 1865 Colored Convention in Charleston, South Carolina, as African Americans imagined a life beyond the bonds of slavery. They insisted on "the right to develop our whole being."

In so many respects, this volume is a scholar's pursuit of a "whole being." As an intellectual autobiography, *The Sankofa University* is Dr. Gallman's fervent and urgent effort to "keep faith with the magnificent company of witnesses" and writings that have shaped his own journey as a conscious, conscientious, and "woke" citizen and public intellectual.

Imagine being the heir of a legacy shaped by a wide circle of educators and physicians who had a passion for knowing and studying the past. Dr. Gallman emerges from a long tradition—a river—of insurgent and gifted minds who gave voice to the history of African people. As Dr. Gallman outlines in the preface "How Did I Get Here?" a mighty river of ancestors ordered his steps and prepared him for the journey ahead.

The river that shaped Dr. Burnett Kwadwo Gallman flowed through **Dr. John S. Rock**, a pioneering nineteenth century medical doctor, lawyer, and abolitionist who was born in New Jersey in 1825. As a child, Rock demonstrated an early fascination with books.

After establishing a reputable record as a teacher, Rock studied dentistry and then attended medical school. Along the way, he maintained an intense interest in history. In Dr. Gallman's intellectual journey, we see Dr. John S. Rock's imprint. On March 5, 1858, Dr. Rock joined others in Boston's Faneuil Hall to honor the memory of Crispus Attucks and to mark the 87th anniversary of the Boston Massacre. An uncompromising "race man," Rock used the occasion to challenge prevailing historical narratives and social commentaries that depicted African people as intellectually, emotionally, and physically deficient. To such ideas, Dr. Rock retorted:

> I would have you understand, that I not only love my race, but am pleased with my color; and while many colored persons may feel degraded by being called negroes, and wish to be classed among other races more favored, I shall feel it my duty, my pleasure and my pride, to concentrate my feeble efforts in elevating to a fair position a race to which I am especially identified by feelings and by blood.

The river that shaped Dr. Burnett Kwadwo Gallman flowed through **Dr. C.V. Roman**, a professor at Meharry Medical College and a talented historian and physician who founded the Journal of the National Medical Association. Dr. Roman, who had a close association with Dr. Carter G. Woodson, attended the first biennial meeting of the Association for the Study of Negro Life and History in Washington, DC in 1917. He authored numerous publications including *A Knowledge* *of History is Conducive for Racial Solidarity* and other writings and *American Civilization and the Negro.* In the latter, he observes: "There is nothing in the blood or beliefs, ancestry or heredity of the Afro-American incompatible with the highest civilization."

As demonstrated in this volume, the river that shaped Dr. Burnett Kwadwo Gallman flowed through **Dr. Matilda A. Evans**, one of the first African American female physicians In South Carolina, a staunch civil rights leader, and a champion of black pride and enterprise who resided in Columbia, South Carolina. A native of Aiken, Evans graduated from the Schofield Normal and Industrial School, where she was mentored by the school's founder Martha Schofield. In 1916, after the passing of Schofield, Dr. Evans published a book entitled, *Martha Schofield, Pioneer Negro Educator: Historical and Philosophical Review of Reconstruction Period of South Carolina.* In some respects, this volume provides a revisionist assessment of Reconstruction, especially as it highlights the brutal violence African Americans witnessed and experienced in the decades following Emancipation. But the work is also an appeal for African self-rule and governance. On the eve of World War I and in anticipation of the platforms of Marcus Garvey and Malcolm X, Dr. Evans remained convinced that the forces of white supremacy would never enable progress among her people. She remarked:

> By every test or qualification and efficiency the Negro, in government, in the science of war, in the art of agriculture, in manufacturing, invention, medicine, law and literature is well prepared to assume the government of his race in a territory of his own. This insures him the same protection from the persecution and injustices of the stronger race that enabled the latter to succeed so famously when they, too, in the course of human events, found it necessary to dissolve the political bonds that united them to a dominant authority that gave them no justice.

These were the words of a black female doctor in South Carolina in the early twentieth century. Who was Dr. Matilda Evans? What shaped her worldview? And how did her medical practice and social activism impact her community? Fortunately, these questions are answered in the impressive archival research that Dr. Gallman showcases in this volume.

The river that shaped Dr. Burnett Kwadwo Gallman flowed through **Dr. J. Max Barber**. Born in Blackstock, South Carolina, in 1878, Barber attended Benedict Institute and earned a bachelor's degree from Virginia Union University. Later, he moved to Atlanta where he edited *The Voice of the Negro*, a brilliant publication that championed civil rights and directly challenged the leadership of Booker T. Washington. When the 1906 Atlanta Race Riot targeted African American institutions and leaders, Barber feared for his life and departed for Chicago. He continued his work in journalism, pursued a dental degree, and helped establish the NAACP.

An astute student of history, Barber published *The Negro of the Earlier World: An Excursion into Negro Ancient History* in 1920. Providing a platform upon which Dr. Gallman and others would build, Barber noted:

> Traditions and history are the background of a people. A race without traditions and without history is most likely to be a race without backbone and without self-respect...We are taught to believe that the history of the race began with slavery...The white man has tried to rob us of Egypt because Egypt is the mother of modern civilization.

Dr. Barber lauded the work of fellow African American historians such as J. A. Rogers, Carter G. Woodson, and W. E. B. Du Bois. "They are digging down around the roots of history and the historical facts which they are unearthing furnish us background of splendid traditions." "The vast majority of Negroes do not know that their race has any history," Dr. Barber wrote. "How could they know? It is not taught in the schools. It is not printed in the newspapers. The white historians and archaeologists have carefully overlaid anything that could possibly be credited to us with lies and doubts."

Over a decade later in a column in the *Pittsburgh Courier*, published by his Virginia Union classmate Robert L. Vann, Dr. Barber underscored the critical importance of reading and researching ancient African history. Contrary to prevailing scholarship and teaching,

Barber reported: "Negroes have distinguished themselves in every age and every land. It is hardly too much to say he rocked civilization in the cradle."

The river that shaped Dr. Burnett Kwadwo Gallman flowed through **Arturo Schomburg**, a dedicated historian and inveterate bibliophile, who amassed an impressive collection of primary sources documenting African and African American history. In Dr. Alain Locke's landmark 1925 volume, *The New Negro*, Schomburg submitted an essay "The Negro Digs Up His Past," which gave marching orders to the future Burnett Gallmans and other students of history. Schomburg writes:

> The African in America must remake his past in order to make his future. Though it is orthodox to think of America as the one country where it is unnecessary to have a past, what is a luxury for the nation as a whole becomes a prime social necessity for the Negro.... History must restore what slavery took away, for it is the social damage of slavery that the present generations must repair and offset."

The river that shaped Dr. Burnett Kwadwo Gallman flowed through **Dr. W. E. B. Du Bois,** the first African American Ph.D. graduate of Harvard University and the author of several canonical works, including *The Souls of Black Folk* and *Black Reconstruction*—a 1935 landmark volume that relied, in part, upon historical research conducted in South Carolina. With *Black Reconstruction* and other publications, Dr. Du Bois provides a canvass for Dr. Burnett Gallman. In a piercing essay entitled "The Propaganda of History," Du Bois took aim at the "libel, innuendo and silence" that "completely misstated and obliterated the history of the Negro in America." Dr. Du Bois observes: "We have too often [made] a deliberate attempt to change the facts of history [so] that the story will make pleasant reading for Americans."

The river that shaped Dr. Burnett Kwadwo Gallman flowed through **Dr. Carter G. Woodson.** Born in 1875, Woodson pursued his educational studies at Berea College, the University of Chicago, and Harvard University, where he received his Ph.D. in 1912. Foregoing a formal career as a college professor, Woodson initiated a life-long crusade to revise and reconstruct African American history. In 1915, he and his colleagues established the Association for the Study of Negro Life and History. *The Journal of Negro History* began publication one year later. Given the limited access African Americans scholars encountered at major libraries, Woodson facilitated research in Negro history by wisely building his own collection.

From the beginning, Woodson entertained clear objectives:

> "This organization publishes a magazine, researches in Negro History, directs studies in clubs and schools, promotes the study of the Negro by mail, produces texts on the Negro for schools and colleges, collects and preserves valuable documents of Negro History, supplies libraries with special collections of rare books on the Negro, and educates promising and enterprising young men for service in historical research."

Woodson also prepared and disseminated Negro History kits that included "pictures of most of the outstanding Negroes in the history of the race in various sizes suitable for the school, the library, or the home."

In addition to the Association and the *Journal of Negro History*, Woodson was a prolific researcher and writer. He published and edited several works, including the iconic 1933 book, *The Mis-education of the Negro.* This volume is amply quoted in Dr. Gallman's *Sankofa University.* As readers will see, both authors share a central thesis. Consider Dr. Woodson:

> To handicap a student by teaching him that his black face is a curse and that his struggle to change his condition is hopeless is the worst sort of lynching. It kills one's aspirations and dooms him to vagabondage and crime.

And now consider Dr. Gallman:

> "Racists hold to the belief of their own superiority despite all evidence to the contrary. Their evidence of their superi-

> ority is usually fabricated information. They stack the deck against others and then blame these others for failing, using this failure as proof of inferiority. Because they control many information systems, they introduce and reinforce the idea of Black inferiority after taking away culture, which is the solid ground upon which all self-respecting people stand."

The river that shaped Dr. Burnett Kwadwo Gallman flowed through **Dr. Mary McLeod Bethune**, a native of Mayesville, South Carolina, who led Bethune-Cookman College and the National Council of Negro Women. Dr. Bethune also served as president of Carter G. Woodson's Association for the Study of Negro Life and History. At a meeting in Chicago in 1935, Bethune declared: "The search for truth is not for timid souls...The great thing to learn is to be unafraid of knowledge." Two years later, while speaking in Washington, D.C. at a meeting of the Association, Bethune delivered an address entitled "Clarifying our Vision with Facts." "If our people are to fight their way up out of bondage we must arm them with the sword and the shield ... belief in themselves and their possibilities, based upon a sure knowledge of the achievements of the past. We must tell the story from the cradle to the grave." Bethune contended that "accurate research and investigation" would "supplement, correct, re-orient and annotate the story."

The river that shaped Dr. Burnett Kwadwo Gallman flowed through **Dr. W. Montague Cobb.** A 1929 graduate of the Howard University Medical School. Dr. W. Montague Cobb led the school's Anatomy Department, served as a president of the National Medical Association, and received a Ph.D. in Physical Anthropology. Described by Gallman as a "staunch integrationist," Dr. Cobb edited the NMA's journal and penned a number of historical reflections. He credited Carter G. Woodson's Association for the Study of Negro Life and History as the "only repository for rescuing the history of the most highly selected element of our population." Battling assertions by scientists and pundits that black people were physically, mentally, and culturally inferior, Cobb documented the grueling exploitation of enslavement and contended "a lesser group would have been destroyed, but the American Negro has survived." "Not only has he survived," Dr. Cobb asserted, "but he has multiplied and so after the last 100 years of brutal treatment and exhaustive labors when one finds a Willie Mays or a Jim Brown, its only representative of the survival of the fittest."

The river that shaped Dr. Burnett Kwadwo Gallman flowed through **James E. Campbell**, a native of Charleston who served as a teacher and administrator in Baltimore, New York City, and Tanzania. He also edited the *Freedomways* magazine and conducted history workshops for the Citizenship Schools organized by Septima P. Clark and for the **Malcolm X's Organization of Afro-American Unity.** The Campbell papers, archived at the Avery Research Center in Charleston, include an original copy of the OAAU's June 1964 newsletter, published months before Dr. Gallman began his junior year at Butler High School in Hartsville, South Carolina. The words and sentiments in the organization's "Statement of Basic Aims and Objectives" read like a blueprint for young Gallman:

> Our history and our culture were completely destroyed when we were forcefully brought to America in chains. And now it is important for us to know that our history did not begin with slavery's scars. We came from Africa, a great continent and a proud and variable people, and which is the new world and was the cradle of civilization. Our culture and our history are as old as man himself and yet we know almost nothing of it.

We must recapture our heritage and our identity if we are ever to be liberated from the bond of white supremacy. We must launch a cultural revolution to un-brainwash an entire people.

The river that shaped Dr. Burnett Kwadwo Gallman flowed through *other young women and men in the mid 1960s* who grew increasingly frustrated with the world they inherited. While Dr. Gallman attended Morehouse College, undoubtedly he heard the fierce declarations of black nationalists, including the **Black Panther Party**. When members of the party debated the basic tenets of their organization, they were determined to challenge and reframe the types of history African Americans read and heard. The fifth demand in the Panther's 10-point program read: "We want education for our people that exposes the true nature of this decadent American society. We want education that teaches us our true history and our role in the present-day society."

The river that shaped Dr. Burnett Kwadwo Gallman flowed through **Dr. Martin Luther King, Jr.** In the spring of 1968, Gallman was a student at Morehouse College. He has vivid memories of the shock and dismay that ensued after Dr. King was assassinated on April 4, 1968. Dr. Gallman also recalls the rage and anger that literally flowed in the streets as he and other black people fought back against systems and histories that killed a prophetic black voice and non-violence champion. Ironically only months earlier, Dr. King travelled to New York to be with James Campbell, members of the *Freedomways* staff, and others in a memorial program marking the fifth anniversary of Dr. W. E. B. Du Bois' death. In the tribute, King hailed Du Bois as a "tireless explorer and a gifted discoverer of social truths" who filled an "immense void" created by previous writers and scholars who "ignored the contribution of the Negro in American history." Like Gallman, King reminded listeners that these dangerous and deceptive works "only served to intensify the Negroes' sense of worthlessness and to augment the anachronistic doctrine of white supremacy."

The river that shaped Dr. Burnett Kwadwo Gallman flowed through his friend and brother **Listervelt Middleton.** Born on a farm in Berkeley County, South Carolina, Middleton received a degree in political science from Benedict College and then made it his life's work to use television as "a tool to educate and liberate the mind." "Every black must see himself as an instrument of his ancestors," Middleton observed. The author of publications such as *Fatback and Caviar* and the host and producer of the widely viewed television series *For the People*, Middleton was emphatic about introducing young African Americans to readings and cultural resources that affirmed their identities. "Watch out for the kinds of information that goes into children's minds.

A battle is going on for the minds of children. If they do not put into their minds a sense of commitment, of mission, then the children will wind up being of no use in the struggle for freedom." In Dr. Gallman, Middleton found a fellow "missionary" and "an instrument of his ancestors" who believed strongly in the curative and healing powers of a liberated history.

Finally, the river that shaped Dr. Burnett Kwadwo Gallman flowed through homes, offices, and schools across the South from Atlanta and Gainesville, Georgia; to Westminister, Pendleton, Seneca, Newberry, Orangeburg, and Hartsville, South Carolina; to Raleigh and Wilson, North Carolina; and on to villages and kingdoms across the sea. *The Sankofa University* is a tribute and a testimony to rivers of influence over many generations that have guided Dr. Gallman through his personal, professional, and intellectual journeys.

His paternal grandfather, George Johnson Gallman, was born in 1871 to Elijah and Rosanna Gallman. He completed the Allen University Normal School in 1893 and worked as an educator. Students and colleagues in Newberry County called him Professor G. J. Gallman.

His maternal grandfather, Dr. Newton Alexander Doyle, graduated from the Leonard Medical School on the campus of Shaw University in Raleigh in 1906. A local newspaper in the Oconee County area described him as the "son of Benjamin Doyle, a highly respected colored citizen of this section." Dr. Doyle, a medical doctor in Gainesville, Georgia, was a church deacon, Sunday school superintendent, trustee at Seneca Junior College, and an active leader in the Georgia State Medical Association of Colored Physicians, Dentists and Pharmacists. When the Association met in Savannah in 1910, Doyle joined other participants including the acclaimed writer, Dr. C. V. Roman. At the 1915 meeting in Augusta, Dr. Doyle was elected the organization's third vice president, and he had an opportunity to meet educator Lucy Craft Laney on the campus of Haines Institute, where she had mentored Mary McLeod Bethune decades earlier.

While enrolled at Leonard, Dr. Doyle met and married Ella Stokes. She had a tremendous influence on Dr. Gallman and his pursuit of a medical career. And, although Dr. Doyle died twelve years before

Gallman's birth, it was clear that these two men had much in common. When Dr. Doyle was featured in the book *History of the American Negro, Georgia*, among other influential "race leaders," his biographical sketch noted, "Apart from his professional reading, Dr. Doyle is very fond of history."

The river that shaped Dr. Burnett William Gallman, Jr. also flowed through his parents Burnett William Gallman, Sr. and Lenora Doyle Gallman. A graduate of Spelman College High School and Benedict College in Columbia, Lenora Doyle, a woman with a "quiet brilliance," developed a strong reputation as an accomplished musician. While teaching in Pendleton, she met and married Burnett Gallman, the principal of the Anderson County Training School in June 1937.

Gallman Sr. graduated from the South Carolina State Agricultural and Mechanical College in Orangeburg in 1929. On campus, Gallman stood out as a talented student, a gifted debater, a civil rights advocate, and a strong champion of Negro history. Writing in the College's newspaper, *The Collegian*, in 1929 Gallman observes: "It is unfortunate that the outstanding achievements of Negroes have not been in American history....Why should we not develop that race pride that has been developed so completely by other nations and races."

While Gallman was on the Orangeburg campus, several accomplished members of the faculty or the alumni body influenced his development and outlook. At the time, the distinguished scholar Benjamin E. Mays served as the president of the alumni and he spoke at Gallman's commencement ceremony. Three years prior to Gallman's graduation, Mays gave the opening remarks for a "Negro Older Boys' Conference" at Benedict College in February 1926. Mays called the young men of Gallman's generation "New Negroes," and he instructed them to cast their gaze "upward to truth, onward to virtue, thru perils to right, and thru bitter experiences to the plain of justice...in order that those who come after us may enjoy a larger freedom and a greater heritage."

One of Gallman's most influential mentors was Professor Asa H. Gordon, a graduate of Atlanta University, a World War I veteran and a protégé of W. E. B. Du Bois; later, Gordon earned his Ph.D. at Columbia

University. Gordon taught history and economics and coached young Gallman on the debate team. In 1921, Professor Gordon instituted Negro History Week on the State campus, five years before Carter G. Woodson developed a national program. In 1927, Gordon attended the annual meeting of the Association for the Study of Negro Life and History in Pittsburgh.

In 1928, State's president Robert Shaw Wilkinson, likely upon Gordon's advice, informed members of the faculty that he expected them to become members of Woodson's Association. During that same year, Professor Gordon publicly attacked the inequities between African American and white educational resources in South Carolina. He described the disparities as "alarming to one who believes in the American principles of democratic education…They are positively and unquestionably disgraceful to the commonwealth of South Carolina." While teaching Gallman and others and speaking out against injustices, Professor Gordon conducted extensive research for his 1929 book, *Sketches of Negro Life and History in South Carolina.*

This publication, rarely discussed now, was a monumental work of revisionist scholarship. With a wealth of archival resources and first-hand accounts, Professor Gordon interpreted and analyzed African American history and culture *"through their own eyes."* As the book was released and Burnett Gallman, Sr. graduated, *Sketches of Negro Life* was met with strong praise from African American readers and educators as it became the primary text for a series of popular summer school courses designed for teachers on the State campus. One reviewer of the book observed:

> The large enrollment in these courses indicates the growing appreciation of Negro teachers for the history and progress of their own race and will result in a widespread propagation of valuable and inspiring information about the colored people of this state and of the nation. This seems to be one of the most significant and inspiring developments of progressive education among colored people. It is also encouraging because of the fact that it gives encouragement to the

> ambition of negro teachers and thinkers to write and publish original, scientific, creative work such as the critics claim Professor Gordon's book and teaching to be.

Undoubtedly, Burnett Gallman, Sr. took the historical and political lessons he learned from Professor Gordon in Orangeburg and applied them during the course of his career as an educator in Newberry, Pendleton, and Hartsville, South Carolina. Writing in the *Palmetto Leader* newspaper in February 1930—only months after graduating from college—Gallman observed: "The so-called race problem of America must be solved by national thinking and controlled emotional or rightly speaking labor problems. In a like manner must war be brought to an end and peace made to triumph."

In December 1932, while teaching in the depths of the Great Depression in a rural "Negro school" in Newberry, Gallman penned a note to W. E. B. Du Bois. He writes:

> I am [a] public school teacher of the state of South Carolina. For quite a number of years I have noted with great interest the wonderful service rendered to my race by the N.A.A.C.P. For this reason I am endeavoring to stress the importance of supporting the organization to everyone coming under my instruction and influence. Now, I confess that I am not fully informed as to the entire history of this organization," Gallman concedes. "For this information or the proper source of the same I am hereby requesting of you. Many thanks in advance. Yours truly, B. W. Gallman.

In response, Dr. Du Bois' secretary sent Gallman a pamphlet that outlined the history and mission of the civil rights organization.

While working in Newberry and later in Pendleton, Gallman strongly advocated for the teaching and recognition of African American history. Following the example of his mentor, Professor Asa H. Gordon, Gallman initiated Negro History Week at the Anderson County Training School. During daily chapel services, students made presentations and Gallman invited "interesting leaders and makers of Negro History" to share their memories and experiences. At the same time, Gallman remained quite active in a number of civic and professional organizations, including the local and state teacher associations. His future wife, Lenora Doyle, was also active. In the summer of 1938, Gallman attended the meeting of the American Teachers Association held at Tuskegee Institute where speakers included Dr. Mary McLeod Bethune, Thurgood Marshall and Dr. Robert C. Weaver. At the meeting the delegates agreed to support NAACP legal plans to challenge inequities in education. The members affirmed that teachers should "receive equal pay for equal service without regard to color or sex."

As the NAACP forged partnerships with national and state teacher organizations to advance a civil rights agenda, progress within South Carolina was gradually slow, especially as teachers realized that their jobs and livelihood could be jeopardized. Frustrated by developments, John H. McCray, the editor of the *Lighthouse and Informer* newspaper complained: "The great mistake our teachers have made, and are making, is that of having a pussyfooting, yowsah boss type of state organization." McCray strongly encouraged new leadership within the organization, and he found a kindred ideological spirit when Gallman—labelled a "radical" by some observers—was elected in 1944 as the president of the Palmetto State Teachers Association. The vice president was H. B. Butler, Jr. of Allen University who declared: "The NAACP is next to the church the best organization we Negroes have. May God bless it."

As the Association president and the principal of the Anderson County Training School, Gallman firmly and openly championed progressive civil rights reform.

In April 1944, the Association agreed to commit $1200 to the NAACP legal campaign for equalization of teacher salaries, the very same campaign that Gallman learned about during the American Teachers Association Meeting in Tuskegee six years earlier.

In addition to the NAACP, Gallman also supported the South Carolina Progressive Democratic Party, an organization journalist John McCray and others established to challenge the pronounced racial discrimination of white Democrats who refused to permit African

Americans to vote in the primaries. In a June 1944 message to party treasurer J.C. Artemus, Gallman remarked: "We feel that your movement will add an important page to the history of our race and nation." He included a $2.00 contribution.

During Gallman's tenure, the Association adopted the following platform:

We urge that the Association fully support the democratic ideal of equality of educational opportunity for all citizens to include:

1. Equal salaries for all teachers with the same or equal qualifications.
2. Availability of equal elementary and secondary education for every child in South Carolina.
3. The same enforcement of the S.C. Compulsory School
4. Attendance Law for children of all races and religions.
5. Provision for equal facilities on the undergraduate and graduate levels for all persons qualifying for and desiring the same.

To achieve these goals, Gallman understood the critical value of collective action among African Americans. In a January 1946 message, he noted that "the time is at hand when all organizations working for the full citizenship of the South Carolina Negro unite their forces for the common cause."

When the Palmetto State Teachers Association executive committee gathered for a meeting at Allen University in March 1946, members began to sharpen their focus on the adverse impact of racial inequities among African American schools, including teachers' salaries, facilities, operational funding, and transportation. To underscore the critical link between equity and education, Gallman and his committee adopted "Education for Peace and Economic Security" as the theme for the April 1946 annual meeting in Columbia, and they invited NAACP executive secretary Walter F. White to deliver the keynote address before 3,000 audience members at the Township Auditorium.

The rules of the Association were such that Gallman could only serve a two-year stint, culminating in the spring of 1946. John McCray, one of Gallman's strongest admirers and champions, commended him for his progressive ideas and his effective stewardship of the organization. "It is my belief that you have [challenged] forthrightly the positive means by which teachers can unify themselves and advance their organization and working problems and for this service we are indebted to you. I certainly hope your influence and interest with the organization will be continued in some executive capacity."

In response, Gallman thanked McCray for his cooperation "in trying to help bring about democracy in education." He also wrote to remind McCray that the Association, under his leadership, was unerring in their support of the right to vote and committed to urging the "6000 teachers to press their claim for democracy at the polls." He also informed McCray that the "small village" of Pendleton was working to establish a NAACP chapter "with a goal of 200 members." "Hence you may feel assured," Gallman concluded, "that we are 100% behind all of your efforts for full citizenship in S.C."

In the aftermath of World War II, B.W. Gallman was part of that "greatest generation" of black folk who were steadfastly committed to "victory at home and victory abroad." As Gallman prepared to end his tenure as president of the Palmetto Teachers Association, young people in South Carolina, across the nation, and around the world, under the tutelage of educators such as Modjeska Monteith Simkins, Ethel Williams Wilson, and Dr. Annie Belle Weston, planned to convene a meeting of the Southern Negro Youth Congress (SNYC) in Columbia, South Carolina, in October 1946. With speakers including W. E. B. Du Bois and famed singer and activist Paul Robeson, the SNYC issued a blueprint, designed by young dynamic minds, for the Modern Civil Rights Movement.

The Congress' culminating program, featuring renowned activist, historian, and NAACP founder Dr. W. E. B. Du Bois, took place at the Antisdel Chapel on the Benedict College campus on Sunday October 20, 1946. Du Bois delivered a powerful and hotly debated speech entitled *Behold the Land.* A loudspeaker carried his long-awaited message to those eager to hear him outside of the sanctuary. "I trust then that an organization like yours is going to regard the South as the battle-ground of a great crusade," the aged scholar declared." "This is the firing line not simply for the emancipation of the African Negro and the Negroes of the West Indies; for the emancipation of the colored races and for the emancipation of the white slaves of modern capitalistic monopoly." Du Bois issued a powerful charge to young people. "Grit your teeth and make up your minds to fight it out right here," he said, "if it takes every day of your lives and the lives of your children's children."

To date, my research has not verified if B.W. Gallman attended the Columbia SNYC meeting. But given his politics and his outlook on the world, I suspect he was front and center. And I have no doubt that he would have endorsed Dr. Du Bois' sentiments. Asè!! Ironically, a chapter of the SNYC was established in Anderson in 1947, led by Alvin Rucker. Three years later, a charter for a NAACP youth council in Pendleton was granted. Undoubtedly, Gallman laid the foundation for these developments before he and his wife moved to Hartsville, South Carolina.

It is no small irony that it was against this backdrop and within this hopeful and troubled climate that B. W. Gallman and Lenora Doyle Gallman witnessed the birth of their son in 1948. This is the river that nurtured Dr. Burnett Kwadwo Gallman's ideological and intellectual journey. This is the river that awakened his consciousness and inspired him to gift this book to us.

Out of these rivers of tradition and upon this legacy, Dr. Gallman has placed on paper an array of topics pulled from his deep well of knowledge. Quite literally, this volume provides readers a language and a vocabulary to understand the past. It is an incisive and provocative analysis that compels all of us to dig deeper and to question long-standing assumptions about the Afrikan journey.

This is not a conventional book. It provides both serious historical analysis and social commentary. It builds upon existing literature and adds substantive new angles, context, and background. It is a manual, a tool kit, an encyclopedia, a quilt—multiple topics all stitched together into a collective whole by Dr. Gallman's brilliant insights on the glorious, tragic and triumphant history of our people.

For those who wish to follow a grand tradition, for those who wish to stand a little taller to see the distant horizon of full liberation and freedom, and for those who seek a deeper and richer history of African Americans *through their own eyes,* Dr. Gallman has provided an imaginative and richly informed road map. Read it. Discuss it. Share it. And journey on!

PREFACE

How Did I Get Here?

Although academic excellence was always stressed during my upbringing, my arrival into the field of medicine and as a student of history may be of some interest. My maternal grandparents, Dr. Newton Alexander Doyle (Newt) and Mrs. Mary Ella Stokes Doyle (Nana) have influenced my choices more than I could have imagined.

"Newt," the son of illiterate, formerly enslaved field hands and sharecroppers from Oconee County, South Carolina, who died twelve years before I was born, was so dedicated to becoming a physician that he worked his way through the Leonard Medical School of Shaw University in Raleigh, North Carolina, by laboring in the fields, laying down railroad tracks and working with practicing physicians (yes, Shaw University had a medical school). Although it took him six years to earn enough money to complete his studies, he earned the respect and admiration of his peers.

"Nana," the proud daughter of impoverished formerly enslaved Afrikan Native Americans (I suspect from the Tuscarora Nation) in Wilson, North Carolina, was so determined to obtain an education that at age sixteen, after the death of her mother and after getting her younger siblings situated with relatives, she walked from Wilson to Raleigh, North Carolina, in order to convince the officials at Shaw University that she be allowed to work her way through college. My grandparents graduated in the class of 1906, he with an M.D. degree and she with a degree in Home Economics. Nana, who was so convinced of the nobility of the medical profession that she married a physician, saw her oldest daughter marry a physician, and saw all three of her grandsons become physicians. In fact, my earliest memories of my grandmother are of her telling me that I was going to be a physician.

With regards to my love for my people and their history, the route was more circuitous.

For most of my life, my father, Burnette W. Gallman, Sr. was bedridden from inadequately treated Parkinson's disease. He transitioned to the Ancestral realm when I was fourteen years old. Because of his inability to physically participate in my rearing, my mother, A. Lenora Doyle Gallman Hunter, made sure that I was aware of what a great man he was. She made sure that I knew that my father came from a family of educators, that he was academically brilliant, and that he loved people of Afrikan origin. She also made sure I knew he was a true Christian man who did not run around with women, did not use tobacco or alcohol, and loved history.

These facts were reinforced by everyone in the community which I interpreted as putting pressure on me to be someone that I did not see myself as being at that time. So, to be able live peacefully in my mother's house, I had to excel academically. I did everything that I was told that he did not do and tried to excel in those activities also. I drank and smoked constantly, chased women, and hated history.

After graduating Valedictorian from segregated Butler High School in Hartsville, South Carolina, I went to Morehouse College in Atlanta, Georgia. I was very immature and inexperienced and started hanging with friends who were from large cities and were far more worldly and experienced. But, the love for reading that my mother had instilled in me prevailed; I started reading historical fiction which, incidentally, benefitted me academically.

Slowly but inevitably, these books whetted my appetite for the real history. I partied a great deal in Atlanta but my life changed when I first heard Stokely Carmichael (later Kwame Ture) speak. I became very Black conscious. I had the opportunity to hear him in Atlanta several more times and then heard him again after I transferred to Benedict College in Columbia, South Carolina. Years later, in 1993, I had the opportunity to meet him personally while traveling in Ghana with Drs. Leonard and Rosalind Jeffries and Professor James Small.

Initially, this new consciousness waxed and waned with my environment. After leaving Benedict, I taught for a year in Hartsville before being admitted into medical school. Many of my old habits came to the forefront again during that year. Carousing with multiple females became a major activity until I left Hartsville for Philadelphia. The racism my Afrikan classmates and I encountered at Hahnemann Medical College and Hospital was eye-opening and aided in my transformation. While at Hahnemann, I was introduced to The Cress Theory of Racism (White Supremacy) and lived several blocks from a Black bookstore. It was there that I became introduced to the poetry of Don. L. Lee, now Haki Madhubuti, and Sonia Sanchez.

After graduating from medical school, I did my internship, residency and fellowship in Washington, D.C. which was then truly "Chocolate City" and where I became familiar with politics from a Black perspective.

Leaving Washington, I landed again in Columbia where I started my medical practice. A major milestone in my life was meeting and spending time with Listervelt Middleton, the host and producer of a major international public television program called *For The People.* Listervelt became one of my best friends and introduced me to cutting-edge Afrikan-centered scholars, with whom I have developed many close relationships. When I proposed starting what, then, I called a book club, Listervelt was extremely encouraging and also introduced the book club/study group to the Association for the Study of Classical African Civilizations (ASCAC). He accompanied Association members on their historic 1984 journey to Kemet (Egypt) when almost 1000 Ausa (Afrikans from the United States of America) traveled there to study the history of our ancient ancestors.

We became active members of ASCAC and, to this day, I am a member of the National Board. Fortunately, I have been supported in my studies and travels by my wife, partner, collaborator and biggest cheerleader, Jodi, and could not have been able to accomplish a fraction of the things that I have been blessed to accomplish without her love and support.

INTRODUCTION

Studying Afrikan-Centered History and Culture

Anthony T. Browder

The Sankofa University: Studying Afrikan-Centered History and Culture is a timely compilation of Afrikan and Afrikan American historical facts, bibliographies, essays and commentaries. It is a thought-provoking publication brilliantly researched and written by Burnett Kwadwo Gallman who is eminently qualified to write on the topic. Brother Gallman has studied alongside some of the most highly respected scholars within the Afrikan-Centered community (Middleton, Hilliard, Clarke, ben-Jochannan, McIntyre, Carruthers, Ani, Welsing, Kambon and others). He has distinguished himself as a learner with a keen intellect and as a teacher with a profound mastery of his subject and a passion for transferring his enthusiastic love of learning to his students.

Brother Gallman is a physician who has had a distinguished career caring for the physical well-being of his patients. But he is also well known throughout his home state of South Carolina and the country as a "Race Man" with a genuine interest in the mental, spiritual and cultural welfare of Afrikan people. Brother Gallman has consistently walked the walk and talked the talk while constructing bridges of cultural awareness across a vast chasm of socially engineered ignorance and apathy.

In the generations to come, *The Sankofa University: Studying Afrikan-Centered History and Culture* will be heralded as essential reading for the restoration of an Afrikan consciousness. In the Introduction, Brother Gallman provides the reader with a basic framework for grasping the critical importance of "history, culture, axiology and epistemology" while introducing the reader to the groundbreaking research of Edwin Nichols and Linda James Myers. He discusses issues of culturally induced ignorance (agnotology); the pervasiveness of the Dunning Kruger Effect; and cognitive dissonance — three components of a world-wide system of racism and white supremacy which hold the minds and souls of Black folk in a debilitating state of suspended animation.

The Sankofa University not only provides readers with a compelling list of atrocities committed against people of Afrikan ancestry for over five millennia, it also provides readers with a path out of the abyss by introducing conceptual frameworks critical to the creation and maintenance of an Afrikan-Centered consciousness. One specific aspect of *The Sankofa University* which makes it an essential publication for every Afrikan household is the carefully curated bibliography and list of scholars that should occupy the hearts, minds and souls of every person seeking to secure and preserve freedom for future generations.

This is not an overtly academic treatise written exclusively for a limited population. To the contrary, *The Sankofa University* has a universal appeal and does not have to be read sequentially like a traditional textbook. Each chapter stands on its own as an independent narrative that fits seamlessly into a comprehensive portrait of the Afrikan and Afrikan-American experience, thus assuring that this book will be heralded as a classic and passed down from generation to generation.

To paraphrase the late, great Ancestor, Dr. John Henrik Clarke, "I conclude something, which has no conclusion" by urging you to purchase, read and study one of the most important books of the new decade. *The Sankofa University* is a book about achievements rather than achievers. It chronicles the enduring legacy of the Mothers and Fathers of humanity, culture and civilization, and leaves the reader with the profound understanding that what our Ancestors have accomplished we have the capacity to replicate…now and forevermore!

It is my sincere desire that *The Sankofa University: Studying Afrikan-Centered History and Culture* stimulates a new generation of Race Men and Women who, with restored consciousnesses, will restore Ma'at and turn the world right side up.

May the Ancestors continue blessing Brother Gallman for faithfully fulfilling his cultural and cosmic obligations.

Hotep,
Anthony (Karakh) Browder
December 21, 2019

CHAPTER 1

Culture, History and Agnotology

"Never forget that intelligence rules the world and ignorance carries the burden. Therefore, remove yourself as far as possible from ignorance and seek as far as possible to be intelligent."

Marcus Garvey

Culture

One definition of "culture" is that it is the behavior and beliefs (both conscious and unconscious) of a particular group. Music, cooking, literature and so forth are expressions of culture and are not the actual culture. The groups that are referred to most frequently as having a culture are racial groups (such as Native Americans, Asians, and Blacks); national or geographical groups (such as Chinese, Japanese, French, or West African); or philosophical and religious groups (such as Western culture or Eastern culture).

The culture of the people who were kidnapped from Afrika and enslaved was intentionally distorted and destroyed. Afrikans, especially Ausa (Afrikans from the United States of America) are the original victims of identity theft. We are in the process of relearning and reclaiming the best of Afrikan culture and marrying it to the best of Ausa culture that was necessary for us to create for our survival. As this process continues, it is interesting how similar these two cultures are which gives more credence to the fact that our culture is carried in our DNA.

Research the work of Dr. Edwin Nichols and Dr. Linda James Myers and you will find excellent discussions of culture and comparisons of all its aspects, such as axiology and epistemology, among Afrikans, Europeans, Asians and others. I strongly urge the reader to research, evaluate and study their work. A brief discussion of their work is included in Chapter 7 on Cheikh Anta Diop's Two Cradle Theory.

All people see the world from a centered position that takes into account their particular history and culture, whether or not they realize it. Ideally, there is tolerance and even understanding of other worldviews, but recognition of and adherence to one's own worldview is of paramount importance. Almost all people who see themselves as white or European have a worldview that is frequently called Western civilization which is frequently synonymous with Christian. Historically, they have attempted to universalize their worldview, often to the exclusion and detriment of others. As we, people of Afrikan origin, relearn our identity, we need to do it in a positive manner that reflects who we truly are and not what others say we are.

We are in a culture war whether we realize it or not. As Baba Asa Hilliard told Professor James Small, unless we win the culture war, economics and politics will not matter. In order to win, we must regain control over our education and the socialization of our children.

Our education has formed our outlook and has been controlled by forces outside of our culture. The works of Asa. G. Hilliard, III, Gloria Boutte, Janice Hale, Django Paris, and Gloria Ladson-Billings provide information on the way that our education has been manipulated and what corrections can be made. The concept of culturally sustaining pedagogy recognizes three approaches. Western education has traditionally embraced *Deficit Approaches*, teaching that all non-western content (history, language and culture) is less valuable than white or European or American. The *Difference Approaches* equate non-western content as equal but the goal is still to encourage the embracing of western content. This Difference Approach is what Diversity and Multiculturalism are about. *Asset/Strength Approaches* see the differences as positive strengths that should not be relinquished even as the student learns the dominant content.

Even if a Black person prefers or adopts white (European), Asian, or Arab culture, realistically, they can never actually be white, Asian or Arab. At best, they can only be honorary white, honorary Asian or honorary Arab. This puts them in a position to be used and manipulated.

As mentioned above, multiculturalism and perhaps also diversity as used today mean knowing other cultures while keeping European/Western culture in a position of superiority over those other cultures or viewing other cultures from a Eurocentric point of view. These ways of seeing the world make Eurocentric culture the standard. Ideally, these words should mean knowing enough about other cultures so that you can be understanding and tolerant of the differences from your own culture without placing them in positions of superiority or inferiority. This cannot be done effectively unless we understand that we are all part of a culture and know our own culture. Only then can we really, truly appreciate other cultures.

The most frequently misunderstood culture (consciously or unconsciously) is the culture of people of Afrikan origin, especially those who live in areas dominated by another culture, such as Ausa and Afrikans in Europe, South America and Asia. Some who claim to know Afrikan American culture not only have wrong ideas about the culture but many of these ideas are negative. There are many reasons for this and one of the main reasons is ignorance of our history.

Everyone is part of at least one culture and many people are part of more than one culture. One of these cultures should be the one native to your people. If you do not know or do not feel a part of your own culture, you must be a part of someone else's culture. Afrikan Americans (Afrikans from the United States of America or Ausa) are frequently bi-cultural at least in order to exist. Some may call this "double consciousness" as did W.E.B. Du Bois; others may call it code switching; Afrofuturists may call it shape shifting; and some may even call it being fake; but, almost all Ausa have become adept at responding to the environment they are in at any particular time. The purpose of this code-switching/shape shifting is almost always to make white people feel comfortable. Unfortunately, too many people will "act the fool" in an attempt to not be "fake," as if acting foolish is their true culture.

Culture (including what is known as "pop culture") influences morality. While it is not the intent of this book to attempt to define, legislate or critique morality, there are some ongoing events that need to be closely examined.

The hip-hop culture started out as a youthful reflection of the reality as seen and experienced by the artists. It was frequently called "conscious rap." Originally, it was based in the gritty reality of the inner cities. At some point, in my opinion, it was hi-jacked by a way of thinking that was based in disrespect and materialism. Every generation rebels against the previous generation in some way but the rebellion has never been based in more disrespectful and vulgar rhetoric than it is in much of what is defined today as hip-hop. Frantz Fanon's words seem especially appropriate here: "Each generation must, out of relative obscurity, discover its mission, fulfill it or betray it." That mission has been usurped by outsiders with unlimited financial resources who care nothing about Afrikan people. I would also add that they intend to do us damage.

Even fictional TV and movie heroes and heroines are too often adrenalin addled, ruggedly individualistic, sociopathic criminals or the wretched (ratchet), self-hating, disrespectful, shameless participants in so-called reality shows. We should always be cognizant of the fact that, with our actions, we are influencing future generations. If this influence is hi-jacked and directed in negative directions (as they appear to be), our future as a people is grim. Again, to quote Frantz Fanon, "The oppressed will always believe the worst about themselves."

History

History is a chronological record of past events often including an explanation or commentary of those events, especially as it pertains to one's culture. It is the branch of knowledge that records and analyzes past events.

Knowledge of history and culture is more than just knowing a bunch of dates and events and biographies. As my brother, Joe Benton, has said, it is a study of the achievements rather than just the achievers. It is knowing what your Ancestors did to influence the course of events of their time and how this affects you today. Knowing history means also knowing enough about the past so that you can influence the future. History must be studied to fully understand culture. From there, traditions are created.

Too frequently, history is taught as a disjointed procession of random events and lives (biography). As a result, the true significance of these experiences is lost. This may be at the heart of what today's youth experience. As their elders we have failed them by not emphasizing the repetitiveness and cause/result aspect of history. The situation of Ausa people today has not been caused by yesterday's events or even by those in the last generation. Our situation has endured since Europeans and their American kinsmen interrupted our Ancestors' daily lives.

Often, we hear we have been civilized by our experiences in slavery and colonization. This logic epitomizes rationalization. European civilizations were able to progress naturally (although there are many who feel that many European-descendant nations are still not truly civilized but only technologically advanced, without the essence of true civility). Those who followed the television series *Star Trek* will remember that the "prime directive" was not to interfere in the development of civilizations that were less technologically advanced. Although there is ample evidence that Afrika was not as technologically backwards as claims have been made, it is safe to say that Afrika was light years ahead of Europe and America in ethics, morals and human relationships.

Everyone should be an expert in their own history and not just depend on someone else to teach them. It should also be understood that this information is not easy to obtain; it requires time and study. However, if you do not know yourself, you can be told almost anything and not truly know whether what you are told is true or false. Many Afrikans have written Afrikan and Diasporan history. Studying Afrikan, Ausa and Afrikan Diasporan history helps us to avoid the mistakes of the past, helps to set the record straight and helps us to understand the world. It is important to study with someone who does not repeat the same story (his-story) given to them by our oppressors.

THE AUSA

The history of the Ausa did not begin with slavery. It began in Africa many thousands of years ago, before any other group of people can trace their history. This is a fact that has been camouflaged and hidden away.

While it is true that all peoples experience significant highs (zeniths) during the course of their history, it is also true that significant lows (nadirs) also occur. One mark of the greatness of a people on the world stage is how willing and effective they are in fighting to regain the zenith while living in the nadir.

The enslavement, colonization and degradation of Ausa was systematic, awfully efficient and tragically effective. Trees that have grown from seeds planted during this time are still bearing fruit, even in today's world.

Since the first Afrikans were kidnapped, enslaved and brought to America, "The Land of the Free," one recurrent discussion has been the method of liberation. Our brilliant ancestor, Dr. Jacob H. Carruthers (Baba Jedi or "Jake from Chicago"), called this "Black talk and the white question." One school of thought was that of "moral suasion." Later called "religious appeal" and "nonviolence," the proponents of this approach believed that the enslavers could be positively influenced by highlighting the immoral aspects of "The Peculiar Institution" of slavery. They felt that the enslaver's consciences would be pricked and they would repent of their evil ways.

Even within the ranks of this approach, "moral suasionists" of Afrikan origin were frequently integrationists, accomodationists, apologists and assimilationists who felt that America was one society and that all people could share in its "greatness." In other words, they wanted to rid themselves of their Afrikanity and become an abstract entity called "American," which was essentially a race-less and a-cultural being. On the other hand, white "moral suasionists" (often called "abolitionists") frequently had anti-slavery views but were openly white supremacists. They were against slavery, sometimes for moral reasons, just as today some people champion animal rights. More often, I believe, they were against slavery for political reasons, that is, what slavery was doing to destroy the new country.

The other school of thought held that Afrikan Liberation should be achieved by any means necessary, including violence if needed. Since the nineteenth century these individuals have always been denounced as crazy and impractical.

Interestingly, one change that has occurred in that dialogue since the early days of this nation is that our self-identification has changed. Until fairly recently, there was no argument as to the fact that we are Afrikan people. Even those who were the result of interracial relationships usually did not hesitate to identify themselves as Afrikan (or Black), even though in some cases, they were made to feel superior because of their "white" blood. Now, it seems many people with Afrikan ancestry appear to be running away from their Afrikanity towards identities that frequently do not welcome them.

Agnotology is the study of culturally induced ignorance. The fact that many Ausa have no or little knowledge of themselves or their history is a monument to the success of the application of Agnotology. Afrikans and Ausa have other conditions related to Agnotology. The Dunning Kruger Effect is a bias in which people of low ability feel superior to others, judging their own ability as greater than it really is. A corollary would be those Ausa who think they know their history but really don't.

Other Ausa suffer from the Stockholm Syndrome, a condition that causes individuals to develop a psychological allegiance with their oppressors. This syndrome is closely related to cognitive dissonance (holding fast to a core belief even when evidence is presented that works against that belief) and frequently gives way to ultracrepidarianism (giving opinions about things that you know nothing about). These entities give rise to the practice of gaslighting, which is psychological manipulation that causes people to doubt their own worth and beliefs.

*****

WHAT IS IN THE BOOK?

This book is a collection of some of my interests over the past 30-plus years. Much of the information is geared towards South Carolina youth because South Carolina is my home and where most of my teaching has occurred. However, most of this information can be used generally, as much of it is intended to be an introduction to the topic and not an exhaustive treatise. References are given at the end of each chapter to be used for further study.

Bibliography

The initial idea for the bibliography came as a result of inspiration from our esteemed Ancestor, one of my most respected *Jegnoch* (see description in Chapter 17, No More Mentors), and someone I am proud to have called a friend, Dr. Asa G. Hilliard, III, who, many years ago, compiled an annotated 300-page bibliography. Later, whenever I spoke to any group, I was (and still am) asked to provide references and reading suggestions. *The Sankofa University* was put together to provide a starting point of study for people of Afrikan origin. It is important to note that, as Baba Asa has said, we must take the time and expend the effort to study. I have read or used most of the books listed as reference for my essays, lectures or projects. The ones that I have not read were recommended by people whose opinions I respect.

YouTube Lectures

YouTube lectures are suggested in *The Sankofa University* but it should be understood that each of those lecturers studied many books and worked hard for their knowledge. We should all have a basic amount of knowledge about ourselves and our Ancestors that is not based just on hearsay. Every teacher I have had has challenged me to not just accept information from them but to do my research to make sure they are correct. If a lecturer/teacher is not willing to be checked and/or questioned or give references, then something is wrong with them. We should also try not to take "short cuts" to knowledge. Do not become a "YouTube scholar," using only YouTube as a source of information. You must read!!

Black History Factsheet

I created the Black History Factsheet for a group of students for Black History Month. It was inspired by my close friend and comrade and now Ancestor, Listervelt Middleton, who had done something similar to advertise his seminal public television program *For The People.* Incidentally, I recommend this YouTube program for study also. Each year the factsheet grew; this chapter is its current iteration. References are given and the reader is encouraged to check each fact.

Study Groups

The idea for study groups blossomed with my association with ASCAC (The Association for the Study of Classical African Civilizations), an international umbrella organization of study groups. We had already started a study group in Columbia, SC, that we named the African American Resource Institute (AARI) before we became aware of ASCAC. As previously mentioned, Listervelt Middleton made us aware of ASCAC after he had returned from a trip to Kemet (Egypt) with ASCAC in 1984 which included almost 1000 Ausa.

With Listervelt's encouragement, Dr. H. Randolph Scott (Maa Kheru) and I, representing AARI-SC, attended an ASCAC Southern Region conference in Fort Lauderdale, Florida. We were impressed and became members. We had become aware of many of the scholars involved in ASCAC thorough Listervelt's involvement with Brother Bill Jones and his wife Sister Kefa Nepthys who were organizers of a lecture series in Harlem called the First World Alliance. All this is being stated to emphasize that a study group is an ideal way to learn and that we must communicate and network with each other for the greater good of all people of Afrikan ancestry.

Quotations

A small number of quotations that the author felt are useful are also included. The idea is to emphasize the importance of using the work of others for inspiration, education and illumination.

Symbols

Symbols are important although their importance is sometimes misunderstood. Hopefully, Chapter 9 on symbols will appeal to our youth and they will stop adopting and using symbols from alien cultures and understand the bottomless well of Afrikan Deep Thought, as taught to us by Dr. Jacob Carruthers and Afrikan culture and its symbols.

The Maafa

The Maafa factsheet hopes to introduce the reader to the Maafa. Dr. Marimba Ani first used this Afrikan concept to describe what has happened to Afrikan people since Kemet was invaded after the 25th dynasty, what our Esteemed Ancestor, Dr. John Henrik Clarke, called Afrika's last walk in the sun.

Biographies

Chapter 23 includes biographies, mostly of men. The author and two of his "brothers from another mother" – Baba Derrick Jackson and Nana Joe Benton – developed a Rites of Passage Program for boys and these biographies were written to illustrate greatness in Black men who are not taught about in school. The chapter also includes lists of men, women and events/organizations that can be used as a basis for research and study. A group of questions this writer feels should be considered with the utmost urgency follows these lists. Hopefully, this work will help answer these questions or guide the reader to resources that will answer these questions.

Context and Frameworks

Chapters 7 and 8 deal with context and frameworks for Pan-Afrikanism. Diop's Two Cradle Theory and Nichol's Philosophical Aspects of Cultural Differences are extremely useful in visualizing reality. Neely Fuller's Nine Areas of Human Activity help create an organizational structure for where we need to be.

Race and Culture

The concept of race is currently in flux because of the newly accessible DNA tests. Culture rather than race has been emphasized although we have not discarded race. In fact, science (or pseudoscience) has been used for generations to inferiorize and demonize people of Afrikan origin. A brief discussion of race and scientific racism is included in order to expose readers to information they do not usually encounter. This discussion is followed by a brief introduction to the whole idea of *blackface*, a topic that has been in the news quite a bit lately.

Later, Chapter 18 explores the Afrikan origin of medical science. My good friend and teacher, Dr. Charles Finch, one of the true living geniuses of our time, introduced this topic to me.

Names

Names are important to Afrikan people and often are given to describe the qualities desired in the person or to illustrate the qualities of an Ancestor. Afrikan people in America have had an almost cyclical relationship with the names that we call ourselves. In our Kemetic Temple, Krst Universal Temple, we have chosen to call ourselves Ausa (tribe or ethnic group). This is "short" for "Afrikans from the United States of America." Ausa is used interchangeably in this book with Black and Afrikan American.

Greeks

The author belongs to several Greek letter organizations and has been frequently asked, "Are you Greek?" The reply is, "No, I'm Afrikan but I belong to a Greek letter organization." This is important because we must know our history so that we can reclaim it and not give others credit for what our Ancestors created and achieved. We provide a framework for a way that Greek letter organizations can aid in the re-ascension of Ausa. This framework was an idea spawned from conversations that the author had had with the brilliant Ancestor, Dr. Ophie Franklin. We had planned a co-authored publication but that never came to fruition.

Reparations

The idea of Reparations is as old as injustice. That some people vehemently oppose Reparations for Afrikan people is not surprising; however, it is important to hold an honest general discussion. This writer authored a pamphlet in the early 2000s entitled *Reparations: Quick and Concise Considerations: Brief, Topical, No-Frills Discussions of Aspects of Reparations, The Maafa, Racism/White Supremacy and White Privilege with References.* It was presented but refused for publication and, at that time, the writer was not in a position to self-publish. The Columba (SC) chapter of the Association for the Study of Classical African Civilizations (ASCAC) sponsored a conference at Benedict College in Columbia, SC, on Reparations in the late 1990s and ASCAC had planned another conference at Benedict for the weekend of September 14, 2001. The events of September 11 effectively cancelled those plans.

Chapter 21 on Reparations contains several points made in that work. Dr. William A. Darity, Jr., of Duke University and Dr. David Swinton, former president of Benedict College in Columbia, have eloquently pointed out the economic bases for Reparations but there are other damages that should be repaired. The chapter attempts to introduce the general argument and multiple references are suggested. Despite the many attempts by right wing organizations to infiltrate and sidetrack the movement, Afrikan people all over the world were damaged by white supremacy and there should not be any attempt to "cherry-pick" who should benefit from reparations. This attempt by organizations and individuals is a direct attack on the concept of Pan Afrikanism, which is the only way that people of Afrikan origin worldwide will shake off the shackles of the white supremacy doctrine.

Twi Language and Customs

When the author made his first trip to Ghana, West Afrika (with Drs. Leonard and Rosalind Jeffries and Professor James Small), he and several others in Columbia who made the trip were given lessons on the Twi language by Professor Kwame Osei-Wusu. Nana Kwame, a native of Ghana, is an Elder in the Columbia Ausa and Ghanaian communities and at Krst Universal Temple. Notes taken during those sessions are included in this volume. Many thanks are due to Nana Kwame for his guidance and availability for corrections to the chapter. Hopefully, this information will prove to be useful to the reader.

This book is offered in the spirit of Beason's *Why We Lose* and Browder's *From the Browder File*. It does not claim to be a complete answer to the problems of Afrikan people or an academic treatise, but it does intend to create, stimulate and continue a discussion among people of Afrikan origin all over the world. Ideally, it will stimulate a desire to do further research and further enlighten Afrikan people worldwide.

It is my desire that this effort will be a major contribution to the intergenerational transmission of knowledge and wisdom. Hopefully, the information that follows will be enjoyable as well as informative.

CHAPTER 2

Black History Factsheet

The facts that follow are interesting bits of African and Ausa history that might be enjoyed and might, hopefully, stimulate the desire to know more.

Did You Know That...

1. Ludwig van Beethoven and his teacher Joseph Hayden have both been described as mulatto?
2. The Ganges River, the sacred river of India, is named after an Ethiopian king?
3. Afrikans had lived and traded in America for about 2000 years before Columbus arrived in the "New World"?
4. France has had at least six Black Cabinet Ministers?
5. There have been at least three Black Popes: Victor (189-199 A.D.), Melchiades (311-312 A.D.), and St. Gelasius (496 A.D.)?
6. The Celestial Saint of Germany is Maurice, an unmixed Afrikan?
7. In 1670, Virginia passed a law forbidding Blacks from buying white people and Louisiana passed a similar law in 1818?
8. The Rock of Gibraltar, a symbol of stability, is named after a Black man? The word "Gibraltar" is a corruption of "Gebel-Tarik" or "The Mountain of Tarik." Tarik was the Moorish general who conquered the Iberian Peninsula (Spain and Portugal) in 711 A.D.
9. The first two Americans to be decorated by France in the first "World War" were Black?
10. The first person killed by John Brown's raiders at Harper's Ferry was a "free" Negro who was running off to warn the white people?

11. Blacks of Seville, Spain, have had a religious procession on the Feast of Corpus Christi since at least 1460 A.D. and have worn white robes and pointed hoods very much like those worn by the Ku Klux Klan, which originated more than 400 years later?
12. The first Black person to be admitted to the bar in America was Macon B. Allen (Worcester, MA, 1845)?
13. John Roy Lynch was the first Black person to preside over a National political gathering (Republican Convention, 1884)?
14. Jane Bolin was the first Black female judge in the United States?
15. Alcorn College in Mississippi was the first Black land grant college in the United States?
16. W.E.B. Du Bois was the first Black person to earn a Ph.D. at Harvard College?
17. Afrikan Americans became full citizens of the U.S. on July 28, 1868?
18. In 1739 in South Carolina, there were at least three revolts of enslaved Afrikans resulting in known deaths of 51 whites and many more Blacks?
19. Benjamin Banneker built a wooden clock in 1754, the first of its kind in America, that kept accurate time for more than twenty years?
20. A South Carolina law in 1834 prohibited the education of any Black child (enslaved or "free")?
21. In 1841, South Carolina forbade Black and white mill hands from looking out the same window?
22. John Rock was the first Black attorney admitted to practice before the U.S. Supreme Court in 1865?
23. The first Kentucky Derby (held in 1875) was won by a Black jockey, Oliver Lewis, riding a horse named Aristides?
24. In 1920, 60% of South Carolina's population was Afrikan American?
25. Martin Delany was the first Black army officer, a physician, a newspaperman, a writer, the "Father" of Black Nationalist theory, and lived in Charleston, SC, after the Civil War?

26. Henry McNeal Turner, a South Carolina native, was an African Methodist Episcopal bishop who was the first Black army chaplain, an elected member of the Georgia state legislature and believed that all Afrikan Americans needed to move back to Afrika in order to realize their full potential?
27. Ida B. Wells Barnett was a newspaperwoman who continued to publicize the lynchings of Black men despite having been thrown off a moving train, having her life threatened constantly, and barely escaping death when her offices were invaded by an angry mob and all her equipment destroyed?
28. Mary Church Terrell was an anti-segregation activist who was a charter member of the National Association of Colored Women, an organizer of the Delta Sigma Theta Sorority and a provocative speaker who spoke three languages? Her message was always the same: equal rights for women and for Afrikan Americans wherever they may be found.
29. Mary McLeod Bethune, the seventeenth child of South Carolina sharecroppers, not only managed to get an education for herself but organized a college from the Daytona City Dump, Bethune–Cookman University, that is still in existence?
30. Paul Robeson, a multi-genius, was a Phi Beta Kappa honor student; an All-American football player who also played professional football; a law school graduate, an accomplished actor; a concert baritone soloist; and a Pan-Afrikan Nationalist theoretician? He spoke and sang in more than nine languages and was an outspoken advocate in asking that Afrikan Americans know and love their Afrikan heritage.
31. An enslaved Afrikan named Cesar was freed by the General Assembly of South Carolina in the 1750s because he discovered a cure for rattlesnake bite?
32. Matilda Arabelle Evans, M.D. was the first Black female physician in Columbia, South Carolina, and founded at least two hospitals, starting in 1901? Born in Aiken, SC, she was the first SC native female physician to practice in SC.

33. The summer of 1919 was called the "Red Summer"; gangs of whites attacked, injured and killed thousands of Ausa and destroyed millions of dollars' worth of property? At least 83 Afrikan Americans were lynched, even in Northern cities like New York City and Washington, DC. These were the original race riots. Thousands of Afrikan Americans were lynched and killed all over the country (north and south, urban and rural) during the period from 1889 through 1922 and the government did not want to officially deal with the problem despite efforts by organizations like the NAACP and individuals like Ida B. Wells Barnett. Fortunately, the Ausa frequently fought back.
34. Cornrowing hair is an ancient Afrikan hairstyle that started in the Afrikan nation of Kemet (Egypt)? It represents the symmetry and beauty of Afrikan women and expressed communication with the universe. Cornrowing was a symbol of status and maturity.
35. Every race or group has its own particular holy days? Six days that should be celebrated by African Americans (without asking permission) are January 15 (Dr. Martin Luther King's birthday), May 19 (Malcolm X's birthday), July 16 (Ida B. Wells Barnett's birthday), August 17 (Marcus Garvey's birthday), and October 6 (Fannie Lou Hamer's birthday). Kwanzaa should be celebrated (December 26-january 1) and the principles of Kwanzaa (the Nguzo Saba) internalized all year long. We may need to create a date for Harriet Tubman's birthday because it is not known.
36. Marcus Garvey founded the Universal Negro Improvement Association (UNIA) in the 1912 which had more than four million members and more than six million followers, most of whom lived in the Southern United States? It was the largest mass movement of Afrikan Americans ever. He also founded a newspaper, *The Negro World*, a steamship corporation, the Black Star Line, and a combination of stores and service enterprises. He organized the African Communities League, was one of the first people to proclaim that "Black is Beautiful" and developed the Red, Black and

Green Liberation Flag. He was also a poet and a brilliant orator. His most famous quotes are, "Africa for the Africans" and "Up you mighty race, you can accomplish what you will."

37. Despite what some history books, historians, television shows, and movies would have the public to believe, most of the enslaved Africans in America never accepted their enslavement and constantly rebelled through different methods, including armed resistance? They also pretended to be stupid and not understand instructions so as to slow down work, pretend to be sick, destroy tools, run away to freedom, and put poison into the food of whites.
38. Nzinga, an Angolan queen, fought so successfully for so long (more than 40 years) against slave traders in her kingdom that slavery could not be fully established in her area until her death on December 17, 1663 at the age of almost 80 years?
39. Many Afrikans were kidnapped from the West Afrikan empire of Songhay, where surgeons in the 1100s were advanced enough to be able to remove a cataract from the human eye, long before surgery in Europe or Asia reached that degree of advancement?
40. Tutmoses III, a Kemetic (ancient Egyptian) Pharaoh, who had dark skin, a wide nose, thick lips, and tightly curled (kinky) hair ruled the entire known world during his lifetime in about 1500 B.C., as did many of his Ancestors and descendants?
41. The Haitian Revolution marked the only time in the history of the western hemisphere when enslaved Afrikans unified and militarily defeated three of Europe's greatest armies, including the army of Napoleon Bonaparte?
42. In what is now Brazil, Palmares, a *quilombo* (a community of escaped fugitive enslaved Afrikans) having a population of up to 30,000 men, women, children and Elders, was the largest and most successful of ten quilombos? It lasted almost the entire seventeenth century, fighting off at least fifteen Portuguese invasions before suffering defeat by an invasion force of more than 3600 soldiers after a two-year siege.

43. The first Afrikan American newspaper was *Freedom's Journal,* which was published by John Russwurm in 1872 in New York City?
44. David Walker, a "free" Afrikan American who moved from North Carolina to Boston, wrote, published and distributed an anti-slavery pamphlet, *Appeal to the Colored People of the World* in 1829? It caused such a furor that the Georgia Legislature offered a reward for him ($10,000 alive, $1,000 dead). His book went into its second printing in 1830 before he died under mysterious circumstances. The book is still available at bookstores.
45. Richard T. Greener was the first Black undergraduate from Harvard and the first Black faculty member of South Carolina College, which is now the University of South Carolina?

*****

References

Adams, Russell L. *Great Negroes: Past and Present.* Chicago: Afro-Am Publishing Company, Inc., 1984.

Clarke, John Henrik. Nzingha, The Warrior Queen. *Journal of African Civilizations,* Volume 9, December 1987, pp. 364-369.

Kunjufu, Jawanza. Lessons from History: *A Celebration In Blackness.* Chicago: African American Images, 1987.

McKissack, Patricia C. and Frederick L. McKissack. *Rebels Against Slavery: American Slave Revolts.* NY: Scholastic, Inc., 1996.

Ploski, Harry A. and James Williams. The Negro Almanac: A Reference *Work on the Afro-American.* NY: John Wiley and Sons, 1983.

Rogers, Joel A. 100 Amazing Facts About the Negro with Complete Proof. St. Petersburg: Helga M. Rogers, 1957.

Trent, Lucia. Zumbi and the Republic of Os Palmatres. *Phylon: The Atlanta University Quarterly Review of Race and Culture.* Volume XIV, 1953, pp. 62-70.

White, Morgan, Jr. *The Black Heritage Book of Trivia.* Boston: Quinlan Press, Inc., 1985.

ALSO: UrbanIntellectuals.com has published a series of Black history flashcards and trivia cards that are excellent and highly recommended for children as well as adults.

CHAPTER 3

AFRIKAN-CENTERED STUDY GROUPS

WHY A STUDY GROUP?

There has been an intentional effort over the last 300 years not only to strip people of Afrikan origin of all knowledge of who they are but also to remove the desire for them to *want* to know who they are. Our history has been kept from us intentionally, and what little has gotten through frequently has been altered. Our esteemed Ancestor teacher, Dr. John Henrik Clarke, said that a consciously historic people cannot be truly enslaved. Many of our Ancestors' accomplishments have been claimed by other people and taught to us as their history. After all, people who do not know their history make excellent slaves, regardless of the type of slavery or the time period (eighteenth century or 21st century).

Many people of Afrikan descent in America, the Ausa people, have realized that they do not know as much about their history as they would like to know or need to know. They are beginning to understand that not only have they been misled but they are Afrikan people with a history that starts thousands of years before our savage kidnapping and enslavement in the Hells of North, Central and South America and the Caribbean (not to mention the so-called "Middle East" and Europe). Various aspects of our history have been well documented by scholars of Afrikan descent who tell our story from our point of view. This method of telling our story from our point of view has been called Afrikancentrism. Studying with people who are like you enhances the learning process. Discussions can point out aspects of the material that you did not consider. The repetition of good analysis aids in the retention of information.

Why Afrikan-centered?

As mentioned previously, all people see the world from a centered position that takes into account their particular history and culture. As we learn our true identity, we need to do it in a positive manner that reflects who we are and who we were. Afrikancentrism is the most promising and profound threat to white supremacy in the last 200 years. The latest incarnation of this philosophy hit the world by surprise. It was not new, but this version had been born of the college rebellions of the 1960s and stimulated by the curiosity of young scholars. They demanded the creation of Black studies programs, and these entities were brought to maturity by dozens of study groups all over the world comprised of "regular" and "ordinary" people.

It was nurtured and guided by the tireless research of several generations of scholars, most recently led by Dr. John Henrik Clarke, Dr. Josef ben-Jochannon, Dr. Adelaide Sanford, Dr. George G.M. James, Dr. Cheikh Anta Diop, Dr. Chancellor Williams, Professor John G. Jackson, Dr. Asa Hilliard, Dr. Wade Nobles, Drs. Leonard and Rosalind Jeffries, Dr. Theophile Obenga, Dr. Molefi Asante, Professor Anthony Browder, Professor William Leo Hansberry, and most recently Dr. Greg Kimathi Carr, Dr. Valethia Watkins-Beatty, Dr. Mario Beatty, Dr. Bobby Donaldson, Dr. Gloria Boutte, Dr. George Johnson, and Dr. Catherine Adams, among others.

Western Culture's Response to Afrikan Centrism?

Afrikan-centered scholars have endured many individual attacks in an attempt to discredit their scholarship. These attacks have failed; other attacks have attempted to identify and boost Black supporters of white supremacy, especially in academia but also in "pop" culture. Attackers have been spread out all over the world but several of the most celebrated individuals were concentrated in one ivory tower of Gottengen-style "classical education" (see Chapter Four of *Black Athena* by Martin Bernal).

Called by many names, including "Black intellectuals," "Black conservatives" and "The Dream Team," their assignments included attempts at taking the attention of Afrikan people away from the Afrikan-centered, Pan-Afrikan Nationalist "upstarts." Although several of these "intellectuals" may be misguided individuals with good intent, many are said to be obnoxiously dogmatic and have adapted well to the role of "attack dog" or "sheep dog" (look up Asa Hilliard's use of this term). They are playing a long-term game in which they plan eventually to capture the minds of the masses of Afrikan people. They constitute a chess move designed to have a replacement ready when (if) Afrikancentrism has been discredited. Their advantage: they have untold millions of dollars supporting them.

One group of scholars posit that Ausa are not culturally related to Afrikans and that our culture started when our Ancestors adapted to the horrendous system of slavery. This theory is called Afro-Pessimism. While I must admit that I am not thoroughly familiar with this theory, it seems it goes against the principle of Pan-Afrikanism (in the service of white dominion). Also, if information that we are getting from the relatively new science of Epigenetics is to be considered, what these Afro-Pessimists posit can be considered an abnormal adjustment to a negative environment.

This intellectual warfare, as described by Dr. Jacob Carruthers in his book, *Intellectual Warfare*) is at least two-pronged. First prong of attack: Charismatic individuals of Afrikan origin have been pressed into traitorous service against their people. In the true spirit of "divide and conquer," they travel throughout the country and exploit and capitalize on the paranoia in the Afrikan community. They widen preexisting gulfs in our community and create new divisions among Afrikan people. They use their charisma in the service of white supremacy against the interests of Afrikan people and spread propaganda designed to heighten mistrust and paranoia.

Second prong of the current attack: Gives attention and credibility to crackpots, pseudo-scholars and misinformed people and allows them to represent the Afrikan-centered movement. Some of the ridiculous claims many of these individuals have made have been publicized, thus "turning off" many Afrikans who otherwise would have been interested in learning more about themselves and their situations. Occasionally, this places serious Afrikan-centered scholars in a bad light when they are mentioned in the same breath with some of these crackpots.

Many of these crackpots are not simply misguided people with a "different" way of seeing things. Many have their own agendas and use ("pimp") our history and culture — and often our spirituality — to achieve these agendas. Frequently, they ask their audiences to "believe" rather than to "know" and offer fantastic sounding "facts" as proof, and they prey on students and youth. They attempt to control our thinking, our labor and our money and, ultimately, because of the divisions they create, they work in the service of white supremacy. Many men use the allure of our history and culture to attract and exploit women. Many African-centered people often greet each other with the ancient Kemetic greeting, Hotep, which means peace, and these exploiters also use that term, generating a negative reaction to anyone who uses that term. In fact, there is a growing stigma to being called a "Hotep brother" (the term hotep will be discussed later in Chapter 9 on symbols).

Unfortunately, some of these exploiters have become prominent which gives further credence to the negative opinions, causing many people to question the well-documented truths of the history of people of Afrikan origin. One way to tell who these pseudo-scholars are is when they disrespect the words and works of their intellectual elders and ancestors. To be truly Afrikan-centered is to respect your elders and teachers, regardless of whether you agree with them 100%.

As a result of these attacks, the Ausa public is bombarded with many voices. This is like the biblical story of the Tower of Babel, except much of the information that the Ausa community is exposed to is mere babble. The latest of these attacks on Pan-Afrikanism and Afrikan-centered thought is ADOS (African Descendants of Slaves), an organization supported by racist right wing groups that seeks to sow seeds of separation between different groups of the Afrikan Diaspora in the United States. I would recommend that everyone interested in Reparations read the document by Jessica Ann Mitchell Aiwuyor entitled, *Understanding ADOS: The Movement to Hijack Black Identity and Weaken Black Unity in America.* It can be Googled and should be read.

If these attacks are successful, the result will be that the true scholars who have a great deal of information to offer our people will be ignored. This is not an accident and we must not allow it to happen.

Who Needs Afrikan-centered Study Groups?

All persons of Afrikan origin need Afrikan-centered study groups, regardless of nationality/ethnicity (for example, American, Brazilian, Afrikan, Indian, Caribbean, British), religion (Traditional, Christian, Muslim, Hebrew, Buddhist, Hindu) or language.

How to Organize and Sustain a Study Group

1. Start with a small group, less than twenty people if possible.
2. Cultivate a strong central leadership, ideally not just one person, and without someone dominating discussion and decision-making.
3. Select a regular meeting place, preferably not someone's home. Several internet platforms are available that can widen the reach of study groups.
4. Create regular rituals and formal activities during meetings, for example, Pledge and/or Libation to start the session and Harambee to complete it.
5. Establish the seriousness of study and distinguish the group from a discussion group (may designate a time during the meeting for discussion of other topics).
6. Start on time and end on time.
7. Institutionalize the existence of the group. If only two people come, have the session. People will come to know that someone will be having study group, no matter what.

8. Try to arrange childcare so that children will not be distractions.
9. Use a variety of means to study subjects: books, articles, slide and PowerPoint presentations, lectures, films, documentaries, audio tapes, seminars, and trips (to museums, conferences).
10. Everyone should lead the discussion at some time.
11. Consider affiliation with a national organization such as the Association for the Study of Classical African Civilizations (ASCAC), which is an international umbrella of study groups found throughout the United States as well as some locations in Europe, the Caribbean, Afrika and Latin America and is an excellent reservoir for scholars.

What to Study?

Begin the study with general discussions of the history and culture of Afrika, starting with and intentionally concentrating on its classical civilization, Kemet (Ancient Egypt). The history and culture of the Diaspora and the history and culture of Europeans, Arabs and Asians and their impact on us is also important. Afrikan people are a spiritual people and seek knowledge about our spirituality. It is because of this fact that many of the charlatans who want to confuse us and prevent us from learning the truth about ourselves find success. They cloak their self-serving messages in spiritual-sounding garments to attract sincere and curious people into their webs of intellectual deceit.

Knowing our history and culture is the best way of knowing our true spirituality. Later, you will find a list of suggested books. If at all possible, consider uniting the group with other like-minded groups to create events such as lecture series, inviting the scholars indicated below, and cultural celebrations, such as Kwanzaa, Juneteenth, and the birthdays of Malcolm X on May 19, Fannie Lou Hamer on October 6, Ida B. Wells Barnett on July 16 and Marcus Garvey on August 17. Unfortunately, we do not have a date of birth for Harriet Tubman so a date can be assigned. She certainly deserves celebrating. Collectively, the group can digest recorded lectures. We suggest also a movie night for watching, discussing and analyzing past and current films.

What Writers and Scholars are Best to Read First?

The name Sankofa comes from a Ghanaian Adinkra symbol that translates literally to "Go back and fetch it." This means that in order to move forward constructively and correctly, we must know our past and use it to frame our future. A more detailed discussion of this concept can be found in Chapter 9 on symbols.

The scholars mentioned below — alive and dead (Ancestors) and their work — make great headway into "Our-story" (not "His-Story"), the HighStory so that we can know what our past is about. Most of their names are listed below and a list of good "start-up" books is given later. The Ancestors, those who have passed away, are denoted by the letter (A) after their names and this work is also dedicated to them.

Any work by any scholar on this list is worth reading. By no means is it suggested that these are the only scholars who are worth reading but these individuals constitute a necessary baseline and starting point. It is believed that their works should be thoroughly understood before branching out to other writers. True knowledge of self and the pride that results works most effectively against white supremacy and awakens the sleeping giant. The books listed below are recommended as the first books to be studied. The chapters after the bibliography (Chapter 4) also have books listed as references.

Many of these scholars' lectures can be seen on YouTube. Although there are many lecturers available on YouTube, I believe that the following scholars' lectures and/or interviews should be viewed first to obtain a firm baseline of information. Any structure under construction must have a firm foundation. The information given by these scholars is vital, like learning the ABCs is vital to reading.

Before overwhelming the reader with a multitude of books, I consider the ones listed below to be the first books to be consumed and digested:

Suggested Reading: First Books

Ani, Marimba. *Let the Circle be Unbroken: The Implication of African Spirituality in the Diaspora.* Trenton: Red Sea Press, 1994.

Bennett, Lerone. *Before the Mayflower: A History of Black America.* NY: Penguin Books, 1984.

Browder, Anthony. *Exploding the Myths, Volume 1, Nile Valley Contributions to Civilization.* Washington: The Institute of Karmic Guidance, 1992.

Browder, Anthony T. *From the Browder File: 22 Essays on the African American Experience.* Washington, DC: The Institute of Karmic Guidance, 1989.

Carruthers, Jacob. Intellectual Warfare. Chicago: Third World Press, 1999.

Diop, Cheikh Anta. *The African Origin of Civilization: Myth or Reality.* Westport, CT: Lawrence Hill and Company, 1974.

Finch, Charles S. III. *Echoes of the Old Darkland: Themes From the African Eden.* Decatur, GA: Khenti, Inc., 1991.

Hilliard, Asa G. III. *Sba: The Reawakening of the African Mind. Gainesville*: Makare Publishing Co., 1997.

Jackson, John G. *Introduction to African Civilizations.* The Citadel Press, 1970.

James, George G. M. *Stolen Legacy.* San Francisco: Julian Richardson Associates Publishers, 1976.

Nobles, Wade W. *The Island of Memes: Haiti's Unfinished Revolution.* Baltimore: Black Classics Press, 2015.

Nobles, Wade W. *African Psychology: Toward Its Reclamation, Reascension and Revitalization.* Oakland: Institute for Advanced Study, 1986.

Rogers, Joel A. *Africa's Gift to America.* St. Petersburg: Helga M. Rogers, 1961.

Stuckey, Sterling. *Slave Culture: Nationalist Theory and the Foundations of Black America.* NY: Random House, 1987.

Van Sertima, Ivan. Any of his works

Welsing, Frances Cress. *The Isis Papers.* Chicago: Third World Press, 1991.

Wilkerson, Isabel. *Caste: The Origins of our Discontents.* NY: Random House, 2020.

Williams, Chancellor. *The Destruction of Black Civilization: Great Issues of a Race From 4500 B.C. to 2000 A.D.* Chicago: Third World Press, 1974.

Wilson, Amos N. *The Falsification of African Consciousness: Eurocentric History, Psychology and the Policy of White Supremacy.* NY: African World Infosystems, 199

Winbush, Raymond and Denise Wright. *The Osiris Papers: Reflections on The Life and Writings of Dr. Frances Cress Welsing.* Baltimore: Black Classic Press, 2020.

Woodson, Carter G. *The Miseducation of the Negro.* Washington: Associated Publishers, 1933.

*****

When all the above have been read and digested, the next five books are:

Ani, Marimba. *Yurugu: An African-Centered Critique of European Cultural Thought and Behavior.* Trenton: Africa World Press, 1994.

Boutte, Gloria Swindler. *Educating African American Students: And How Are the Children?* NY: Routledge, 2016.

Diop, Cheikh Anta. *Civilization or Barbarism: An Authentic Anthropology.* Brooklyn: Lawrence Hill Books, 1991.

Kendi, Ibram X. *Stamped from the Beginning: The Definitive History of Racist Ideas in America.* NY: Hachette Book Group, 2016.

Wilson, Amos N. *Blueprint for Black Power: A Moral, Political and Economic Imperative for the Twenty-First Century.* New York: Afrikan World InfoSystems, 1998.

CHAPTER 4

The Sankofa University and Bibliography

The following people are all brilliant individuals who have frequently been ignored by the mainstream. Their contributions to our knowledge of self are priceless. Whether via electronic means, such as YouTube, or in books, magazines or other articles (popular or scholarly), they are worth digesting. Because of their collective efforts, we call them:

The Sankofa University (YouTube) Scholars

Dr. John Henrik Clarke (A)
Dr. Amos Wilson (A)
Dr. Marimba Ani
Dr. Greg Kimathi Carr
Dr. Valethia Watkins
Prof. James Small
Bro. Anthony Browder
Dr. Jacob Carruthers (A)
Dr. Charles Finch
Prof. Ashra Kwesi
For the People with Listervelt Middleton (A)
Dr. Josef Ben-Jochannon (A)
Dr. Asa Hilliard (A)
Dr. Wade Nobles
Dr. Mario Beaty
Dr. Frances Cress Welsing (A)
Dr. Leonard Jeffries
Dr. Rosalind Jeffries
Dr. Ivan Van Sertima (A)
Prof. Runoko Rashidi
Prof. Merira Kwesi
Dr. Bobby Donaldson

The Sankofa University Authors

First Reads, Group I

Dr. Josef Ben-Jochannan (A)	Dr. Lerone Bennett (A)
Prof. Anthony T. Browder	Dr. Kokia Buuseki-Fukiau (A)
Dr. Jacob Carruthers (A)	Dr. John Henrik Clarke (A)
Dr. Cheikh Anta Diop (A)	Dr. W. E. B. Du Bois (A)
Dr. Frantz Fanon (A)	Dr. Charles S. Finch, III
Dr. Asa G. Hilliard, III (A)	Dr. John G. Jackson (A)
Prof. George G. M. James (A)	Dr. Wade Nobles
Dr. Ivan Van Sertima (A)	Prof. George Wells Parker (A)
Bro. Larry Obadele Williams (A)	Prof. Amos Wilson (A)
Dr. Carter G. Woodson (A)	Dr. Samuel Yette (A)
Mr. Hunter Adams	Dr. Hannibal Afrik (A)
Dr. Na'im Akbar	Prof. Kwame Agyei Akoto
Dr. Marimba Ani /Dr. Dona Richards	Dr. Ayi Kwei Armah
Dr. Molefi Asante	Rev. Ishakamusa Barashango (A)
Prof. Mwalimu Baruti	Dr. Ezra Aharone
Dr. Mario Beatty	Bro. Joe Benton
Dr. Edward Wilmot Blyden (A)	Chinweizu
Prof. James E. Brunson	Prof. Carol Barnes
Dr. Greg Kimathi Carr	Bro. Wayne B. Chandler
Mr. Legrand Clegg, Esq.	Dr. Martin Delany (A)
Dr. Bobby Donaldson	Bro. Neely Fuller
Dr. Burnett W. Gallman	Mr. William Leo Hansberry (A)
Ms. Drusilla Dunjee Houston (A)	Baba Derrick Jackson
Dr. Linda James-Myers	Bro. Ezrah Aharone
Dr. Leonard Jeffries	Dr. Rosalind Jeffries
Dr. Kobi Kambon/Joseph Baldwin (A)	Dr. Maulana Karenga
Dr. Richard King (A)	Dr. Zak Kondo

Bro. Haki Madhubuti
Dr. James C. McIntosh
Dr. Charshee C. McIntyre (A)
Dr. Camille Yarbrough
Dr. Ibram X. Kendi
Mr. Linus A. Hoskins
Dr. Edward Nichols
Prof. Runoko Rashidi
Mr. J. A. Rogers (A)
Dr. Edward Scobie
Dr. Sterling Stuckey
Dr. Anderson Thompson
Dr. Valethia Watkins-Beatty
Prof. Vulindlela Wobogo
Dr. Bobby Wright (A)
Dr. Gloria Boutte
Dr. Tony Martin (A)
David Walker (A)
Bro. Listervelt Middleton (A)
Dr. Rayford Logan
Dr. Kwame Nantambu
Dr. Patricia Newton
Dr. Theophile Obenga
Dr. Walter Rodney (A)
Dr. Adelaide Sanford
Prof. James Small
Dr. Oba T'Shaka
Dr. James Turner
Sir Eric Williams (A)
Dr. Conrad Worrill
Dr. C.L.R. James (A)
Dr. Edward Bruce Bynum

The Sankofa University (Organizations and Periodicals)

- Association for the Study of Classical African Civilizations (ASCAC)
- Association of Black Psychologists (ABPsi)
- National Association of Black Social Workers (NABSW)
- Association for the Study of Afro-American Life and History (ASALH)
- The Nation of Islam
- The Republic of New Afrika
- Institute of the Black World
- Institute of the Black World 21st Century

Bibliography

GROUP 1

Akbar, Na'im. *Visions for Black Men.* Nashville: Winston-Derek Publications, Inc., 1991.

Ani, Marimba. *Yurugu: An African-Centered Critique of European Cultural Thought and Behavior.* Trenton: Africa World Press, 1994.

Ani, Marimba. *Let the Circle Be Unbroken: The Implications of African Spirituality in The Diaspora.* Baltimore: Afrikan World Books, 1980.

Banks, Nancy Turner. *AIDS, Opium, Diamonds, and Empire: The Deadly Virus of International Greed.* New York: Universe, Inc., 2010.

Barashango, Ishakamusa. *African People and European Holidays: A Mental Genocide.* Washington, DC: IV Dynasty Publishing Co., 1980.

Baruti, Mwalimu K. Bomani. *Homosexuality and the Effeminization of Afrikan Males.* Atlanta: Akoben House, 2003.

Bay, Mia E., Farah J. Griffin, Martha S. Jones, Martha D. Savage (Editors). *Toward an Intellectual History of Black Women.* Chapel Hill: University of North Carolina Press, 2015.

Ben-Jochannon, Yosef. *Black Man of the Nile and His Family.* Baltimore: Black Classic Press, 1972.

Ben-Jochannon, Yosef. *Africa, Mother of Western Civilization.* Baltimore: Black Classic Press, 1988.

Benton, Joe, Derrick Jackson, Burnett Gallman. *Project Sankofa: A Rites of Passage Program: Philosophy, Theory, and Overview.* Columbia, SC: Our Community Organization, 1998.

Benton, Joe, Tanya Brice, Burnett Kwadwo Gallman, Baba Derrick Jackson. *Should Black Organizations and Institutions Be Afrikancentered?: The Quest for Self-Determination. Joint Ventures,* Columbia, SC, 2014.

Browder, Anthony T. From the Browder File: *22 Essays on the African American Experience.* Washington, DC: The Institute of Karmic Guidance, 1989. **Must read!**

Browder, Anthony T. *From the Browder File, Volume II: Survival Strategies For Africans in America: 13 Steps To Freedom.* Washington, DC: The Institute of Karmic Guidance, 1996.

Browder, Anthony T. *Exploding the Myths, Volume I: Nile Valley Contributions to Civilization.* Washington, DC: The Institute of Karmic Guidance, 1992. **Must-read!**

Carruthers, Jacob H. *Essays in Ancient Egyptian Studies.* Los Angeles: University of Sankore Press, 1984.

Carruthers, Jacob H. *The Irritated Genie: An Essay on the Haitian Revolution.* Chicago: The Kemetic Institute, 1985.

Carruthers, Jacob. *Intellectual Warfare.* Chicago: Third World Press, 1999. **Must-read!**

Clarke, John Henrik. *African People in World History.* Baltimore: Black Classic Press, 1993.

Clarke, John Henrik and Yosef ben-Jochannan. *New Dimensions in African History.* Trenton, NJ: Africa World Press, 1991.

Clarke, John Henrik. *Notes For an African World Revolution: Africans at the Crossroads.* Trenton, NJ: Africa World Press, Inc., 1991. **Must-read!**

Clarke, John Henrik. *Christopher Columbus & the Afrikan Holocaust.* Brooklyn: A & B Books Publishers, 1992.

Clarke, John Henrik (Editor). *Critical Lessons In Slavery and the Slave Trade: Essential Studies and Commentaries On Slavery, In General, and the African Slave Trade, In Particular.* Richmond: Native Sun Publishers, 1996. **Must-read!**

Coates, Ta-Nehisi. *We Were Eight Years in Power: An American Tragedy.* NY: One World Publishing Co., 2017.

Diop, Cheikh Anta. *The African Origin of Civilization: Myth or Reality.* Westport, CT: Lawrence Hill and Company, 1974. **Must-read!**

Fanon, Frantz. *The Wretched of the Earth.* NY: Grove Press, 2005. **Must-read!**

Finch, Charles S. III. *Echoes of the Old Darkland: Themes From the African Eden.* Decatur, GA: Khenti, Inc., 1991. **Must-read!**

Hilliard, Asa G. III, Larry Williams, and Nia Damali. *The Teachings of Ptahhotep: The Oldest Book in the World.* Atlanta: Blackwood Press and Company, 1987.**Must-read!**

Hilliard, Asa G. *The Maroon Within Us: Selected Essays on African American Community Socialization.* Baltimore: Black Classic Press, 1995.

Hilliard, Asa G. III. *SBA: The Reawakening of the African Mind.* Gainesville, FL: Makare Publishing Co., 1997. **Must-read!**

Hilliard, Asa G. III. *African Power: Affirming African Indigenous Socialization in the Face of the Culture Wars.* Gainesville: Makare Publishing Company, 2002. **Must-read!**

Jackson, John G. *Introduction to Black Civilizations.* Secausus, NJ: The Citadel Press, 1970.**Must-read!**

James, George G. M. *Stolen Legacy.* San Francisco: Julian Richardson Associates Publishers, 1976. **Must-read!**

Johnson, J. C. deGraft. *African Glory: The Story of Vanished Negro Civilizations.* Baltimore: Black Classic Press. (Originally published in 1954),1968.

Karenga, Maulana. *Selections From the Husia: Sacred Wisdom of Ancient Egypt.* Los Angeles: Kawaida Publications, 1984. **Must-read!**

Kondo, Zak. *The Black Student's Guide to Positive Education.* Washington, DC: Nubia Press, 1987.

Kunjufu, Jawanza. *Lessons From History: A Celebration in Blackness.* Chicago: African American Images, 1987.

Madhubuti, Haki R. *Enemies: The Clash of Races.* Chicago: Third World Press, 1978.

McIntyre, Charshee C.L. *Criminalizing A Race: Free Blacks During Slavery,* Queens, NY: Kayode Publications, Ltd., 1992.

Nobles, Wade W. *African Psychology: Towards Its Reclamation, Reascension, and Revitalization.* Oakland: Black Family Institute Publication, 1986. **Must-read!**

Nobles, Wade W. *The Island of Memes: Haiti's Unfinished Revolution.* Baltimore: Black Classic Press, 2015.

Obenga, Theophile. *Ancient Egypt and Black Africa: A Student's Handbook For the Study of Ancient Egypt In Philosophy, Linguistics, & Gender Relations.* Chicago: Karnak House, 1992.

Richards, Dona Marimba. *Let the Circle Be Unbroken: The Implications of African Spirituality in the Diaspora.* Trenton, NJ: The Red Sea Press, 1980. **Must-read!**

Rogers, J. A. *Africa's Gift to America.* Helga M. Rogers, 3806 48th Ave South, St. Petersburg, Florida, 1961.

Shujaa, Mwalimu. *Too Much Schooling, Too Little Education: A Paradox of Black Life in White Societies.* Trenton, NJ: Africa World Press, 1998.

Stuckey, Sterling. *Slave Culture: Nationalist Theory and the Foundations of Black America.* New York: Oxford University Press, 1987. **Must-read!**

Van Sertima, Ivan (Editor). *They Came Before Columbus: The African Presence in Ancient America.* New York: Random House, 1976.

Van Sertima, Ivan (Editor). *Blacks in Science: Ancient and Modern.* New Brunswick: Transaction Books, 1986.

Van Sertima, Ivan (Editor). *Nile Valley Civilizations.* New Brunswick: Transaction Books, 1984. **Must-read!**

Van Sertima, Ivan (Editor): *Black Women In Antiquity.* New Brunswick: Transaction Books, 1988. **Must-read!**

Van Sertima, Ivan (Editor). *Egypt Revisited.* New Brunswick: Transaction Books, 1989. **Must-read!**

Van Sertima, Ivan and Rashidi, Runoko (Editors). *African Presence in Early Asia.* New Brunswick: Transaction Books, 1988. **Must-read!**

Van Sertima, Ivan (Editor) (1986): *African Presence in Early Europe.* Transaction Books, New Brunswick. **Must-read!**

Walker, Robin. *When We Ruled: The Ancient and Medioeval History of Black Civilizations.* Baltimore: Black Classic Press, 2011.

Welsing, Frances Cress (1991): *The Isis Papers: The Keys to the Colors.* Third World Press, 7524 South Cottage Grove Avenue, Chicago, IL, 60619. **Must-read!**

Williams, Chancellor. *The Destruction of Black Civilization: Great Issues of a Race From 4500 B.C. to 2000 A.D.* Chicago: Third World Press, 1976. **Must-read!**

Wilson, Amos N. *The Falsification of Afrikan Consciousness: Eurocentric History, Psychiatry and the Politics of White Supremacy.* New York: Afrikan World InfoSystems, 1993. **Must-read!**

Wilson, Amos N. *Blueprint for Black Power: A Moral, Political and Economic Imperative for the Twenty-First Century.* New York: Afrikan World InfoSystems, 1998. **Must-read!**

Woodson, Carter G. *The Mis-Education of the Negro.* Washington, DC: The Associated Publishers, 1933.**Must-read!**

Yette, Samuel F. *The Choice: The Issue of Black Survival in America.* Cottage Books, 1982.

It is important to realize that the preceding works do not even scratch the surface of fulfilling the edict, "Man, Know Thyself." However, it is a start. It is equally important that real attempts be made to stem the anger and impatience that will occur as one starts on the road to self-rediscovery. Those emotions are probably inevitable and should be anticipated so that they can be dealt with appropriately.

GROUP 2

The following books are excellent and extremely important but, I believe, are not necessarily first-line reads for the beginner. Read the first-line suggested books first and the books that follow can be evaluated in what I believe is the proper perspective.

First-tier Reading:

Alexander, Michelle. *The New Jim Crow: Mass Incarceration in the Age of Colorblindness.* New York: The New Press, 2012.

Akbar, Na'im. *Chains and Images of Psychological Slavery.* Jersey City: New Mind Productions, 1984.

Akbar, Na'im. *Light from Ancient Afrika.* Tallahassee: Mind Productions & Associates, Inc., 1994.

Akoto, Kwame Agei. *Nationbuilding: Theory and Practice in African Centered Education.* Washington, DC: Pan Afrikan World Institute, 1992.

Anderson, Carol. *White Rage: The Unspoken Truth of Our Racial Divide.* NY: Bloomsbury, 2016.

Bonilla-Silva, Eduardo. *Racism Without Racists: Color-Blind Racism and the Persistence of Racial Inequality in America,* New York: Bowman & Littlefield Publishers, Inc., 2014.

Burrell, Tom. *Brainwashed: Challenging the Myth of Black Inferiority.* Carlsbad, CA: Smiley Books, 2010.

Carew, Jan. *Fulcrums of Change: African Presence in the Americas.* Trenton: Africa World Press, 1988.

Carruthers, Jacob and Leon Harris (Editors). *African World History Project: The Preliminary Challenge.* Los Angeles: Association for the Study of Classical African Civilizations, 1997.

Chinweizu. *Decolonizing the African Mind.* London: Sundoor, 1987.

Diop, Cheikh Anta. *Black Africa: The Economic and Cultural Basis For A Federated State.* Westport, CT: Africa World Press Edition, Lawrence Hill and Company, 1987.

Diop, Cheikh Anta. *Precolonial Black Africa: A Comparative Study of the Political and Social Systems of Europe and Black Africa, from Antiquity to the Formation of Modern States.* Westport, CT: Lawrence Hill & Company, 1987.

Diop, Cheikh Anta. *Cultural Unity of Black Africa.* Chicago: Third World Press, 1978.

Diop, Cheikh Anta. *Civilization or Barbarism: An Authentic Anthropology.* Brooklyn: Lawrence Hill Books, 1991.

Fanon, Frantz. *Black Skin, White Masks.* New York: Grove Press, 1967.

Freire, Paulo. *Pedagogy of the Oppressed.* New York: Continuum, 1992.

Jackson, John G. *Christianity Before Christ.* Dallas: The American Atheist Press, 1985.

Jones, Norece T. *Born a Child of Freedom, Yet a Slave: Mechanisms of Control and Strategies of Resistance in Antebellum South Carolina.* Hanover: University of New England Press, 1980.

Kambon, Kobi Kazembe Kalongi. *The African Personality in America: An African-Centered Framework.* Tallahassee: Nubian Nation Publications, 1992.

Kambon, Kobi Kazembe Kalongi. *Cultural Misorientation: The Greatest Threat to the Survival of the Black Race in the 21st Century.* Tallahassee: Nubian Nation Publications, 2003.

Karenga, Maulana and Carruthers, Jacob (Editors). *Kemet and the African Worldview: Research, Rescue, and Restoration.* Los Angeles: University of Sankore Press, 1986.

Obenga, Theophile: *A Lost Tradition: African Philosophy in World History.* Philadelphia: The Source Editions, 1995.

Rodney, Walter. *How Europe Underdeveloped Africa.* Washington, DC: Howard University Press, 1982.

Williams, Eric. *Capitalism and Slavery*. London: Andre Deutsch, (First published in 1964) 1990.

Wright, Bobby. *The Psychopathic Racial Personality and Other Essays.* Chicago: Third World Press.

*****

Group 2:

Aharone, Ezrah. *Sovereign Evolution: Manifest Destiny From "Civil Rights" To "Sovereign Rights."* Bloomington: AuthorHouse, 2008.

Anderson, Claud. *Black Labor, White Wealth: The Search for Power and Economic Justice.* Edgewood MD: Duncan & Duncan, Inc., Publishers, 1994.

Anderson, Claud. *PowerNomics: The National Plan to Empower Black America.* Bethesda: PowerNomics Corporation of America, 1998.

Barnes, Carol. *Melanin: The Chemical Key to Black Greatness.* Bensenville, IL: Lushena Books, 2001.

Beason, Jake Patton. *Why We Lose: Why the Black Man/Woman Rest Firmly on the Bottom in America, Africa and Elsewhere.* Milwaukee: Col D'var Graphics, 1989.

Berry, Daina Ramey and Kali Nicole Gross. *A Black Women's History of the United States.* Boston: Beacon Press, 2020.

Berry, Daina Ramey and Leslie M. Harris. Sexuality & Slavery: Reclaiming Intimate Histories in the Americas. Athens: The University of Georgia Press, 2018.

Better, Shirley. *Institutional Racism: A Primer on Theory and Strategies For Social Change.* Chicago: Bunham, Inc. Publishers, 2002.

Blain, Keisha N. *Set The World On Fire: Black Nationalist Women and the Global Struggle for Freedom.* Philadelphia: University of Pennsylvania Press, 2018.

Bynum, Victoria E. Unruly *Women: The Politics of Social &. Sexual Control in the Old Sout*h. Chapel Hill: The University of North Carolina Press, 1992.

Carmichael, Stokely. *Stokely Speaks: From Black Power to Pan+Africanism.* Chicago: Lawrence Hill Books, 1971.

Carmichael, Stokely and Charles V. Hamilton. *Black Power: The Politics of Liberation in America.* NY: A Vintage Book, 1967.

Carruthers, Jacob H. *Critical Commentaries: Carruthers On Schlesinger.* Silver Spring, MD: ASCAC Foundation, 1992.

Carruthers, Jacob H. *Critical Commentaries: Carruthers On Yurco.* Silver Spring, MD: ASCAC Foundation, 1992.

Chandler, Wayne. *Ancient Future.* Baltimore: Black Classic Press, 2000.

Chinweizu. *The West and the Rest of Us: White Predators, Black Slavers and the African Elite.* Lagos: Pero Press, 1987.

Chinweizu. *The West and the Rest of Us: White Predators, Black Slavers and the African Elite.* London: Vintage Books, 1975.

Darity, William A. Jr. and A. Kirsten Mullen. *From Here to Equality: Reparations for Black Americans in the Twenty-First Century.* Chapel Hill: The University of North Carolina Press, 2020.

Drake, St. Clair. *Black Folk Here and There: An Essay in History and Anthropology.* Los Angeles: Center for Afro-American Studies, 1987.

Feelings, Tom. *The Middle Passage: White Ships/Black Cargo.* NY: Dial Books, 1995.

Fermin, Anténor. *The Equality of the Human Races.* NY: Garland Publishing, Inc., 2000. (First published in 1885)

Greenidge, Kerri K. *Black Radical: The Life and Times of William Monroe Trotter.* NY: Liveright Publishing Corporation, 2020.

Hilliard, Asa G., *Fifty Plus Essential References on the History of African People.* Baltimore: Black Classics Press, 1993.

Horne, Gerald. *W. E. B. DuBois: An Encyclopedia.* Westport: Greenwood Press, 2001.

Horne, Gerald. *Race Woman: The Lives of Shirley Graham DuBois.* NY: New York University Press, 2002.

Horne, Gerald. *Black and Brown: African Americans and the Mexican Revolution, 1910-1920.* NY: New York University Press, 2002.

Horne, Gerald. *The Counter-Revolution of 1776: Slave Resistance and the Origins of the United States of America.* NY: New York University Press, 2014.

Jeffries, Hasan Kwame (Editor). *Understanding and Teaching the Civil Rights Movement.* Madison, Wisconsin: The University of Wisconsin Press, 2019.

Jeffries, Leonard. *Critical Commentaries: Our Sacred Mission.* Silver Spring, MD: ASCAC Foundation, 1991.

Jeffries, Rhinda Baines (Editor). *Queen Mothers: Articulating the Spirit of Black Women.* Teacher-Leaders. Charlotte: Information Age Publishing Co., 2019.

Jones, Del. *The Black Holocaust: Global Genocide.* Philadelphia: Hikeka Press, Inc., 1992.

Karenga, Maulana. *Introduction to Black Studies.* Los Angeles: University of Sankore Press, 2010.

Karenga, Maulana. *The Book of Coming Forth By Day: The Ethics of the Declarations of Innocence.* Los Angeles: University of Sankore Press, 1990.

Karenga, Maulana (Editor). *Reconstructing Kemetic Culture: Papers, Perspectives, Projects.* Los Angeles: University of Sankore Press, 1990.

Keto, C. Tsehloane. *An Introduction to The African-Centered Perspective of History.* Chicago: Research Associates School Times Publications. Distributed by Frontline Distribution International, Chicago, 1994.

Kunjufu, Jawanza. *Countering the Conspiracy to Destroy Black Boys.* (Volumes 1, 2, and 3). Chicago: African American Images, 2004.

Madhubuti, Haki R. *Enemies: The Clash of Races.* Chicago: Third World Press, 1978.

Muhammad, Khalil Gibran. *The Condemnation of Blackness: Race, Crime and the Making of Modern Urban America.* Cambridge: Harvard University Press, 2010.

Nantambu, Kwame. *Decoding European Geopolitics: Afrocentric Perspectives.* Kent, OH: Imhotep Publishing Company, 1994.

Nunnally, Shayla C. *Trust In Black America: Race, Discrimination, and Politics.* New York: New York University Press, 2012.

Rhoden, William C. *Forty Million Dollar Slaves: The Rise, Fall and Redemption of the Black Athlete.* NY: Broadway Books, 2010.

Rogers, J.A. *World's Great Men of Color* (Volumes One and Two). New York: Collier Books, 1972.

Samudzi, Zoe and William C. Anderson. *As Black as Resistance.* Chico, CA: AK Press, 2018.

Thiong'o, Ngugi wa. *Something Torn and New: An African Renaissance.* New York: Basic Books, 2009.

Weik, Terrance M. *The Archaeology of Antislavery Resistance.* Tallahassee: The University Press of Florida, 2012.

White, Deborah Gray. *Ain't I a Woman?: Female Slaves in the Plantation South.* NY: W.W. Norton & Company, 1999.

Wilder, Craig Steven. *Ebony & Ivy: Race, Slavery, and the Troubled History of America's Universities.* New York: Bloomsbury Press, 2013.

Williams, George Washington. *The History of the Negro Race in America, 1619-1880.* CreateSpace Independent Publishing Platform, 2016.

Williams, Larry Obadele and Asa G. Hilliard, III. *Critical Commentaries: The Struggle to Bring True African History into Being.* Silver Spring, MD: ASCAC Foundation, 1992.

Wilson, Amos N. The Developmental Psychology of the Black Child. NY: Africana.

X, Malcolm (as told to Alex Haley. *The Autobiography of Malcolm X.* NY: Grove Press, 1965.

*****

Some writers of Non-Afrikan Ancestry have written works of use to Afrikan people. This next list is not an exhaustive list, but it is a good start and it covers a broad but important range of topics.

Group 3:

Aptheker, Herbert. *American Negro Slave Revolts.* NY: International Publishers, 1983.

Baptist, Edward E. *The Half Has Never Been Told: Slavery and the Making of American Capitalism.* New York: Basic Books, 2014.

Bernal, Martin. *Black Athena: The Afroasiatic Roots of Classical Civilization, Vol. 1, The Fabrication of Ancient Greece, 1785-1885.* London: Free Association Books, 1987.

Bradley, Michael. *The Iceman Inheritance: Prehistoric Sources of Western Man's Racism, Sexism and Aggression.* New York: Kayode Publications Ltd., 1978.

Note: *Bradley's other works are also excellent.*

DiAngelo, Robin. *White Fragility: Why It's So Hard for White People to Talk about Racism.* Boston: Beacon Press, 2018.

Forbes, Jack D. *Africans and Native Americans: The Language of Race and the Evolution of Red-Black Peoples.* Chicago: University of Illinois Press, 1993.

Ginzburg, Ralph. *100 Years of Lynchings.* Baltimore: Black Classic Press, 1988.

Graves, Kersey. *The World's Sixteen Crucified Saviors: Or Christianity Before Christ.* The Cleage Group, Inc., 1991. (First published in 1885)

Greenberg, Gary. *101 Myths of the Bible.* Chicago: Sourcebooks, 2002.

Greenberg, Gary. *The Moses Mystery: The African Origins of the Jewish People.* A Birch Lane Press Book. Secaucus, NJ: Carol Publishing Group, 1996.

Hochschild, Adam. *King Leopold's Ghost: A Story of Greed, Terror, and Heroism in Colonial Africa.* NY: Houghton, Mifflin, Harcourt. 1998.

Katch, Danny. *Socialism...Seriously.* Chicago: Haymarket Books, 2015.

Koestler, Arthur. *The Thirteenth Tribe: The Khazar Empire and Its Heritage.* New York: Random House, Inc., 1976.

Kuhn, Alvin Boyd. *Shadow of the Third Century.* Elizabeth, NJ: Academy Press, 1949.

Kuhn, Alvin Boyd. *Who Is This King of Glory?* Elizabeth, NJ: Academy Press, 1941. **Must-read!**

Leaming, Hugo Prosper. *Hidden Americans: Maroons of Virginia and the Carolinas.* New Jersey: Garland Publishing, Inc., 1995.

Loewen, James W. *Lies My Teacher Told Me: Everything Your American History Textbook Got Wrong.* New York: A Touchstone Book Published by Simon & Schuster, 1996.

Massey, Gerald. *Ancient Egypt: Light of the World.* New York: Samuel Weiser, Inc., 1976.

Note: His other works, *Book of Beginnings* and *Natural Genesis* are also excellent and must-reads for those interested in Kemet/ancient Egypt.

McLaughlin, Terence. *Dirt: A Social History as Seen Through the Uses and Abuses of Dirt.* New York: Dorset Press, 1971. **Must-read!**

Group 3, Tier 2

Assman, Jan. *The Mind of Egypt: History and Meaning in the Time of the Pharoahs.* Cambridge: Harvard University Press, 2003.

Bauval, Robert and Thomas Brophy. *Imhotep the African: Architect of the Cosmos.* San Francisco: Disinformation Books, 2013.

Blackmon, Douglas A. *Slavery by Another Name: The Re-Enslavement of Black Americans from the Civil War to World War II.* New York: Anchor Books, 2008.

Blum, Edward J. and Paul Harvey. *The Color of Christ: The Son of God and the Saga of Race in America.* Chapel Hill: The University of North Carolina Press, 2012.

Bradley, Michael. *Chosen People from the Caucasus: Jewish Origins, Delusions and Historical Role in the Slave Trade, Genocide and Cultural Colonization.* Chicago: Third World Press, 1992.

Budge, E.A. Wallis. *The Gods of the Egyptians.* Mineola, NY: Dover Publications, 1969.

Note: *Budge has written several excellent books about Kemet (ancient Egypt) but we must bear in mind his era and orientation.*

Davidson, Basil. *The Lost Cities of Africa.* NY: Back Bay Books, 1987.

Note: *Has done good work on Afrika.*

Davies, David. *The Last of the Tasmanians.* London: Frederick Muller, Ltd., 1973.

de Lubicz, R.A. Schwaller. *Symbol and the Symbolic: Ancient Egypt, Science, and the Evolution of Consciousness.* Rochester, VT: Inner Traditions, 1981. He and his wife, Ischa, have done excellent and insightful work on Kemet.

Freud, Sigmund. *Moses and Monotheism.* London: The Hogarth Press, Ltd., 1951.

Goldstone, Lawrence. *Inherently Unequal: The Betrayal of Equal Rights by the Supreme Court, 1865-1903.* NY: Walker and Company, 2011.

Hacker, Andrew. *Two Nations: Black and White, Separate, Hostile, Unequal.* NY: MacMillan Publishing Co., 1992.

Higgins, Godfrey. *Anacalypsis, An Attempt to Draw Aside the Veil of the Saitic Isis or an Inquiry into the Origins of Language, Nations and Religions.* NY: University Books, 1965. (Originally published in London in 1833.)

Huntington, Samuel P. *The Clash of Civilizations and the Remaking of World Order.* New York: A Touchstone Book Published by Simon and Schuster, 1996.

Isenberg, Nancy. *White Trash. The 400-Year Untold History of Class in America* NY: Viking, 2016.

Kochman, Thomas. *Black and White: Styles in Conflict.* Chicago: University of Chicago Press, 1981.

Koning, Hans. *Columbus, His Enterprise: Exploding the Myth.* New York: Monthly Review Press, 1991.

Lindqvist, Sven. *"Exterminate All the Brutes": One Man's Odyssey into the Heart of Darkness and the Origins of European Genocide.* New York: The New Press, 1996.

Loewen, James W. *Sundown Towns: A Hidden Dimension of American Racism.* NY: The New Press, 2018.

O'Reilly, Kenneth. *Nixon's Piano: Presidents and Racial Politics from Washington to Clinton.* New York: The Free Press, 1995.

Osman, Ahmed and Robert Bauval. *Breaking the Mirror of Heaven: The Conspiracy to Suppress the Voice of Ancient Egypt.* NY: Simon and Schuster, 2012.

Parenti, Michael. *Make Believe Media: The Politics of Entertainment.* New York: St. Martin's Press, 1992.

Parenti, Michael. *Inventing Reality: The Politics of News Media,* New York: St. Martin's Press, 1993.

Parenti, Michael. *Dirty Truths: Reflections on Politics, Media, Ideology, Conspiracy, Ethnic Life and Class Power.* San Francisco: City Lights Books, 1996.

Reiss, Tom. *Black Count: Glory, Revolution, Betrayal, and the Real Count of Monte Cristo.* NY: Broadway Books, 2012.

Volney, Count: *The Ruins of Empires.* Publication information missing
Note: *Excellent book by this 19th century European who saw Kemet before the European Egyptologists.*

Weisenthal, Simon. *Sails of Hope: The Secret Mission of Christopher Columbus,* New York: MacMillan Publishers, Inc., 1973.

West, John Anthony: *Serpent in the Sky: The High Wisdom of Ancient Egypt.* Wheaton: Questbooks, 1993.

Zinn, Howard. *A People's History of the United States.* New York: HarperCollins Publishers Inc. 2003.

Zinn, Howard: *SNCC: The New Abolitionists.* Chicago: Haymarket Books, 1964.

*****

Articles

Books are always good; however, we have found it useful also to study and discuss articles from periodicals. Chapters and introductions in books may be more pertinent to the topic discussed than the entire book. Examples of periodicals that have published excellent articles include those on the list that follows, to name a few:

- *The Compass: Journal of the Association for the Study of Classical African Civilizations*
- *Black Books Bulletin*
- *Black World/Negro Digest*
- *Freedomways*
- *Journal of Black Psychology*
- *Western Journal of Black Studies*
- *Black Scholar*
- *Journal of Black Studie*s

Pertinent articles can also be found occasionally in Black mainstream periodicals as *Jet, Ebony, Essence* and *The Crisis.* It should also be noted that much of Ivan Van Sertima's work (except *They Came Before Columbus*) was part of a journal called *The Journal of African Civilizations.* For a more extensive listing and examination of these publications, please see Greg Kimathi Carr's Editor's Notes in *The Compass: Journal of the Association for the Study of Classical African Civilizations, Volume 1, Issue 1.* An excellent article that should also be studied is "Mentacide: The Ultimate Threat to the Black Race," a timeless, unpublished document written by Bobby E. Wright, Ph.D. Below is a list of some of these articles.

Akbar, Na'im. The Challenge of Implementation. *The Black Collegian*, September/October, 1991.

Amini, Johari. Redefinition: Concept as Being. *Black World*, May, 1972.

Baldwin, Joseph A. aka Kobi Kambon. Black Psychology and Black Personality. *Black Books Bulletin*. Volume 4, Number 3, Fall, 1976.

Bennett Jr., Lerone. *Why Black History Is Important to You*. Ebony Magazine, February, 1982.

Bennett Jr., Lerone. *A Historical Detective Story: Part 1, The Mystery of Mary Ellen Pleasant*. *Ebony*, June, 1993.

Bethune, Mary McLeod. "My Last Will and Testament". *Ebony*, November, 1990.

Black 'White" Man Challenges Federal Race Identity Law. *Jet*, January 7, 1991.

Burt, Della. The Legacy of the Bad Nigger. *Journal of Afro-American Issues*, Volume 5, Number 2, Spring, 1977, pp. 101-124.

Carlisle, Rodney. Black Nationalism: An Integral Tradition. *Black World*. February, 1973.

Carruthers, Jacob H. Futurity and the Black Race in the Western Hemisphere. *Black Books Bulletin*, Volume 4, Number 2, Summer, 1976.

Clarke, John Henrik. Cultural Continuity and Slave Revolts in the New World: (Parts One and Two). *The Black Scholar*. September, 1976, pp. 41-49.

Clarke, John Henrik. In Our Image. *Essence Magazine*, September, 1989, p.158.

Clarke, John Henrik. "The Black Woman in History". *Black World*, February, 1975.

Clarke, John Henrik. *The Black Family in Historical Perspective*. Journal of Afro-American Issues. Vol.3, No. 3 & 4, Summer/Fall, 1975.

Clarke, John Henrik. The Meaning of Black History. *Black World*, February, 1971.

Clarke, John Henrik. Why Africana History? *The Black Collegian*, January/February, 1987.

Clarke, John Henrik. Balancing History. *Black World*. February, 1973.

Dekenu-Arlantch. Interview with Michael Bradley: The Rise of Western Power and World Domination Through Violence, Religion and Sex. *Afrikan Business and Culture*. Volume 3, Number 20.

Dekenu-Arlantch. Interview with Dr. Frances Cress Welsing: White Supremacy and Black Survival in the 21st Century. *Afrikan Business and Culture.* Volume 3, Number 20.

DeLeon, Monica. Don't Be Thrown by Casual Appearance of "The Toss." *Emerge.* April, 1994.

Diop, Cheikh Anta. Africa: Cradle of Humanity. *Nile Valley Civilization,* 1985.

Fairchild, Halford H. From Bleeding to Healing: "Wealth Creates Culture?" *Psyche Discourse,* Volume 32, Number 1, January, 2001.

Falk, Leslie A. Black Abolitionist Doctors and Healers: 1810-1885. *Bulletin of the History of Medicine* 54(2): 258-272, Summer, 1980.

Finch, Charles S. Race and Evolution in Prehistory. *African Presence in Early Europe,* 1986.

Genetic Researchers say 'Mother Of Us All' in Africa. *The State,* September, 27, 1991.

Ghee, Kenneth L. The Psychological Importance of Self-definition and Labeling: Black vs. African American. *The Journal of Black Psychology,* volume 17, number 1, Fall 1990, pp. 75-93.

Gross, Bella. The Roots of the National Negro Convention Movement. *The Negro History Bulletin.* November, 1946, pp. 40-44.

Hall, Ronald. The Bleaching Syndrome: African Americans' Response to Cultural Domination vis-à-vis Skin Color. *Journal of Black Studies.* Volume 26, Number 2, November, 1995.

Henry, Charles P. The Political Role of the "Bad Nigger." *Journal of Black Studies,* June, 1981.

Hilliard, Asa G. III. Introductions to *From the Browder File* and *Stolen Legacy* (1976 Reprint)

Hoskins, Linus A. Eurocentrism vs. Afrocentrism: A Geopolitical Linkage Analysis. *Journal of Black Studies.* Volume 23, Number 2, December, 1992, pp. 247-257.

Interview with Chancellor Williams. *Black Books Bulletin,* Volume 1, Number 4, 1973.

Kahn: Robert M. The Political Ideology of Martin Delany. *Journal of Black Studies,* June, 1984.

King, Richard D. Black History Review: Part 1. *The Black Psychiatrists of America Quarterly.* [n.d.]

Lawrence-McIntyre, Charshee Charlotte. The Double Meanings of the Spirituals. *Journal of Black Studies*, June, 1987.

Lowe, Christopher. Talking About "Tribe' Moving from Stereotypes to Analysis. *Africa Action* (formerly the Africa Policy Information Center). November, 1997.

Montagu, M.F. Ashley. The Negro's Problem: The White Man. *The Negro History Bulletin*, Volume 8, Number 8, May, 1945.

Myers, Linda James. The Deep Structure of Culture: Relevance of Traditional African Culture in Contemporary Life. *Journal of Black Studies*, vol. 18, no. 1, September, 1987, pp. 72-85.

Newsinger, John. Lord Greystoke and Darkest Africa: The Politics of the Tarzan Stories. *Race & Class*, Volume XXVIII, Number 2, 1986, pp.59-71.

Nobles, Wade W. Africanity: Its Role in Black Families. *Black Scholar*, June, 1974, pp. 10-17.

Oliver, William. Black Males and Social Problems: Prevention Through Afrocentric Socialization. *Journal of Black Studies*, vol. 20, no. 1, September, 1989, pp. 15-39.

Pease, Jane H. and William H. Pease. Negro Conventions and the Problem of Black Leadership. *Journal of Black Studies*, Volume 2, Number 1, September, 1971, pp. 29-44.

Perkins, Eugene. Benevolent Racism: The Oppressor as Messiah. *Black Books Bulletin. Volume* 3, Number 4, Winter, 1975.

Peterson-Lewis, Sonja and Afesa Adams. "Television's Model of the Quest for African Consciousness: A Comparison with Cross' Empirical Model of Psychological Nigrescence". *Journal of Black Psychology*, volume 16, number 2, Spring, 1990, pp. 55-72.

Reed, Harry A. Slavery in Ashanti and Colonial South Carolinax. Black World, February, 1971, pp. 37-40, 70-74.

Richardson, Sharon. Resurrection of the Black Mind. *Richardson Educational Information Distribution Center Newsletter*, Volume 2, Number 2.

Sanders, Edith R. The Hamitic Hypothesis: Its Origin and Functions in Time Perspective. *Journal of African History*. Volume X, Number 4, 1969, pp. 521-532.

Seraile, William. David Walker and Malcolm X: Brothers in Radical Thought. *Black World*, October, 1973.

Schomburg, A.A. and Dr. James McCune Smith. *Negro History Bulletin*, November, 1945.

Schoor, Joel. The Rivalry Between Frederick Douglass and Henry Highland Garnet. *Journal of Negro History*, Volume 64, Number 1, Winter, 1979, pp. 30-38.

Sherwood, Henry Noble. Paul Cuffee. *Journal of Negro History*. Volume VIII, Number 2, April, 1923.

Staples, Robert and Terry Jones. Culture, Ideology and Black Television Images. *The Black Scholar*, May/June 1985.

Sutherland, Marcia E. Individual Differences in Response to the Struggle for the Liberation of People of African Descent. *Journal of Black Studies*, vol. 29, no. 1, September, 1989, pp. 40-59.

Wallace, Douglas. The Search for Adam and Eve. *Newsweek*, January 11, 1988.

Walton, Jr., Hanes. Toward a Theory of Black African Civilization: The Problem of Authenticity. *Journal of Black Studies*, Volume1, Number 4, June, 1971.

Young, Lawrence W. Isn't She Pretty? *Black Issues in Higher Education*, January 19, 1989.

Other Reads

My brother, Listervelt Middleton (Maa Kheru), and I debated frequently the importance of fiction to the internalization of history. His position was that fiction and poetry were vitally important in teaching history. I was of the opinion non-fiction was the best way to learn and internalize history. As was frequently the case, Listervelt was right. I have found some fiction very instructive in solidifying history and below are a few books and authors that I have found useful and stimulating.

Armah, Ayi Kwei. (anything by him is absolutely awesome, especially *Two Thousand Seasons*)

Bascile, Natalie. *Queen Sugar: A Novel*

Bell, Derrick. *Faces at the Bottom of the Well: The Permanence of Racism*

Butler, Octavia (especially her *Parable* Series)

Dickey, Eric Jerome (especially his later works)

Gallman, Kwadwo. *To Be Human: The Conflict Continues.* Columbia:Imhotep-The Drum, 2020

Gyasi, Yaa. *Homegoing: A Novel.* NY: Alfred A. Knopf, 2016.

Moore, Weyetu, *She Would Be King.* Minneapolis: Graywolf Press, 2018.

Okorafor, Nnedi. *Who Fears Death.* NY: Daw Books, Inc., 2010 (also her *Binti* series)

Walter Mosley (his fiction and non-fiction works are awesome)

Schuyler, George S, Black Empire. Boston: Northeatern University Press, 1991 (first written in 1936).

Wright, Richard. *Native Son.* NY: Harper and Row Publishers, 1966.

And the body of work by these authors:

- James Baldwin
- Toni Cade Bambara
- Gwendolyn Brooks
- Ta-Nehisi Coates
- Tananarive Due
- Ralph Ellison
- Zora Neale Hurston
- Toni Morrison
- Sister Souljah
- Colson Whitehead

Other writers, such as Carl Weber, Zane, Omar Tyree, Tina McElroy Ansa, Kimberla Lawson Roby, Mary B. Morrison and Damon Tweedy, are entertaining and interesting and perhaps instructive on certain aspects of Ausa life but do not always portray a positive view.

Frequently, I am asked to recommend children's books and I depend greatly on my good friend Dr. Gloria Boutte for recommendations. The following books are a partial list taken from her recommendations (Adapted from Boutte, 2016 and Jackson & Boutte, 2008) plus some that were suggested by others. Please note that many of the listed authors have written other books for children.

Websites

African American Literature Book Club https://aalbc.com/books/children.php

Ifeoma Onyefulu A collection of contemporary books about African culture. http://www.ifeomaonyefulu.co.uk/index.htm

Books for Younger Students (Preschool – 5th Grade)

Adero, Malaika. *A Black Woman Did That: 42 Boundary-Breaking, Bar-raising, World-Changing Women.* Auburn, NY: Downtown Books Publishing, 2020.

Agusi, A. *Dear future history maker.* Atlanta, GA: Cultivated Roots Media, 2017.

Amadi, P. and N. Amadi. *Chichi and Didi love their names.* Columbia, SC: Independent Publisher, 2020.

Brann, S. K. and C. Morales-James. *The ABCs of the Black Panther Party.* USA: Decolonizing Education Publishing, 2017.

Braswell, Kenneth. *Daddy, There's a Noise Outside.* Dunwoody, GA: Fathers Inc., 2015.

Ellis, V. F. *Afro-Bets First Book About Africa.* Orange, NJ: Just Us Books, 1989.

Chbosky, S. *Who Owns the Sun?* Kansas City, MS: Landmark Editions, 1988.

Cline-Ransome, L. *Light in the Darkness: A Story About How Slaves Learned in Secret.* NY: Little Brown Books for Young Readers, 2013.

Cook, M. *Our Children Can Soar: A Celebration of Rosa, Barack, and the Pioneers of Change.* NY: Bloomsbury USA, 2012.

Cooper, Melrose. *Getting Through Tuesday.* NY: Lee and Low Books, 2000.

Daly, Niki. *Happy Birthday, Jamela.* NY: Farrar, Straus, Giraux, 2006. **Note:** *One of a series of books about Jamela*

Friedman, M. *Africa.* NY: Scholastic, 2009.

Hest, Amy. *Jamaica Louise James.* Massachusetts: Candlewick Press, 1997.

Holman, Sandy Lynne. *Grandpa, Is Everything Black Bad?* Davis, CA: Culture C.O.-O.P., 1998.

Knight, M. B. and M. Melnicove. *Africa is Not a Country.* Minneapolis, MN: Millbrook, 2000.

Lester, J. *From Slave Ship to Freedom Road.* NY: Dial Books, 1998.

Littlesugar, Amy. *Freedom School, Yes.* NY: Philomel Books, 2001.

Lucas, Eileen. *Cracking the Wall: The Struggle of the Little Rock Nine.* Minneapolis: First Avenue Editions, 1997.

McDermott, G. *Anansi the Spider. A Tale from the Ashanti.* NY: Henry Holt, 1972.

McKissick, Patricia C. *Ma Dear's Aprons.* NY: Aladdin Paperbacks, 2000.

Miller, William. *The Bus Ride.* NY: Lee and Low Books, 2001.

Mitchell, R. *The Talking Cloth.* NY: Orchard Books, 1997.

Musgrove, M. *The Spider Weaver: A Legend of Kente Cloth.* NY: Scholastic, 2011.

Myer, S. L. *New Shoes.* NY: Holiday House, 2015.

Parker, Toni Trent. *Sienna's Scrapbook: Our African American Heritage Trip.* San Francisco: Chronicle Books, 2005.

Pinkney, Andrea Davis. *Alvin Ailey.* NY: Little, Brown Books for Young. Readers, 1995.

Rahaman, Vashanti. *Read for Me, Mama.* Westminster, MD: Boyds Mills Press, 1997.

Ringgold, F. *The Invisible Princess.* NY: Dragonfly Books, 1991.

Ringgold, F. *If a Bus Could Talk. The Story of Rosa Parks.* NY: Aladdin Paperbacks, 1999.

Roberts, Brenda C. *Jazzy Miz Mozetta.* NY: Farrar, Straus and Giroux, 2004.

Seward, Angela. *Goodnight, Daddy.* Morning Glory Press, 2000.

Shelf, A. *Our People.* Greensboro: Carson-Dellosa Publishing, LLC. 2002.

Steptoe, J. *Mufaro's Beautiful Daughters. An African Tale.* NY: Lothrop, Lee & Shepard Books, 1987.

Smalls, Irene. *Ebony Sea.* Ann Arbor: Borders Press, 1996.

Tarpley, Natasha Anastasia. *Destiny's Gift.* NY: Lee and Low Books, 2010.

Tchana, K. Sense *Pass King. A Story from Cameroon.* NY: Holiday House, 2002.

Trice, Linda. Kenya's Word. Watertowne, MA: Charlesbridge, 2006.
Williams, Sheron. *Imani's Music.* NY: Atheneum, 2002.
Winter, Jeanette. *Follow the Drinking Gourd.* NY: Dragonfly Books, 1992.
Winter, Jonah. *Dizzy.* NY: Arthur A. Levine Books, 2006.
Yarbrough, Camille, *Cornrows.* NY: Puffin Books, 1997.
Youme. *Selavi, That is Life: A Haitian Story of Hope.* El Paso: Cinco Puntos. Press, 2005.

Books for Older Students (Middle/High School)

Achebe, C. *Things Fall Apart.* NY: Anchor Books, 1994.
Crowe, Chris. *Getting Away with Murder: The True Story of the Emmett Till Case.* NY: Dial Books, 2003.
Curtis, Christopher Paul. *Bud, Not Buddy.* NY: Delacorte Books for Young Readers, 2001.
Davis, Sampson, George Jenkins, Rameck Hunt, Sharon M. Draper. *We Beat the Street: How a Friendship Pact Led to Success.* NY: Puffin Books, 2006.
Dooley, Norah. *Everybody Cooks Rice.* Minneapolis, MN: First Avenue Editions, 1991.
Douglass, F. *The Life of Frederick Douglass.* Mineola, NY: Dover Publishers, 1995.
Draper, S.M. *Copper Sun.* NY: Simon and Schuster, 2006.
Du Bois, W.E.B. *Souls of Black folk.* NY: Bantam Books, (1903/1989).
Ferguson, Dwayne J. *Kid Caramel Private Investigator: Case of the Missing Ankh.* US: Just Us Books, 1997.
Flake, Sharon. *The Skin I'm In.* NY: Little, Brown Books for Young Readers, 2018.
Haley, A. *The Autobiography of Malcolm X: As Told to Alex Haley.* NY: Ballantine Publishing Group, 1964.
Hansberry, Lorraine. *A Raisin in the Sun.* NY: Vintage (Reprint), 2004.
Hansen, J. *The Amazing Lives of Africa's Royal Women.* NY: Jump at the Sun, 2004.
Hansen, Joyce. *I Thought My Soul Would Rise and Fly.* NY: Scholastic, 1997.

Hunter, LaToya. *The Diary of LaToya Hunter: My First Year in Junior High.* NY: Vintage (Reprint), 1993.

Kunjufu, Jawanza. *Lessons from History: A Celebration in Blackness. Chicago: African American Images: Elementary ed.*, 1987.

Krass, P. *Sojourner Truth. Antislavery Activist.* NY: Chelsea House Publishers, 1988.

McGovern, A. *Runaway Slave. The Story of Harriet Tubman.* New York, NY: Scholastic, 1965.

McKissack, P. and F. McKissack. *The Royal Kingdoms of Ghana, Mali, and Songhay: Life in Medieval Africa.* NY: Henry Holt and Company, 1994.

Myers, Walter Dean. *Slam!* NY: Scholastic Paperbacks, 2008.

Myers, W.D. *At Her Majesty's Request: An African Princess in Victorian England.* New York, NY: Scholastic, 1999.

Price, L., and D. Dillion. *Aida.* NY: Gulliver Books. 1990.

Reynolds, J. and I. X. Kendi. *Stamped. Racism, Antiracism, and You.* NY: Little, Brown and Company, 2020.

Smith, Hope Anita. *The Way a Door Closes.* NY: Square Fish (Reprint Edition), 2011.

Thomas, Velma Maia. *No Man Can Hinder Me: The Journey from Slavery to Emancipation Through Song.* NY: Crown, 2001.

Welch, Catherine A. *Children of the Civil Rights Era. (1950s to 1960s)* Minneapolis, MN: Carolrhoda Books, 2001.

Woodson, C. G. *The Mis-Education of the Negro.* Trenton, NJ: Africa World Press, 1933/1990.

Woodson, Jacqueline. *Miracle's Boys.* NY: Puffin Books, 2010.

Books That Can Be Used Across Age Groups

Adero, Malaika. *A Black Woman Did That: 42 Boundary-Breaking, Bar-raising, World-Changing Women.* Auburn, NY: Downtown Books Publishing, 2020.

Crowe, C. *Getting Away with Murder: The True Story of the Emmett Till Case.* NY: Random House, 2003.

Hansen, Joyce. *I Thought My Soul Would Rise and Fly.* NY: Scholastic, 1997.

Haskins, J. and K. Benson. *African Beginnings.* New York, NY: Lothrop, Lee & Shepard, 1998.

Hilliard, Asa G. III, Larry Williams and Nia Damali. *The Teachings of Ptahhotep: The Oldest Book in the World.* Atlanta: Blackwood Press, 2012.

O'Dell, Scott. My Name is Not Angelica. NY: Houghton, Mifflin, Harcourt, 2011.

Thompson, C. *African Civilizations. The Asante Kingdom.* NY: Franklin Watts, 1998.

CHAPTER 5

Quotations and Thoughts on History and Other Topics

1. "What is History, but a fiction agreed upon?"

   NAPOLEON BONAPARTE

2. "History is the struggle and record of humans in the process of humanizing the world, i.e. shaping it in their own image and interests. To shape the world in a human image is to give it a human form and character and to shape it in human interests is to make it serve humans rather than threaten, deform or destroy them."

   MAULANA KARENGA

3. "The hard fact is that most of what we now call world history is only the history of the first and second rise of Europe…more than five thousand years had unfolded before what was to become Europe was a political factor in world affairs."

   JOHN HENRIK CLARKE

4. "…our own reality, however fine and attractive the reality of others may be, can only be transformed by detailed knowledge of it, by our own efforts, by our own sacrifices."

   AMILCAR CABRAL

5. "We need…to understand our past defeats if we want to avoid the deadly shocks our future seems to be holding in ambush for us. And to do so, it is imperative that we revise our understanding of the history of which we are products…. Africans, especially, must endeavor to see clearly the larger system of things in which we

are enmeshed or be irretrievably lost in catacombs of irrelevant details; and that we must understand the awful predicament that binds us together or we shall be repeatedly manipulated to fight one another and so hasten the march of disaster upon ourselves."

CHINWEIZU

6. "Our concern with the connection to our African past is really future oriented. It is not merely for sentimental or aesthetic reasons that we return. While it is true that no one can or should live in the past, it is equally true that all futures are created out of some past."

   ASA G. HILLIARD, III

7. "History, I have often said, is a clock that people use to tell their political time of day. It is also a compass that people use to find themselves on the map of human geography. History tells a people where they have been and what they have been. It also tells a people where they are and what they are. Most importantly, history tells a people where they still must go and what they still must be."

   JOHN HENRIK CLARKE

8. "If a race has no history, if it has no worthwhile tradition, it becomes a negligible factor in the thought of the world, and it stands in danger of being exterminated."

   CARTER G. WOODSON

9. "Knowledge of our history and culture is the glue that bonds us together and gives us a sense of purpose in life."

   JACOB CARRUTHERS

10. "When we classify mankind by color, the only primary race that has not made a creative contribution to any civilization is the Black race."

    ARNOLD TOYNBEE

11. "To be denied historical achievement is to be placed outside of humanity, for only humans make history."

    MAULANA KARENGA

12. "The way to right wrongs is to turn the light of truth upon them."

    IDA B. WELLS

13. "In my music, my plays, my films, I want to carry always this central idea — to be African, multitudes of men have died for less worthy ideals; it is even more eminently worth living for."

PAUL ROBESON

14. "To be African, or not to be!"

ASA G. HILLIARD, III

15. "Power is the ability to define reality and have other people respond to your definition as if it were their own."

WADE W. NOBLES

16. "Struggle is a never-ending process. Freedom is never really won, you earn it and win it in every generation."

CORETTA SCOTT KING

17. "...Powerful people never have to prove anything to anyone. And by extension, powerful people never apologize to powerless people for the actions they take in order to remain in power... Powerful people never teach powerless people how to take their power away from them."

JOHN HENRIK CLARKE

18. "The greatest fear of our oppressors is that we will become conscious, independent, and unified. When this happens, we will therefore be able to mount effective resistance, gain freedom, mobilize for development, and become serious competitors. This is why, although the African enslaved in the western hemisphere was fully clothed in a rich cultural heritage, the leaders of the slave society set about systematically to strip Africans of all the culture they retained. Those who enslaved us wanted us to be either culturally naked or dead. They wanted to take us out of the human historical and cultural process. They wanted to say that we had never done anything that mattered. They wanted us to think that we were wholly dependent on Europe for everything. They wanted us to view the European as the only creator of culture and the African only as spectator."

ASA G. HILLIARD, III

19. "When you control a man's thinking you do not have to worry about his actions. You do not have to tell him not to stand here or go yonder. He will find his "proper place" and will stay in it. You do not need to send him to the back door. He will go without being told. In fact, if there is no back door, he will cut one for his special benefit. His education makes it necessary."

CARTER G. WOODSON

20. "Each generation must out of relative obscurity discover its mission and having discovered it either betray it or fulfill it."

FRANTZ FANON

21. "It is of no use for us to wait any longer for a generation of well-educated men to arise. We have slumbered and slept too long already; the day is far spent; the day of death approaches; and you have sound sense and good judgement sufficient to begin with, if you feel disposed to make a right use of it."

MARIA STEWART

22. "It may be of no importance to the race to be able to boast today of many times as many educated members as it had in 1865. If they are of the wrong kind the increase in numbers will be a disadvantage rather than an advantage. The only question which concerns us here is whether these educated persons are actually equipped to face the ordeal before them or unconsciously contribute to their own undoing by perpetuating the regime of the oppressor."

CARTER G. WOODSON

23. "Hate has caused a lot of problems in this world, but it has not solved one yet."

MAYA ANGELOU

24. "History shows that it does not matter who is in power or what revolutionary forces take over the government, those who have not learned to do for themselves and have to depend solely on others never obtain any more rights or privileges in the end than they had in the beginning."

CARTER G. WOODSON

25. "The true worth of a race must be measured by the character of its womanhood."

MARY MCLEOD BETHUNE

26. "Our children must never lose their zeal for building a better world. They must not be discouraged from aspiring towards greatness, for they are to be the leaders of tomorrow. Nor must they forget that the masses of our people are still underprivileged, ill housed, impoverished and victimized by discrimination. We have a powerful potential in our youth, and we must have the courage to change old ideas and practices so that we may direct their power toward good ends."

MARY MCLEOD BETHUNE

27. "To embrace one's culture is not to 'go back to the 1500's'. It is not to reject technology. It is not to reject appropriate social and cultural change. It is not to reject categorically 'Western Civilization'. It is not to disrespect the culture of anyone. To embrace one's culture is to do merely what any healthy group does."

ASA G. HILLIARD, III

28. "It is better to build a child than to repair an adult."

FREDERICK DOUGLASS

29. "A people without the knowledge of their past history, origin and culture is like a tree without roots."

MARCUS GARVEY

30. "We are at war but only the enemy knows."

MARIMBA ANI

31. "Those who do not remember the past are condemned to repeat it."

GEORGE SANTAYANA

32. "People are trapped in history and history is trapped in them."

JAMES BALDWIN

33. "A small body of determined spirits fired by an unquenchable faith in their mission can alter the course of history."

MAHATMA GANDHI

34. "The most potent weapon of the oppressor is the mind of the oppressed."

STEVE BIKO

35. "Life's most persistent and urgent question is 'What are you doing for others?'"

MARTIN LUTHER KING, JR.

36. "If we don't know who we are, then we are whoever somebody says we are."

AMOS WILSON

37. "Nobody's free until everybody's free."

FANNIE LOU HAMER

38. "The principle of self-defense, even involving weapons and bloodshed, has never been condemned, even by Gandhi."

MARTIN LUTHER KING, JR.

39. "Our deepest fear is not that we are inadequate. Our deepest fear is that we are powerful beyond measure. It is our light, not our darkness that most frightens us."

NELSON MANDELA

40. "There is nothing more dangerous than sincere ignorance and conscientious stupidity."

MARTIN LUTHER KING, JR.

41. "The basic tenet of black consciousness is that the black man must reject all value systems that seek to make him a foreigner in the country of his birth and reduce his basic human dignity."

STEVEN BIKO

42. "Knowledge trumps belief every time."

PROJECT SANKOFA

43. "I'm sick and tired of being sick and tired."

FANNIE LOU HAMER

44. "In this country, American means white. Everybody else has to hyphenate."

TONI MORRISON

45. "You can never know where you are going unless you know where you have been."

AMELIA BOYNTON ROBINSON

46. "For I am my mother's daughters, and the drums of Africa still beat in my heart."

MARY McLEOD BETHUNE

47. "History belongs to she who holds the pen...if we don't tell our stories, they won't be told."

JULIANNE MALVEAUX

48. "Pan-Africanism or perish"

DR. JOHN HENRIK CLARKE

CHAPTER 6

About the Maafa

What is the Maafa?

"Maafa" is an Afrikan (Ki-Swahili) word that means disaster and is pronounced Mah-ah-fah. First used by Dr. Marimba Ani in her book *Let the Circle Be Unbroken*, Maafa is the word to describe the Afrikan Holocaust. During this period Afrikan people were killed (physically, spiritually and mentally) through enslavement, colonization, torture, murder and South Afrikan/North American Apartheid/segregation. The cold, cramped, damp overcrowded stay in the "slave dungeons" located on the coast of West Afrika where our Ancestors were warehoused while waiting for ships to the "New World" was beastly. The "Middle Passage" — the actual trip from Afrika to the so-called "New World" — alone was torture.

Although the word "holocaust" is not specific to any one event or series of events, it has come mostly to be identified with one group of people. Although there have been many holocausts in history, the Maafa is not only the worst (in excess of 100 million people lost, displaced or killed) and the longest (almost 1400 years) but was the best organized and most complex. The perpetrators of this horror are still not willing to acknowledge their fault through reparations or even an apology, which would be inadequate but at least a step in the right direction. Interestingly, Hitler is rightfully condemned as a monster because of his inhuman treatment and murder of at least six million European Jews, gypsies and other peoples of color while little, if anything, is said of King Leopold of Belgium who killed more than 10 million people in the Congo and maimed many more.

When Did the Maafa Occur?

The Maafa is generally thought to have begun in 1492, the year Columbus arrived in the Caribbean, which was the start of European enslavement and colonization of Native Americans and Afrikans. The end of the Maafa in America has been generally accepted as 1865, the end of the Civil War and overt American physical enslavement. It is important, however, to realize that the conquest, the physical and mental enslavement, mass murder and colonization of Afrikan people on a large scale actually started about 640 A.C.E. by the Western Asiatic people we now call Arabs, who were determined to spread their new religion by force throughout the world. This period of the Maafa is too frequently ignored but is important and possibly more barbaric.

We must also not forget that the Maafa may not be over even now, more than 150 years after the Emancipation Proclamation and the end of the Civil War in 1865. Although Reconstruction in the U.S. was a lull in the Maafa, the post-Reconstruction period, called the "nadir" by historian Rayford Logan, was notable by brutally enforced American Apartheid. Terrorism marked this period: lynching and other terrible mechanisms of torture and death were a constant threat to Afrikan men and women and stimulated a mass migration as well as popular songs of the era (for example, *Strange Fruit* by Billie Holliday). During this same post-Reconstruction era, European countries scrambled for Afrika, culminating in the carving up of Afrika in Berlin in 1884. These European countries wanted the continent's riches and natural resources of Afrika without paying fairly for them. We should realize that Europe, the wealthiest group of nations in the world today, would be among the poorest if they had had to survive on their own riches and natural resources. This scramble for Afrika was played out in military conquests throughout the continent; the low point was Belgium King Leopold's savage repression of the Congo and his massacres and mutilation of the population from 1885 to 1908. Approximately ten to fifteen million Afrikan lives were lost during this time period. The high point of this scramble was Ethiopian Emperor Menelik II's successful military defense of Ethiopia and defeat of Italy at Adwa in 1896.

Who Were the Participants in the Maafa?

The victims of the Maafa have been Afrikan people no matter where they have found themselves. The victimizers have been the Arabs, the Europeans, and the Euro-Americans. There were then, as there are now, Afrikan and Ausa collaborators with our oppressors.

Every holocaust known to the world has been perpetrated, directly and indirectly, by these groups — from the little-known complete genocidal elimination of the natives of Tasmania by the British to the Afrikan genocidal holocaust in Rwanda. The only thing missing in understanding the Burundi/Rwanda situation and the so-called xenophobic killings in South Afrika (Azania) is in not knowing the right questions to ask in order to get to the correct answers and analyses. The first question is, "How did these people get along BEFORE they came in contact with the Europeans?" And the second question is, "What happened to bring this relationship to such violence and ferocity?"

Where and Why Did It Occur?

The Maafa took place wherever Afrikan people are found — in Afrika, in the Americas, in the Caribbean, in Asia, in India (that is another whole story that is still being played out), and in Europe. Several theories have been advanced as to why this happened. These theories deal mostly with the origins of racism and an explanation of the worldview of Europe that is so different from the worldviews of the rest of the world.

One of the best known theories is the Two Cradle Theory as posited by Dr. Cheikh Anta Diop. His main thesis is that the origins of Humanity/Afrikans in the tropics of Afrika near the equator and the emergence of modern Europeans during the last Ice Age in Europe created not only differences in appearance but differences in worldview. Europeans were individualistic, aggressive and materialistic; Afrikans (and much of the rest of the world) were communal, spiritual and peaceful.

Dr. Frances Cress Welsing posits another theory: racism/white supremacy was/is simply a mechanism for white genetic survival since, generally speaking, those physical traits that define whiteness are usually genetic recessive traits and those physical traits that define Blackness are usually genetic dominant traits. In her book, *Yurugu*, Dr. Marimba Ani gives an in-depth analysis of the European worldview and European culture in all its major aspects from an Afrikan-centered perspective. *Yurugu* is believed by many to be one of the most important books written during the twentieth century.

How Did the Maafa Occur?

Again, there are several schools of thought. History suggests that Arabs had conquered much of North, East and West Afrika which weakened Afrika so much that it was much easier for the Europeans to be victorious. A comparative study of West Afrika and Europe during the eleventh through the thirteenth centuries would suggest that, at that time, Afrika might have defeated Europe in an all-out war.

Europeans went to Afrika first as "explorers" and were guests of the people. When their presence was relatively institutionalized, they brought in the two groups whose efforts sealed the fate of Afrikans: teachers and priests. They offered to educate the Afrikan children (especially the children of kings and nobles) and made massive attempts to convert the people to their brand of Christianity. Through this they created a group of people (along with the mulatto offspring of European men and Afrikan women) who were not really of their people.

The Europeans did not take women on their voyages of "exploration"; they had sex and children with the native women they found at their destinations. Many of these "Afropeans" or "Black Anglo-Saxons" became traitors. It was through these Afrikans that the so-called "slave trade" prospered. Yes, Afrikan people participated in and sold their own people into chattel slavery. But, these were people who were tainted by the European in some way — they were "educated," Christianized, or were addicted to something they had been introduced to by Europeans, such as alcohol or raw power, which was unknown to Afrikan royalty during that time. The natural xenophilia, spirituality and cosmopolitan attitudes of the Afrikans were used as weapons against them to their near destruction.

Final Thought

Although painful, Afrikan people all over the world must unite and create a unified memorial to the Maafa and to those lost during the Maafa. Some groups have set aside July and October to commemorate the Maafa.

*****

References and Suggested Reading

Allen, James, Hilton Als, Congressman John Lewis, Leon F. Litwack. *Without Sanctuary: Lynching Photography in America.* Santa Fe: Twin Palms Publishers, 2000.

Ani, Marimba. *Yurugu: An African-Centered Critique of European Cultural Thought and Behavior.* Trenton: Africa World Press, 1994.

Brent, Linda. *Incidents in the Life of A Slave Girl: An Authentic Historical Narrative Describing the Horrors of Slavery as Experienced by Black Women.* NY: A Harvest/HBJ Book, Harcourt Brace Jovanovich Publishers, 1973.

Butler, Alfred J. *The Arab Conquest of Egypt and the Last 30 Years of the Roman Dominion.* Brooklyn: A & B Books Publishers, (First published in 1902), 1992.

Carew, Jan. *Fulcrums of Change: Origins of Racism in the Americas and Other Essays.* Trenton: Africa World Press, Inc., 1988.

Clarke, John Henrik. *Christopher Columbus and the African Holocaust.* Brooklyn: A & B Books. 1992.

Davies, David. *The Last of the Tasmanians.* London: Frederick Muller, Ltd., 1973.

Diop, Cheikh Anta. *The Cultural Unity of Black Africa.* Chicago: Third World Press, 1978.

Du Bois, W.E.B. *The Suppression of the African Slave Trade to the United States of America 1638-1870.* Baton Rouge: Louisiana State University Press (First published in 1896), 1968.

Finch, Charles S. III. *Echoes of the Old Darkland: Themes from the African Eden.* Decatur, GA: Khenti, Inc., 1991.

Ginsburg, Ralph. *100 Years of Lynching.* Baltimore: Black Classic Press, 1988. Hochschild, Adam. *King Leopold's Ghost.* NY: Houghton Mifflin Co., 1998.

Jones, Del. *The Black Holocaust: Global Genocide.* Philadelphia: Hikeka Press, Inc., 1992.

Jones, Norece T. *Born a Child of Freedom, Yet a Slave: Mechanisms of Control and Strategies of Resistance in Antebellum South Carolina.* Hanover: University Press of New England, 1990.

Lewthwaite, Gilbert A. and Gregory Kane: Witness to Slavery: Where Children Live in Bondage. *The Baltimore Sun* (three-part series), June 16-18, 1996.

Lindqvist, Sven. *"Exterminate All the Brutes": One Man's Odyssey into The Heart of Darkness and the Origins of European Genocide.* NY: The New Press, 1992.

McIntyre, Charshee C. *Criminalizing a Race: Free Blacks During Slavery.* NY: Kayode Publications, Ltd., Queens, 1992.

Stuckey, Sterling. *Slave Culture: Nationalist Theory and the Foundations of Black America.* NY: Oxford University Press, 1987.

UNESCO. *The African Slave Trade from the Fifteenth to the Nineteenth Century*: Paris: Studies and Documents 2, United Nations. 1978.

Welsing, Frances Cress. *The Isis Papers: The Keys to the Colors.* Chicago: Third World Press, 1991.

Williams, Chancellor. *The Destruction of Black Civilization: Great Issues of a Race From 4500 BC to 2000 AD.* Chicago: Third World Press, 1976.

Williams, Eric. *Capitalism and Slavery.* London: Andre Deutsch, London. 1990 (First published in 1964)

Wobogo, Vulindlela I. *Cold Wind from the North: The Prehistoric European Origin of Racism Explained by Diop's Two Cradle Theory.* Charleston, SC: Books On Demand, 2011.

CHAPTER 7

Two Cradle Theory and Philosophical Aspects of Culture

Dr. Cheikh Anta Diop put forth a schema (see below) to explain how climate not only influenced the physical appearance of human populations but also influenced their culture, worldview and outlook. He held that the gentle climate in temperate areas like Afrika gave birth to populations that had not needed to struggle for survival. On the other hand, Afrikans who migrated to Europe and experienced the last Ice Age (the Wurm Interglacial), went through physical, emotional and cultural adaptations that resulted in the aggressive, chauvinistic and violent aspects of what we call Western Civilization. Dr. Charles Finch furthered the argument with medical and biochemical explanations of the processes involved in these mutations.

Arikan/Southern Cradle	Aryan/European/Northern Cradle
Matrilineal	Patrilineal
Sedentary	Nomadic
Burial funeral rites	Cremation funeral rites
Wife keeps legal status	Wife loses legal status
Matrilocal marriage	Patrilocal marriage
Matrilineal succession	Patrilineal succession
Wife keeps family name	Wife loses family name
Inheritance from maternal uncle	Inheritance from father

Arikan/Southern Cradle	Aryan/European/Northern Cradle
Wife can divorce	Wife cannot divorce
Land is collective property	Land is private property
Communalism is special virtue	Individualism is supreme virtue
All children raised	Excess children killed
Cosmologically optimistic	Cosmologically pessimistic
No notion of original sin	Original sin is fault of woman
Peace-loving morality	War-like mentality

Psychologists Dr. Edwin Nichols and Dr. Linda James Myers applied the schema detailed below to philosophical aspects of the culture of different populations. Nichols applied his Philosophical Aspects of Cultural Difference to Europeans/EuroAmericans, Afrikans/Ausa, Asians/AsianAmericans and Native Americans and Mediterranean/ Middle Eastern people but we will concentrate on Afrika and Europe.

Cultural Comparisons

Afrikan/Ausa	Euro/EuroAmerican
Epistemology: Way of knowing is through symbolic imagery and rhythm, feeling and intuition	Knowledge is through counting and measuring.
Axiology: Highest value is in interpersonal Relationships.	Highest value is in the object or in acquiring the object (size and monetary value). Conflict of opposing forces representing a continual struggle.
Ontology: All things have spirit and worth and value	Worth is measured by utility and Materialism
Cosmology: All things in the universe are interconnected and interdependent.	Humans are apart and separate from nature.

Cultural Comparisons (continued)

Afrikan/Ausa	Euro/EuroAmerican
Worldview: The universe is alive and has inherent order and divine laws.	Order is imposed by the stronger force then gains the advantage by ordering the universe as it wishes. "Survival of the fittest."
Ideology: Oneness of all things. Group maintenance, collectiveness and sharing are essential. Life is primary and must reflect divinity.	Drive for mastery and control of nature and the accumulation of possessions.
Identity: We are, therefore I am; I am therefore we are.	I think, therefore I am.
Ethos: All things are with and in harmony with nature.	Control and mastery of all life.

Asian/Asian American	Mediterranean/Middle Eastern
Value System: The highest value lies in identity with the group. Self-worth associated with oneness with nature and Earth	Highest value lies in adherence to sacred text and scripture. Self-worth determined by adherence to divine the relevation
Epistemology: Knowledge gained by direct transcendental experience by entering meditative or altered states of consciousness, then applied to people and situations in the world	Knowledge gained by spiritual teaching passed from generation to generation
Logic: Relative (knowing)	Prescribed

References

Diop, Cheikh Anta. *Cultural Unity of Black Africa.* Chicago: Third World Press, 1978.

Finch, Charles S. III. *Echoes of the Old Darkland: Themes From the African Eden.* Decatur, GA: Khenti, Inc., 1991.

Nichols, Edwin. Philosophical Aspects of Cultural Differences. www.afrometaphysics.org

Van Sertima, Ivan (Editor). *African Presence in Early Europe.* Transaction Books, New Brunswick, 1986.

CHAPTER 8

Nine Areas of Human Activity

In her book *The Isis Papers: The Keys to the Colors*, Dr. Frances Cress Welsing identifies nine areas of human activity in her article, "The Cress Theory of Color Confrontation and Racism (White Supremacy)." As the origin of this information, she cites Neely Fuller, Jr. in his book *The United-Independent Compensatory Code/System/Concept Textbook: A Compensatory Counter-Racist Code.* Too often, we get hung up in arguments about what Black people must do to get "there." If our destination is freedom and sovereignty, there is no one area that is more important. It is essential that we understand that we must address all these areas. Some of us are more interested in one or more areas than in others. But, we must not become so tunnel-visioned that we negate or reduce the importance of the other areas. We must also pay heed to people who have a more holistic vision and who are able to put the pieces together.

These nine areas are all vitally important. Each of us has preferences in our own areas of concentration and I have added two more. I feel these additions are extremely important and that we must reclaim and control them. These areas are:

1. **ECONOMICS.** We do not use our own economic systems. We are forced to use systems that were designed by people with a radically different culture and worldview. Often, we are asked to defend capitalism and/or socialism/communism. We have to ask ourselves the following questions.

a. Can an alien economic system really work for us as a people?

b. Does the system that we find ourselves in really benefit us?

c. Can we mobilize resources for the common good?

d. Can we relearn and reinstitute the economic system that our ancestors created?

2. **EDUCATION.** We have demonstrated, sacrificed, suffered torture and even died for the "right" to send our children to our enemies to be educated. We forced our children onto people who wanted nothing to do with them and did not love or respect them. We are now experiencing the results of that decision with so many young people embracing anti-Afrikan philosophies or who are just confused. It has been shown repeatedly that many of our children have different learning styles that are not addressed in most classrooms. Schools that use systems natural to our children display remarkable success. We must educate our children and give them, the information that is withheld from them in Eurocentric schools and also the love and respect they deserve.

3. **ENTERTAINMENT.** This is one area where we could dominate if we had the will. Only relatively recently have we started to control our destinies in this area to any extent. We should consider the pathology of wanting to entertain those who continue to oppress us. Interestingly, some innovative young people have combined numbers 2 and 3 and have created a system that they call "edutainment." This can help to educate us without the "baggage" of studying, although, there is no adequate substitute for disciplined reading and studying. We need to understand the weapon that the entertainment industry has been. We should analyze and discuss the content and intent of films, TV and sports, much as Professor Anthony Browder has done. In discussing entertainment, we should not neglect the role of sports in distracting us and the general public away from serious thought about our plight.

4. LABOR. We control little, if any, aspect of our labor. We have had to struggle to join organizations that were created to help other

people. We need to create organizations designed for us. Short of that, we should support each other in our different occupations and professions. Better still, we should create businesses that employ and support our brothers and sisters and not rely on others for our sustenance. We should produce our own food, create our own clothes and supply all human needs — food, shelter, clothing, safety and security.

5. **LAW.** Despite the existence of brilliant attorneys, too many of us have bought into the pseudo-rugged individualism dogma that criminalizes our people. Legal organizations could be formed primarily to help our people who continue to be railroaded by overworked public defenders. Not only must we become expert in Western law, we must be authorities in Afrikan systems of justice.
6. **POLITICS.** We have felt it most prudent to join political organizations that were created for the benefit of non-Afrikans. Why not create a huge party that votes on issues and not on personalities? If we were able to organize such a party and fund it, we would be power brokers instead of beggars for crumbs from the tables of democrats and republicans.
7. **RELIGION.** We have been made to fear and ridicule Afrikan spirituality. We do not bother to learn the history of the religions that have been forced upon our Ancestors and passed on to us. The media, especially films and television, have made us shun the spiritual systems that are the parents of the ones that we now claim. We do not realize that today's religions are variations of the spiritual systems that our Ancestors created but with modifications made to fit the worldview of the culture that modified it. Also, in terms of where we are now, churches do not supply the needs of our community. If all Ausa churches banked with Ausa banks and used Ausa vendors, the economic situation of the Ausa community would be greatly improved.
8. **SEX.** Too frequently we lose sight of the beauty of sexual relations with someone that we love and respect. We have become male and

female whores or guilt-ridden souls, fearful of our own sensuality. The sexually repressed oppressors have passed on their sickness to us.

9. **WAR.** At present, we have no means of successful self-protection as a people, so the idea of armed struggle is ridiculous. Even if we identified a concrete enemy, we have no way of waging a successful war. The Black Panthers tried to provide self-defense (as well as meals and healthcare) and systematically were hunted down and murdered. At the same time, we must understand the theory and philosophy of warfare.
10. **HEALTH.** We lead the country and, indeed, the world in most if not all of the negative health statistics. This health disparity is not only due to poor access to healthcare and/or the racism of healthcare providers. It is not only related to the forced segregation through red-lining in housing causing frequently crowded living conditions. This health disparity is greatly related to the fact that we do not take care of ourselves and too many of us do not live healthy lives. We do not eat correctly. We consider "soul food," a survival diet, a delicacy, and many of us live lives that are detrimental to health. And, we live in an atmosphere of racism/white supremacy that adversely affects our health also, as is being made clearer by the new science of Epigenetics.
11. **ENVIRONMENT.** Our Ancestors revered the Creator and the Creator's creations. They considered the aspects of nature (the Creator's Creations) as a part of the Creator. They called them *ntrs* (which some would argue is where our word "nature" comes from). As a result, they kept their surroundings clean and livable. Our exposure to anti-Afrikan philosophies and the resulting self-hatred has caused us to become lax in our upkeep of our surroundings. In addition, our enemies have turned too many of our communities, and other communities of non-white people, into toxic waste dumps. Some of the results of these poisonings are that Ausa die at younger ages than other people. An excellent example of this

occurring is the water supply crisis in Flint, Michigan. The water has been poisoned with lead since 2014 and, as of this writing, nothing definitive has been done and no one has been held accountable. Unfortunately, Flint is not unique. Cities and towns in states as far apart as Wisconsin, Texas, Pennsylvania and South Carolina have reported problems with their water.

CHAPTER 9

SYMBOLS

Rituals and symbols are important to all people, especially to Afrikan people. Rituals are a grounding force that makes up the essence of spirituality. As Sister Louisah Teish has taught us, if the first three and last three letters of the word spirituality are removed, we are left with the word ritual. The repetitious aspect of ritual keeps us in the proper frame of mind in our relationship with the Creator and the Creator's Creations.

In *Ritual: Power, Healing, and Community*, Malidoma Patrice Some says,

> ...ritual is, above all else, the yardstick by which people measure their state of connection with the hidden ancestral realm, with which the entire community is genetically connected...Where ritual is absent, the young ones are restless or violent, there are no real elders, and the grown-ups are bewildered. The future is dim.

ABOUT SYMBOLS

Symbols are letters, figures, emblems, pictures, tokens, words, phrases, images or other objects that represent ideas or concepts that have value. This chapter is not intended to be an in-depth exploration of the topic of symbols; rather, it is hoped that it will stimulate the reader to dig deeper and study more about themselves.

The first symbol used is the **Ankh**, which is familiar to many people. It is a triliteral from ancient Afrika and is discussed below. The next four symbols used here are among the more than 500 **Adinkra** symbols that originate from Ghana. Adinkra are symbols that represent concepts and are used in fabric, pottery and furniture. They are extremely profound in their symbolic meanings and can be helpful to Ausa. Many of these symbols are becoming more familiar to us but, too frequently, we only look at them in one dimension. They have the potential to revolutionize our view of ourselves and can be a potent tool in combating the mental slavery and psychological misorientation that has become an epidemic among our people.

The five symbols that follow are called triliterals in MDW NTR (medu netcher), the sacred writing of our Kemetic (ancient Egyptian) Ancestors, which the Greeks called hieroglyphics. Triliterals are three-letter words and concepts that are important to us and are part of the first written language known to man — an Afrikan language. We are an oral people and a people of letters.

We do not seek to romanticize or idealize Afrikan culture. Although it is the oldest of the world's cultures, it does and did have many faults. Despite these faults, however, we still feel that the deep structure of Afrikan culture is the template upon which all futures should be built. We Afrikans need to check ourselves, to realize that many life-sustaining things have been taken away from us, and to relearn who we were and are. We need to readopt those things that were positive and worked for us; we need to redefine those things that were ambiguous; and, we need to eliminate those things that were/are negative and destructive.

During our contact with other people we have been dominated psychologically, spiritually, and militarily, even though we are not physically or mentally inferior. Our dominators have more sophisticated methods of aggression but have not reached the cultural maturity or spiritual potential that Afrikans have reached.

We must rediscover, reclaim, relearn, reinstitutionalize and reincorporate those things about us that made us the guardians of the

Creator's Creations before the world is destroyed by violence, pollution, greed, environmental poisoning and sheer hypocrisy. We must not actively participate in our own destruction.

One example of that cultural destruction is the current style many Afrikan youth and adults wear in which Asian characters appear on caps and tee shirts and even tattoos. Hopefully, people who wear that style will not reject symbols from their own Ancestral culture. That, partially, is what prompted this chapter. The reader is strongly encouraged to examine and study the references for these symbols.

The Ankh

ANKH

More than 5000 years old, the Ankh is an ancient Afrikan symbol of life. It is NOT an Afrikan cross. It is DEFINITELY NOT a sign of the devil or of Satanism or of the occult.

The Ankh symbolizes the sacred joining of the female and male to create life. The top part, the oval loop, symbolizes the female; the bottom part, the vertical line, symbolizes the male. It makes several profound statements that come to us through the symbolism of our ancient ancestors:

1. The act of joining, intercourse, should not be trivialized, sensationalized, and cheapened (as with pornography). Our Ancestors were not repressed prudes and they definitely enjoyed and explored their sexuality but within defined bounds set by their society.

2. Because children, the fruit of intercourse, were believed to be the reward of life, creation of children indiscriminately, without being able, or responsible enough, to take care of them was frowned upon.
3. Life is created by male and female and is sacred. It should not be taken lightly and snuffed out without hesitation.
4. Life can only be created by female and male and not male and male or female and female. Those other combinations were considered aberrations and abominations and were frowned upon.

If we are to understand who and what our ancestors were, and listen to their voices through the words and images that they left us, we could cure many of the ills that we have suffered while trying to adapt ourselves to an alien culture with radically different values, ethics and morals. Studying and understanding the symbol of the Ankh alone could help us approach solutions for cheap recreational sexual intercourse, pornography, rampant illegitimate births, child neglect and abuse, Black on Black violence and murder, spousal abuse and homosexuality.

Before listening to other peoples' interpretations of our symbols — people who frequently do not know what they are talking about or who have an anti-Afrikan agenda — we should take time to find out ourselves because our ancient Ancestors can still offer us enough guidance to correct ourselves.

Gye Nyame

GYE NYAME (GIN-YAH-MEH)

gye-except
Nyame-God
gye Nyame-I am afraid of none, except God

Gye Nyame is one of the most common Adinkra symbols known in America and one of the most respected and profound Akan spiritual symbols. The Akan are a large ethnic group in Ghana that includes the Asante, who are the primary creators of Adinkra. Gye Nyame is a symbol of power, representing the power and supremacy of the Creator and the power and courage of man.

In the King James Version of the Christian Bible, Psalm 23:4 states, "Yea, though I walk through the valley of the shadow of death, I will fear no evil: for thou art with me; thy rod and thy staff they comfort me." My interpretation of Gye Nyame parallels this verse. To paraphrase the Psalm: Yea though I walk through the valley of the shadow of death, I will fear no evil because, except for the Creator, I am the baddest, meanest and smartest entity in the valley and am afraid of no one but God.

So, except God, I fear no one defines courage and bravery against the forces of confusion, evil and disorder that we face.

Another word that can be used in this regard is *confidence.* We should have the confidence in ourselves to do whatever needs to be done for ourselves and our people and only shy away from doing things that the Creator would not want us to do.

It is also important to note that the concept of formally fearing or being afraid of the Creator is not a common one in Afrika. To Afrikans, the Creator was kind, beneficent and forgiving, not jealous, vengeful and cruel.

FUNTUMMIREKU-DƐNKYƐMMIREKU

FUNTUMMIREKU-DƐNKYƐMMIREKU
Foon-too-mee-ray ku   den-cheh-mee-ray-ku

This two-headed crocodile with one stomach is perfectly symbolic of the concept of Pan Afrikanism. Despite the fact that Afrikan people all over the world have differences, Dr. Cheikh Anta Diop proved convincingly in *The Cultural Unity of Black Africa* that Afrikan people all over the world have one culture. This culture has minor differences that mostly account for the differences in customs that are found in different geographical locations. These differences can also be traced to adaptations to the cultures of the oppressors. However, in the deep structure of culture, Afrikan people are basically the same all over the world.

Other Afrikan words or phrases that describe this concept and all meaning unity are as follows:

- *Umoja*, a ki-Swahili word from East Afrika that means *unity*
- *Harambee*, a ki-Swahili word that means *pull together*
- *Ifo wo su wo po*, a Yoruba phrase from Nigeria that means *coming together*
- *Oganihu* (Oh-gah-nee-hue), an Igbo word from Nigeria
- Ajosepo (ah-jah-sheh-paw), another Yoruba word from Nigeria
- Nkabom (en-kah-bahm), a Twi word from Ghana

To regain our traditional place in the world we must all pull together instead of using our energies and genius to keep other people in positions of superiority over us.

Funtummireku Dɛnkyɛmmireku also tells us that all Afrikan people share one destiny. Whatever is bad for one of us ultimately is bad for all of us and whatever is good for one of us ultimately is good for all of us. All of us must contribute to the common good.

Within this common destiny are many different opinions, philosophies and goals. We should not fight or do damage to each other. The only thing that should remain constant is the recognition that we do share one destiny and are hence our brother's keeper.

Sankofa

SANKOFA
san-ko-fah
san - to return to the roots, to the source
ko – to go
fa – to take or seize

Sankofa means, literally, *go back and fetch it.* This symbol is profoundly educational in what it teaches the Ausa and other Diasporan Afrikan peoples: it reinforces the fact that the past is the only effective building block for the future.

If we would only open our eyes, we would see that we are the only people who do not build our future based on our past. Anyone who thinks any future is built without considering the past is, unfortunately, delusional.

We simply MUST take the time to rediscover our ancient and archetypical selves. We must actively, persistently and diligently dedicate ourselves to the quest for knowledge. Without that knowledge, we are poor imitations of our oppressors, who are frequently badly imitating our Ancestors. We become our own greatest oppressors — at all levels of socioeconomic and political realities.

To paraphrase Sun Tzu, an ancient Chinese warrior-philosopher, in a conflict: *Those who know themselves and not their enemy will win 50% of the time; those who know their enemy and not themselves will win 50% of the time; but those who know themselves and their enemy will win 100% of the time.* Sadly, many of us have been so incorporated into the mindset, value system, and standard of beauty of our enemies that we do not recognize who our enemies are or know them. To paraphrase Dr. Marimba Ani, we are in a war but only the enemy knows.

It is a matter of controlling our destiny as a people. As Tony Browder quoted George Orwell:

> Whoever Controls the Past
> Controls the Future
> Whoever Controls the Present
> Controls the Past.

The past is the key! We must go back and rediscover the missing details of our Ancestral heritage that were intentionally and strategically taken away from us. It would follow that if our past had to be taken away from us to make us slaves, then there must be great power in our past. If much time, energy and money are spent to keep us from learning about ourselves or being socialized into beings non-threatening to the status quo, then what we do not know about ourselves must be truly powerful.

To quote W. Bruce Willis in *The Adinkra Dictionary*:

> Sankofa is a realization of self and spirit. It represents the concepts of self-identity, redefinition, and vision. It symbolizes an understanding of one's destiny and the collective identity of the larger cultural group. Sankofa is the repossession of something that was forgotten and the initiation of a process to return to the place where the object was lost in order to fetch it and then move forward into the future.

Two symbols are commonly used for Sankofa. One is a bird looking backwards. The other is in the shape of what we commonly call a heart. We can be sure that many of the enslaved ironworkers who created the decorations for grills and doors all over the South were Akan, especially in coastal areas like Charleston, South Carolina, Savannah, Georgia, and New Orleans, Louisiana. It is like they were telling us not to forget who they were and who we are.

Akoben

AKOBEN (AH-KOH-BANE)

Akoben – a war horn

An *akoben* is an ivory horn that was blown through a cut near the smaller end and used by the Akan people as a symbol of readiness for war or a call to action, according to Willis. Traditionally, among the Akan people, it was used to alert people who were scattered throughout the fields and forests that they should assemble for a common task or to prepare for a nearby enemy. In modern Ghana, the akoben is used to represent a communal readiness to perform a task for the common good.

This is the ultimate challenge for all Afrikan people, it is what we all should be about. We should all be activists. The time is getting short and we are rapidly approaching extinction as a people who have a distinctive culture and worldview. The world is significantly at-risk from pollution of values, ethics, morals, noise, violence, toxic waste and trash. Establishing and institutionalizing the documented Afrikan worldview is one of the few methods by which the world will survive for our grandchildren's grandchildren.

We must all answer the call to action and become activists for our own survival. We must become mentally healthy enough to at least stop actively participating in our own destruction.

In order to become subscribers of Akoben, we must embrace Sankofa to know what and who we are and to know that knowledge of self is worth saving; we must understand and embrace Funtummireku-Dɛnkyɛmmireku so that we will know that we are one; and we must embrace and understand Gye Nyame so that we will internalize the knowledge of the Creator's omnipotence and the necessity of our own courage.

Hotep

HOTEP

Peace

Hotep is the earliest greeting that Afrikan people have offered each other. The quest for the state of inner and outer peace seems to have always been a human characteristic. Perhaps warlike societies had not quite reached the state of being human. In Christian churches worldwide today, the phrase, *peace be with you* is a frequent greeting. A similar phrase in Islamic/Arabic culture, *as-salaam alaikum,* is a common greeting. In Hebrew culture, Shalom, which also means peace, is a common greeting. This greeting also suggests that, as we search for peace, we wish for peace for those whom we meet in a day. True spiritual and mental maturity can only come in an atmosphere of peace.

The negative connotation of hotep in today's world is a result of the misguided and frequently intentionally misleading but charismatic individuals who have used that word while scamming and seducing unsuspecting and well-meaning people who are seeking knowledge. It is important to know that the positive use of the term hotep preceded by thousands of years the current negative light that surrounds it.

Khepra

KHEPRA

Being and Becoming

The significance of *Khepra* came from the dung beetle in Kmt. They

laid their eggs in the mud and later, as fully functional beetles, flew from this mud. At a basic level, being and becoming means being the best that you can be while continually striving to be even better. If you shoot for the sun and miss, you will still be among the stars. We must also consider resurrection and the continuous cycle of moving from one stage of life to another. We must always be the best that we can be and always seek perfection.

Sia

SIA

siA-(sia)

Perception, Insight and Knowledge

Sia was the Kemetic *ntr* (aspect of the Creator or part of nature) symbolizing complete understanding of one's environment and relationships. It meant "to know." There are several ways of knowing. In fact, with the Mali ethnic group the Dogon, there is a progression of scientific, cultural, historical, symbolic and spiritual knowledge.

Level 1 is *giri so* (gear-ee so), which means *sight without understanding* or *understanding words at face value.* This is the immature and childish approach to the world.

Level 2 is *benne so* (been-ee so), or *sight with perspective* which refers to the understanding of some of the meaning associated with words. The Dogon way of saying this is *word from the side,* or being able to understand some nuances in communication.

Level 3 is *bolo so* or *insight* which refers to vision beyond the words. This refers to the ability to correctly interpret spoken word.

Level 4, *so dayi* (clear word), is the highest level of knowledge and refers to understanding the true meaning behind words. It is the latter-day equivalent of sia, to which all Afrikans should aspire. This allows the acquisition of what has been called *sacred wisdom.*

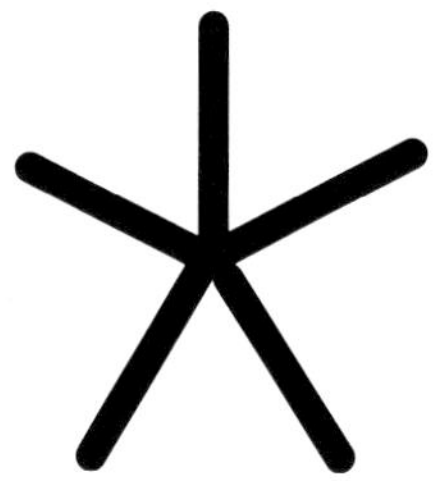

SEBA

SEBA

Teaching and Wisdom

Once sia is achieved, it is the duty of all to pass that knowledge and wisdom to others. Teachers (the *sebait*) were valued, honored and highly respected, as they still should be. For effective transmission of knowledge, there must be effective communication or Mdw Nfr (good speech), as well as effective hearing in an atmosphere of respect. We must once again earn the respect of our Elders, peers and youth in order to teach and learn from them. Students should not only trust the teachers but trust themselves to learn and use appropriately what is taught.

Other Concepts

Other concepts that are of importance to people of Afrikan origin are considered here also. The words are important although we have not included actual symbols.

WHEM (Repetition and Reawakening)

Despite the individual advances of Afrikan people in foreign cultures, our greatest times as a people are long past. We must have, as a goal, the reascension of our culture: our values, morals, standards of beauty, and unique sense of fairness. We must repeat our glory days. In fact, our Kemetic Ancestors had a concept called *Whmy Msw*, or *repetition of the birth.* We must recreate our glory days because our survival is at stake.

AGOO (Ah-go)

Agoo is an important term that comes from the Twi language of the Akan people of Ghana. It is frequently used in a ritualistic manner in two circumstances: When someone wants to enter a home, a room or another building and when someone wants to get the attention of others.

First circumstance: It is used when visiting. When standing at the entrance, Agoo is spoken in a firm voice. If the person can enter, the response is *Amee* (Ah-may), which means, come in. If entrance is not desirable or advisable, the response is gyina haɔ— (gin-a-haw), which means *hold it or don't come in right now.*

Second circumstance: Frequently, it is used to get the attention of others, as in opening a meeting or in a crowded room, bus, or classroom. When a person says, Agoo loudly, the people will respond by saying Amee and becoming silent. Rarely should it be necessary to repeat this more than once. In this circumstance, Amee means, *You have my attention, I am listening.*

All good language teachers make their students use new words and concepts in sentences or practical situations to test their grasp of the material. In terms of the things that we have discussed here, our esteemed Ancestor, Dr. Asa Hilliard, in his book, *Sba: The Reawakening of the African Mind* gives us methods of using and understanding some of the concepts:

> Proper sba is a prerequisite for sia... But before sba, we must remember sankofa...Part of understanding what is happening to us in the maafa (Great disaster--our holocaust) requires that we know where we came from...Study is a requirement for our redemption. All African people must be students. Greater understanding was earned through sba, the study of mdw ntr (divine speech) and mdw nfr (good speech). Jacob Carruthers (1995) has referred to the combination of mdw ntr and mdw nfr as African deep thought. Without African deep thought, the whmy msw (whemy mesue) (reawakening and rebirth) would be impossible. The healing process for people of African descent can only be initiated as a consequence of our engagement in deep thought.
>
> Our whmy msw requires deep thought about our cultural essence, our cosmology and metaphysics, our geopolitics, and our strategies for long-range development, among other things. We cannot evade our responsibility to study. We have a massive task before us. This time we must get it right.
>
> The perception and insight into MAAT (truth, justice, righteousness, harmony, balance, order, propriety, reciprocity) brings heka (power)...It is heka that will ultimately fuel the whmy msw. African teachers must help students realize their heka. Students must be walked through the process of learning that will take them from sba to sia to MAAT to heka.
>
> The only agenda for us that will ensure our renewal is sankofa for whmy msw.

Finally, there appears to be little disagreement among thoughtful and knowledgeable Ausa that the Confederate battle flag is symbolic of a terrible time in our history. The Confederate battle flag is symbolic of a time in our history when we were lower as a people than we have ever been — before or since our Maafa.

When considering the question of the flag, we must again be aware of the power of symbols, especially on the subconscious mind. That flag is insulting (or should be, I think) to all Ausa. What it represents for Afrikans in America is a time when degradation was the norm. This was a time when Afrikan women (and men) could be beaten or raped or even killed by white men and women (and frequently they were), and there was nothing that they or their husbands, wives, fathers, mothers, sons, daughters, brothers, sisters, or other concerned Afrikans could do.

The fact that so many white Americans are supportive of that symbol of the enslavement, rape, beating, torture, and hatred of Afrikan people is proof of their disrespect and dislike of Afrikan people as well as their lack of and disdain for sensitivity of our feelings. If their "reasoning" is that the flag represents a proud Southern heritage, we must remember that there was no such thing as the Confederate battle flag until the "peculiar institution" of slavery (The Maafa) was threatened. The flag was created to symbolize that group of people who were willing to destroy the country their forefathers had died to create in order to continue the enslavement, debasement and degradation of Afrikan people. Even more interesting, many "flag supporters" claim to be patriotic Americans yet they honor and defend the symbol of their ancestors' attempt to destroy the very country they claim to love. This is treasonous.

There may be some Afrikan Americans who are not insulted by the flag and do not feel strongly that it should be banned. However, these individuals are probably victims of the miseducation that our honored Ancestor, Dr. Carter G. Woodson, speaks about in his book, *The Miseducation of the Negro.* Individuals of Afrikan origin who do feel strongly in favor of prominently displaying the flag either are confused or are collaborators with our historical and current oppressors and, therefore, our enemies.

The study of our Maafa is necessary for all Afrikan people in the world and especially for those of us in America. We must learn the truth and not just the whitewashed versions (no pun intended) given to us in popular books, in movies and on television. Our story has never been told in movies. *Gone with the Wind* was the southern white woman's version and *Glory* was the northern white man's version. By the time *Roots* got to the television screen, it was diluted, softened and not even historically accurate.

These are the books we must read to even begin this study:

- *Born a Child of Freedom, Yet a Slave* by Norece T. Jones
- *Slave Culture* by Sterling Stuckey
- *Christopher Columbus and the Afrikan Holocaust* by Dr. John Henrik Clarke
- *The Black Holocaust by Del Jones*
- *Criminalizing a Race* by Charshee C. L. McIntyre
- *Incidents in the Life of a Slave Girl* by Linda Brent.

Then, we can get deeply into the other so-called "slave narratives" and books by people like Walter Rodney, Eric Williams, Asa Hilliard, Jacob Carruthers, Wade Nobles, John G. Jackson, Chancellor Williams, Ivan van Sertima, Charles Finch, Theophile Obenga, Cheikh Anta Diop and many others. If you wonder about the mentality of a people or a worldview that can commit terrible atrocities, such as our Maafa, read *Yurugu* by Marimba Ani.

BIBLIOGRAPHY AND SUGGESTED READING

Benton, Joe, Derrick Jackson, and Burnett Gallman. *Project: Sankofa: A Rites of Passage Program: Philosophy, Theory & Overview.* Columbia: Our Community Organization, 1998.

Carruthers, Jacob H. MDW NTR: *Divine Speech: A Historiographical Reflection of African Deep Thought from the Time of the Pharaohs to the Present.* Lawrenceville, NJ: Red Sea Press, 1995.

Diop, Cheikh Anta. *The Cultural Unity of Black Afrika: The Domains of Matriarchy and of Patriarchy in Classical Antiquity*, London: Karnak House Publishers, 2000.

Hilliard, Asa G. III. *SBA: The Reawakening of the African Mind.* Gainesville: Makare Publishing Company, 1997.

Karenga, Maulana. *The African American Holiday of Kwanzaa.* Los Angeles: University of Sankore Press, 1989.

Ra, Ankh Mi. Let the Ancestors Speak: *Removing the Veil of Mysticism from Medu Netcher: A Guide to the Grammar of the Language of KEMET.* Temple Hills: JOM International Inc., 1995.

Rossini, Stephane. *Egyptian Hieroglyphics: How to Read and Write Them.* NY: Dover Publications, Inc., 1989.

Some, Malidoma Patrice. *Ritual: Power, Healing and Community.* Portland: Swan/Raven & Company, 1993.

Tzu, Sun. *The Art of War.* (Translated by Thomas Cleary), Boston: Shambhala, 1991.

Willis, W. Bruce. *The Adinkra Dictionary: A Visual Primer on the Language of ADINKRA.* Washington: The Pyramid Complex, 1998.

CHAPTER 10

Race, Health and Scientific Racism

Introduction

The question of race and racism in America has long been a special topic, sometimes taboo, frequently antagonistic but always sensitive. Repeatedly, Ausa and European Americans have demonstrated that they see questions of race frequently from diametrically opposite vantage points. Many of the reasons for this are steeped in the pseudo-scientific prattle used to justify the enslavement of human beings by other human beings and to provide a way for one group to feel superior to another.

Drs. W. Michael Byrd and Linda Clayton have been researching and writing on this topic for many years. This very gracious "dynamic duo" have gifted us with the definitive look at the problem with their two-volume work, *An American Health Dilemma*, which is the standard reference in this area and their findings predate the Institute of Medicine report by at least ten years. It has become a timeless classic and is necessary reading for every healthcare provider.

The Institute of Medicine (IOC) report, published in 2003, researched, analyzed and reported on the current racial health disparities. Before this report, there had been no *official*, universal agreement on the existence of disparities, despite a multitude of anecdotal evidence and Byrd and Clayton's earlier major work.

The IOC identified several areas that they called "variables" that contribute to racial health disparities:

1. Patient level variables such as preferences, treatment refusal and the clinical appropriateness of care
2. Healthcare systems-level factors, which involve institutional racism
3. Care process level variables such as bias, stereotyping and uncertainty

In this chapter we will deal with the bias or racism in existence in America and especially in South Carolina, the state where the first shots of the Civil War were fired. South Carolina was also the first state to indulge in the treason of secession from America and had an abysmal record of lynching African American men and women from the 1880s until the 1950s. Regarding the latter, at least two governors and several other well-known political figures took every opportunity to publicly and unapologetically endorse the idea of black inferiority or to encourage violence against Ausa.

What the IOC report did not say is that these racial health disparities have been in existence in America since the Ancestors of most of today's Afrikan Americans were kidnapped and brought to America, as dealt with effectively in Byrd and Clayton's contribution in the IOC report and in their other work. The IOC "variable" contributes to the disparity evidenced in the "prejudice" (or racism) of providers that is directed against patients and physicians of color and in the inadequate numbers of Afrikan American providers.

When the research on this study was started, I was surprised by the sheer volume of research that had been done and was being done on this topic. The researchers represented several fields. I became disappointed that most healthcare workers, including and especially physicians, give so little attention to this research. Obviously, this is an extremely uncomfortable subject. I would invite all readers of Byrd and Clayton's article to peruse the references, paying special attention to their works, as well as to those of Drs. David R. Williams, Nancy Kreiger, Camara Jules Harrell, Camara Phyllis Jones, Thomas LaVeist,

Raj Bhopal, Kwame McKenzie, Shawn Bediako and Sherman James, who is one of the sources of pride of Hartsville, South Carolina, my home town.

Before going any further, I must state that racism is only one of the "-isms" associated with white supremacy (dominion); the others are *imperialism, sexism, age-ism* and *classism.* Volumes could be written about each of these "-isms" and their relationship to white supremacy (dominion) but because race is such a profound factor in the world today, the concentration will be on racism.

Racism has been a festering abscess in the vital organs of America since its birth. Its presence in the world is very problematic especially when placed into context of reality. Individual and cultural negation due to racism probably has cost the world many scientific discoveries from geniuses who had failed to reach their potential. Many lives have been lost, from those taken savagely by racist murderers to those wasted by substance abuse fueled by the frustration felt by victims of different forms of racism. Even white lives have been lost that may have been saved by medical advances not achieved because the potential discoverer never had the opportunity to make the discovery. These facts do not take into consideration fully the loss of advances caused by institutional racism.

Although the word "racism" represents a very real concept, it has meant different things to different people. Unfortunately, the word has been overused and used inappropriately. Nevertheless, racism is alive, well and thriving. It is my belief that racism is prevalent among all healthcare providers.

Today, racism is frequently unrecognized, unacknowledged or ignored by medical practitioners as well as by many of their patients. These practitioners refuse, or are unable to see the problem from any perspective other than their own which too frequently is very narrow or filled with defense mechanisms. Despite occasional, inappropriate accusations of racism, this is a major problem and not enough energy or other resources have been used to study racism in a useful manner.

Healthcare workers, including physicians, are not immune from being racist, even though many would deny it. I would suggest that those individuals who are angered most by this discussion probably need the most self-assessment. We live and participate in the American aspect of the Western world and many of the existing negative notions about race were either developed or perpetuated by Western physicians.

Some feel that racism was created to justify slavery. These physicians formulated myths of superiority and some created diseases peculiar to Black people. The most ridiculous "disease," *Drapetomania*, was created by Dr. Samuel A. Cartwright, a Louisiana physician, a discussion of which was reprinted in a respected medical journal in 1851. Drapetomania was the disease that caused enslaved Africans to run away from slavery. We also cannot forget J. Marion Sims, the South Carolina native who is called the "Father of Gynecology" because he surgically experimented on enslaved black women *without anesthesia*. Apparently, he did not think Black people felt pain.

This chapter is intended to explore and discuss racism, and especially scientific racism, so light can be shed on the topic for the uninformed reader. We want to provide nourishing food for thought, especially since so many people, especially young people, are unable to recognize racism even when they are experiencing it. Race relations in America are fascinating. Blacks and whites see the same events frequently from vastly different vantage points.

One example of this phenomenon was the O.J. Simpson verdict. Many whites were shocked at the joyous reaction of most Blacks at O.J.'s acquittal. What whites did not realize was that most of the Black reaction was not based on a feeling of solidarity with O.J. The reaction was based on the fact that, after centuries of inequality in the American court system in which whites always won, even when it was obvious that they were guilty, a Black man finally "beat" the system. It was a truism in this writer's community that if a Black person was accused of the murder or rape of a white person, they would die (by lynching or legal execution) while whites who killed or raped blacks usually went free, if they were arrested at all, as with the Emmitt Till case.

In treating addictive disorders and other mental illness, one of the first steps is to help the patient realize that they do have a problem (help develop insight). It is hoped that the reader will benefit from the information presented in this chapter.

Definitions

In every discussion there are terms that tend to recur. In this discussion, it is important to expose and discuss the terms that will be used as well as the context for their use. The section that follows is an attempt to define and contextualize these terms.

- **RACE**: Race is a concept that has been used since before Europeans needed to justify slavery and imperialism and attempted to define human types by appearance. It is a social construct and was said not to be a biological reality. However, the new discipline of epigenetics is suggesting that there may be some validity to the concept. The original creation of race, however, was definitely a European invention. The concept placed those people now described as white at the top of the human family in terms of intelligence, culture and beauty. Since that time, and despite the fact that, now, race is seen as unscientific, it is still the basis of many important decisions and actions.

Although it is probably true that race, as a scientific concept, is unsound, most of western culture, including the health and social sciences, have been built on a foundation of which race is a prominent part. In America, racism thrives in virtually every area of endeavor and exists in the air, the water and the soil. The races that have traditionally resided at the bottom of the so-called evolutionary tree now have tremendous disparities in health and healthcare, as well as in education, economics, incarceration and the use of death sentence. If suddenly we were to become color blind, however, there would be no way to measure and track the health and other status markers for those groups. The current genocide could not be demonstrated, proven or tracked.

- **EUGENICS:** Eugenics is a pseudoscientific discipline originating in the late nineteenth century that developed and spread theories supporting genetic engineering to produce "superior" humans and eliminate "inferior" humans by forced sterilization, euthanasia, abortion or mass murder (Hitler). It was felt that the superior humans were of Northern or Western European stock. Poor whites and people of color were said to have genes for feeblemindedness which caused misery, poverty and crime. The solution for U.S. social problems was believed to be forced sterilization of the poor and prevention of the immigration of poor and colored people. Planned Parenthood, originated by Margaret Sanger, is an example of the institutions created by Eugenics supporters.

Interestingly, the American Eugenics movement was supported financially by very wealthy and influential people, like the Kelloggs, Rockefellers Carnegies, Henry Ford, Alexander Graham Bell, and Charles W. Eliot (a president of Harvard College). Sweden, Italy and Prussia also supported Eugenics. Using Eugenics textbooks, Eugenics was taught in colleges and medical schools all over the world, especially in Germany and the United States.

Eugenics also impacted religion in that it rejected science and the theory of evolution, and Eugenics principles were often coupled with religious beliefs. It appears that today's conservative Christians share some Eugenic principles.

- **PREJUDICE:** Prejudice, according to the IOC, is "an unjustified negative attitude based on a person's group membership."
- **RACISM**: The United Nations uses the term "racial discrimination" to describe "any distinction, exclusion, restriction or preferences based on race, color, descent or national or ethnic origin which has the purpose or effect of nullifying or impairing the recognition, enjoyment or exercise, on an equal footing, of human rights and fundamental freedoms in the political, economic, social, cultural or any other field of public life." We

have come to call this racism.

Interestingly, racism has been described frequently in mental health terms as a chronic mental health illness. Symptoms include acting out, denial of reality, projection, transference of blame, delusions of grandeur, disassociation, and justification. People affected (infected?) with racism are paranoid, delusional (they have false beliefs contrary to truthful wellness that do not change when evidence is presented to the contrary) and psychopathic (they are unable to experience guilt, are completely selfish and callous, have total disregard for the rights of others, and are constantly in conflict with other persons or groups). Also, they exhibit maladaptive narcissism and sadism in their relationships with other groups.

Another good general psychiatric definition of racism is that it is a defense and adjustment mechanism that not only helps individuals and groups deal with insecurity but forms a systematic method of control of one group by another for the purposes of exploitation and control.

Racism could also be considered a public health problem as well as a chronic mental health illness. However, the problem in defining racism as a mental illness is that racists conceivably could take an insanity plea after committing a heinous crime and escape punishment.

The concept of power is important in distinguishing racism from prejudice. As we discuss racism, it is important to note the racism present in physicians who have immigrated to this country. Frequently, this is noted in the way many African American patients are treated by some of these immigrants. Although many come from countries with rigid systems of caste, class and race stratification and although American style racism has been exported quite well, much of this racist behavior has to do with the images of African Americans that have been broadcast on television, in books and in film. These images create negative stereotyping which frequently translates into racist behavior and can be seen in physicians from India, the Philippines, Pakistan, Saudi Arabia, Korea, Japan, China and even in some physicians from African countries such as Nigeria, Ghana and Egypt.

Indeed, this writer's medical school roommate, who was from Nigeria, stated that upon arrival in this country he had been cautioned by immigration officials to avoid contact with African Americans as much as possible. He was told that African Americans were violent, lazy and hated Africans from the continent. Fortunately, he had been exposed to many negative aspects of white American officials in Nigeria before he left home. He went directly to contact African Americans and found that he had been lied to again.

This story has been repeated to the author by other continental Afrikans. At that same time, this writer and many Ausa have been told just the opposite, that continental Africans hated and felt superior to African Americans. It is interesting that a document purporting to originate with the National Security Council decries the cooperation of "black Africa and the U.S. Black movement." If this document is real, it tells us what is feared by those who historically have oppressed us.

- **ENVIRONMENTAL RACISM:** The targeting of a specific population for abnormal exposure to harmful material (Benjamin Chavis, 1983).
- **REPARATIONS:** The root word of reparations is "repair." Reparations refers to attempts to repair, to make amends, retribution, or compensation for the commission of an injustice or crime. Reparations will be explored more fully in Chapter 21.
- **SCIENTIFIC RACISM:** This term is used to describe publications, pronouncements and propaganda with scientific sounding content (pseudo-science) used for a political or self-serving purpose that is represented as scientific fact based on research but is distorted by racist ideology and supports a racist paradigm. It can create fear, inflame racism and is intended to create a racially divided and racially hierarchical society. It does not even conform to the Western ideology of objectivity. Eugenics is an excellent example of pseudoscience and scientific racism.
- **STEREOTYPING:** The Institute Of Medicine (IOM) defines stereotyping as "...the process by which people use social

categories (e.g., race, sex) in acquiring, processing, and recalling information about others." The important points from the IOM for the purpose of this paper is the work of Dovidio, et al. "In the United States, because of shared socialization influences, there is considerable empirical evidence that even well-meaning whites who are not overtly biased and who do not believe that they are prejudiced typically demonstrate unconscious implicit racial attitudes and stereotypes."

- **WHITE PRIVILEGE:** No discussion of racism is complete without examining the other side of racism, one of the "desirable" end results of, and the reason for, racism: the phenomenon of "White Privilege." This topic is being looked at and discussed more frequently now than ever before. Numerous websites deal with this topic and it is even taught as a college course. While it is important that all people understand the phenomenon of white privilege, it is a topic that people of European ancestry, who call themselves "white" need to understand.

The good news is this: a large literature on the subject exists. The bad news is many racists really do not care. Admittedly, people who are classified as intentional racists would be unmoved by allegations of white privilege.

Current criticisms of "Affirmative Action" are really a joke. Affirmative action has existed in America since its existence; the difference is that, for the bulk of that time, it benefited only white males. This has been called "the other side of racism": unearned advantage and conferred dominance based on race. Individuals who state that their ancestors did not own slaves or had no prejudice have benefited, nevertheless, from white privilege (see discussion as follows).

White Privilege and Racism

Of all the results of the Maafa, perhaps the ones least discussed and most debated are the concepts of white privilege and racism. Both concepts arise from the myth of white supremacy that was necessary to make it easier to kidnap, enslave, mistreat and disorient Afrikan people, intentionally alienating them from their heritage and homeland.

White privilege is the frequently subconscious feeling of entitlement and superiority that many whites, even some that are "well meaning," feel towards people who do not look like them. It enables them to take advantage of situations that favor them and ignore (or be oblivious of) the fact that they are receiving special treatment not afforded to people of color simply by being white in a world controlled by white people.

This privilege is manifested in many ways, including the attempt to universalize their experiences and opinions by saying "all people do this" or "feel like this." Another way whites see this privilege is their refusal (or inability?) to understand what Afrikan Americans mean when they say discrimination is still a problem. They do not seem to be able to understand that white culture, opinions and visions of reality are considered "normal" and other cultures, opinions and visions are the "other" and are positioned outside of what is right and normal for them. One example of this is the term, "classic." Classical music refers to early European music and the word almost always refers to something European.

Mere mention of "white privilege" (and racism) frequently makes many white people very uncomfortable, much the same as many whites feel uncomfortable in situations in which they are not in the majority and are not the dominant people in situations. Unfortunately, too many whites see the loss of this privilege as oppression. Loss of privilege is not oppression!!

This "cognitive dissonance" is at its most ridiculous when otherwise reasonably intelligent whites say they oppose affirmative action because they believe in a "level playing field" where all people are equal and no one has any advantages. This would be laughable if the results were not so tragic for Afrikan Americans. Equality is not equity.

Again, it must be stated that racism is only one of the "-isms" included in white supremacy; the others are sexism, ageism, classism and imperialism. Racism is a mental illness caused by the delusion of white supremacy and is fed and supported in a symbiotic relationship by white privilege.

Racism is delusional. Racists hold to the belief of their own superiority despite all evidence to the contrary. Their evidence of their superiority is usually comprised of fabricated information. They stack the deck against others and then blame them for failing, using this failure as proof of inferiority. Because they control many information systems, they introduce and reinforce the idea of Black inferiority after taking away culture, which is the solid ground upon which all self-respecting people stand.

Racism is psychopathic. Psychopaths are in constant conflict with others. They are selfish, callous, unable to experience guilt and have a total disregard for the rights of others. They are violent. In photographic and written accounts of lynchings and other atrocities, women and children are often present. The present-day equivalents of being hung, burned alive, or having body parts cut off while conscious have become the beheadings, beatings, sodomizing in police stations, shootings, and being dragged behind trucks until the body fragments that we hear about in today's new, modern and "better" world.

Racism is an abnormal defense and adjustment mechanism against insecurities. These insecurities might be psychological or social. They might also be physical and related to the state of relative deficiency of melanin. Insecurity is manifested in the fact that many whites believe that Afrikan Americans are getting too many privileges since many Blacks are making material strides in this society. This insecurity borders on paranoia. It also may be an insecurity based on a relative genetic deficiency, an inability to produce melanin in significant amounts. Racism (and white privilege) are public health hazards because they are contagious delusions that affect masses of people. These insecurities have heightened since it has become common knowledge that whites in America will soon be in the minority.

Racism is not merely color prejudice. It is a sick, power-mediated ability to negatively influence the lives of others based on color, hair texture and other physical features. It has profoundly affected the world for the worse and shows no sign of dying out. It is responsible for many of the troubles in today's world and is rapidly drawing the world toward a cataclysmic end.

Origins and History of Racism

The physical differences that define race were noted as long as humanity has been in existence. The differences were not given value, however, so the concepts of race and racism that we are dealing with in this work are relatively modern inventions.

There are many theories that deal with the origins of racism/white supremacy. We will briefly discuss a few of those theories.

The late Senegalese scholar, Dr. Cheikh Anta Diop, an Egyptologist, Cultural Anthropologist, Linguist and Nuclear Physicist, was an advocate of the monogenetic theory of man's origins. He posited that the Africans who migrated North from Africa and got caught in Europe during the Wurm Interglacial Era (the last Ice Age) not only went through environmentally stimulated adaptive physical mutations resulting in what we now call a "white" or "Caucasoid" appearance but also experienced cultural and psychological adaptations that resulted in individual and societal aggressiveness, chauvinism, patriarchy, materialism and xenophobia.

According to Diop and one of his many disciples, Charles Finch, M.D., those mutated Afrikans, now called Europeans and some Asians, encountered societies that had not needed to struggle against nature to survive. These people were peaceful and xenophilic; European aggressiveness led them to inferiorize and subjugate these peaceful people.

In another theory, Frances Cress Welsing, M.D., a psychiatrist, posited that racism is a subconscious survival mechanism of whites based on the recessive genetic patterns of many characteristics that are associated with racial whiteness. She states that whiteness is a relative deficiency of melanin and that white people are a numerical minority worldwide. She stated that whites see people of color as a threat to their genetic survival since most of the characteristics that define blackness are genetically dominant and those that define whiteness are recessive. The result, she felt, is hostility towards pigmented people and the imposition of white supremacy or domination. She defined racism as white genetic survival which was reinforced recently by the chants of racists at the 2017 Charlottesville, Virginia, rally, "You will not replace us." Some historical theorists, like Ibram X. Kendi, believe racism was a theory promulgated to justify Europe's enslavement and severe mistreatment of Afrikan people.

Types of Racism

Racism is one of America's imperfections that contributes to the country's unfulfilled promises. Because many people have chosen to ignore the racism and pretend that it has suddenly magically disappeared, it has continued to fester and threatens to become more of a problem.

Table 1: Types of Racism (Jones, James: *Prejudice and Racism.* McGraw Hill, NY, 1972)

Individual Racism	Occurs when a person believes in the racial superiority of one group over another and engages in practices that reinforce the inferiorization of that group.
Institutional Racism	There are two manifestations: 1) Conscious manipulation of institutions or situations to achieve racist objectives. 2) Occurs as a by-product or natural extension of the practices of institutions that impinge on the rights and access of particular racial groups.
Cultural Racism	Occurs when there is, "differential access to the goods, services and opportunity of society by race. It is normative, sometimes legalized and often manifests as inherited disadvantage. It is structural, having been codified in our institutions of custom, practice and law so there need not be an identifiable perpetrator. Institutional racism is often evident as inaction in the face of need.

Table 2: Types of Racism (Jones, Camara Phyllis: Levels of Racism: A Theoretic Framework and a Gardener's Tale. The American Journal of Public Health, 90 (8): 1212-1215, 2000.

Institutionalized Racism	Occurs when there is differential access to quality education, housing, employment, medical facilities, healthy environment, information (including your own history), resources and political voice.
Personally Mediated Racism	This is prejudice and discrimination where prejudice means differential assumptions about the abilities, motives and intentions of others according to their race, and discrimination means differential actions towards others according to their race. It can be intentional as well as unintentional and it includes acts of commission as well as omission. It manifests as lack of respect, suspicion, devaluation, scape-goating and dehumanization.
Internalized Racism	Acceptance by members of the stigmatized races of negative messages about their own abilities and intrinsic worth. Internalized racism is characterized by their not believing in others who look like them and not believing in themselves. It involves accepting limitations to one's own humanity. It manifests as an embracing of "whiteness," self-devaluation, and resignation, helplessness and hopelessness.

Table 3: Types of Racism (Kovel, Joel: *White Racism: A Psycho History*. Vintage, NY, 1971)

Dominative Racism	Bigoted beliefs are acted out and the person openly seeks to keep Black people down and is willing to use force to further his ends.
Aversive Racism	This person believes in white race superiority and is more or less aware of it. He/she avoids the issue of race and tries to ignore the existence of Black people, tries to avoid contact with them and to be polite, correct and cold in whatever dealings are necessary between the races. There are two subtypes: 1) Those who lapse into dominative racism if a Black person gets too close. 2) Those who consider themselves to be liberals and have a strong social conscience. Despite their aversion (which may even be unconscious), they do their best within the given structure of society to improve the conditions of the Negro. He has a pronounced willingness to undertake social reform via remote, impersonal means and by a corresponding reluctance to engage in any kind of intimacy with Black people.
Unconscious Racism	This person does not reveal racist tendencies except as the unconscious persistence of what may be considered mass fantasies but organize them in different combinations, differing relative intensities and different mode of realization.

Table 4: Types of Racism (Farley, John E.: Majority-Minority Relations)

Attitudinal Racism	The same as prejudice, people's attitudes and beliefs that favor one group over another.
Ideological Racism	Set beliefs and theories that state directly some races are superior to others.
Individual Discrimination	Individual behaviors that lead to unequal treatment based on race.
Institutional Racism	Racism that goes beyond individual thoughts and actions, in which social institutions such as family, church, school and government create patterns of racial injustice and inequality and reinforce racist ideas. Individuals involved in the institutions may be unaware that they are participating in racism.

Table 5: Types of Racism (Halstead, Mark: *Education, Justice and Cultural Diversity: An Examination of the Honeyford Affair, 1984-85*, London, Falmer Press, 1988, pp139-55.)

Pre-Reflective Gut Racism	Emotional racial hatred. Observed in individuals and groups. Deep psychological roots traced to 3 factors: 1) feelings of fear, anxiety, insecurity and suspicion around people or groups that are "different." 2) fundamental human motivational feelings such as rejection, aggression, dominance and superiority and 3) ignorance of other races which makes easier the acceptance of myths and stereotypes and gossip.
Post-reflective Gut Racism	Justifies racial privilege and involves the creation of ideology of racial superiority and domination. Rationalizes acts of racism by 1) establishing an unfounded system of belief that would justify racism (if the system was true) and 2) using misapplication of accepted scientific theories to provide support for racist ideology. Rationalizations may be conspiracy and/or self-deception.
Cultural Racism	Shifts the focal point of racism from physical characteristics to cultural characteristics, e.g., beliefs, practices, customs, activities, values and behavior. The culture of blacks is seen as inferior and preventing blacks from progressing to the point of whites. Holds that the biological capacity to change is present and encourages blacks to ignore their own native culture and be absorbed by white culture.

Institutional Racism	Deals with the way that institutions and the distribution of resources reinforce the advantages of whites. It is the failure to adapt long-standing practices to new needs. It involves four steps: 1) creation of an institution that is non-racist in intent, designed for a homogenous society, 2) changing the context within which the institution exists. Examples include preferential employment or school admission to children of members or seeing only white faces in schoolbooks, 3) power of whites over the institution (this may be intentionally for racist reasons, intentionally for non-racist reasons or unintentionally or unthinkingly), and 4) despite awareness of racist practices of the institution, perpetuating them is racist. "Business as usual" is racist.
Paternalistic Racism	Implies that whites have the right to interfere in the lives of Blacks for "their own good" and have the power to define that good.
Color-Blind Racism	Corresponds to unintentional racism. It involves injustice when treating people the same when in relevant respects they are different. It ignores or marginalizes the distinctive needs, experiences and identities of blacks. When a colorblind approach is adapted to any social policy, usually whites are able to dominate because the common experiences are defined in terms which whites can more easily relate to than blacks.

Table 1 describes the attempts of four researchers (two Black and two white) to analyze and describe the types of racism. In those types of racism, almost everyone is covered. The types that I feel are most common are the Individual, Aversive, and Institutional types. Many physicians and nurses have paternalistic attitudes towards patients who are unlike them and their accepted societal "norms." Frequently, many of these physicians and nurses are unaware that any of their attitudes and opinions are racist. Most likely, many of the non-Black people reading this chapter feel that these descriptions are about someone else.

This unconscious racism exists throughout Western society. The Eugenics Movement of the early twentieth century unleashed much false information to the public that has influenced negative stereotypes of Black people that many people accept as real even to this day. It is being described in physicians only because it appears to adversely affect the overall health of Afrikan people in America.

The statistics and observations of the court system and criminal justice system as well as the educational system are significant examples of racism in action, conscious and unconscious.

One expression of racism I have not seen discussed in the many works dealing with racism that were used in this work is a group I call "Talk Radio Racists." Frequently, they do not consider themselves racist but do not care if someone else does. Most of them think of themselves as "conservatives" and accept the label "racist" as a natural course of events based on their choices. It is my belief that the rise of conservative talk radio during the Reagan years played an important part in the development of these racists.

These talk show hosts, many of whom have achieved cult status, made many unconscious racists or racists-in-denial comfortable with their racism and gave them the ability to openly deny it while spouting racist opinions. The current administration in Washington, D.C. has provided further comfort to racists. While they concede freely that many whites fall onto their lists of negative traits, they take comfort and satisfaction in their belief that the majority of the objects of their scorn are Blacks and other "nonwhites" and immigrants.

Transmission of Racism and More about Eugenics

In antiquity, physical differences were noted but were not given value.

Herodotus, the so-called "Father" of history mentioned this fact several times. The most direct quote is:

> It is in fact manifest that the Colchians are Egyptian by race...Several Egyptians told me that in their opinion, the Colchians were descended from soldiers of Sesostris. I had conjectured as much myself from two pointers, firstly because they have black skins and kinky hair (to tell the truth this proves nothing for other peoples have them too) and secondly, and more reliably, for the reason that alone among mankind, the Egyptians and the Ethiopians have practiced circumcision since time immemorial.
>
> Herodotus, Book II, 104

As early as the seventeenth century, attempts were made in Europe to classify and categorize mankind. Carl Linnaeus, the Swedish scientist who created the classifications of organisms, formulated a classification of humans that had very uncomplimentary descriptions of non-Europeans and especially of Afrikans. Subsequent European "thinkers" added to the negative theories of Afrikans, thinkers with names like Hume, Montesquieu, Marx, Bacon, Locke, Hobbes, Weber and Blumenbach. These racist theories were continued by Americans, such as Benjamin Rush, a signer of the Declaration of Independence, who felt that the dark skin of Afrikans was due to a hereditary skin disease but intermarriage should be prohibited to eradicate the disease. Thomas Jefferson, a proven pedophile, even published his beliefs about the inferiority of Afrikans.

Physicians in the eighteenth and nineteenth centuries inferiorized the enslaved Afrikans. This helped to justify the institution of slavery. Samuel George Morton was a leading physician from Philadelphia and is felt to be the originator of American scientific racism. He created the pseudoscience of craniometry, which held that the intellectual capacity of a race could be determined by their skull size. In his book, *Crania Americana*, Morton divided humanity into four races: Europeans, Asians, Native Americans and Africans and assigned qualities and characteristics to each. Not surprisingly, Europeans placed themselves at the top of the vertical hierarchy and Africans were at the bottom. Using these criteria, he claimed that the ancient Egyptians were European.

Josiah Clark Nott was a South Carolina-born physician who practiced in Alabama and was a follower of Morton. He and George Robbins Gliddon, another follower of Morton, wrote *Types of Mankind or Ethnological Research* (1854), a book that popularized the polygenetic theory of separate origins of the different races of humanity. Nott was a founder of the Medical College of Alabama and served as a Confederate surgeon during the Civil War.

During that same time Arthur de Gobineau, a French diplomat and aristocrat, wrote his book, *An Essay on the Inequality of the Human Species*, a white supremacist book. A study of Germany during this time would be enlightening also, especially of the professors at the University of Gottingen, such as Johann Joachim Winckelmann and J.F. Blumenbach.

The Eugenics Movement

The Eugenics movement was quite dominant in the early twentieth century. Many medical schools taught their students the principles of Eugenics, much of which was pseudoscientific stereotyping. The infamous Tuskegee Study in which Black men infected with syphilis had had treatment withheld to observe the effects of the disease has been opined to be the result of Eugenics courses the three principal researchers and organizers of the study took at the University of Virginia Medical School where Eugenics theory was included in the curriculum. Prominent racist eugenicists in this movement are noted below.

Madison Grant, a New York City-born attorney wrote in 1916 one of the best-known books of scientific racism, *The Passing of the Great Race.* Adolf Hitler wrote to Grant that "The book is my Bible." Tremendously popular in the United States, it had multiple printings and was translated into many other languages. Grant singlemindedly dedicated his life to Eugenics. He never married and had no children. His Nordic Theory divided humans into three races: Negroids,

Mongoloids and Caucasoids. Caucasoids were divided further into three groups:

- Nordics (Scandinavia, northern Germany, England, Scotland, Ireland, Holland, Flanders, parts of northern France and northern Poland)
- Alpines (Central France through Switzerland, northern Italy, Austria, southern Germany, southern Poland, central Russia and into central Asia); and
- Mediterraneans (southern France, the Iberian Peninsula, southern Italy, Greece and parts of Wales).

Grant was a eugenicist who advocated exterminating "undesirable" traits and "worthless race types" from the human gene pool. He believed in environmental influence in evolution but assigned a superior role to survival in cold and ice as the Nordics were supposed to have done. He played an active role in creating strong immigration restrictions and anti-miscegenation laws in America.

Charles Davenport was a Brooklyn-born, Harvard-educated biologist and eugenicist. In 1911, he wrote *Heredity in Relation to Eugenics,* which was used as a college textbook for many years. His book, *Race Crossing in Jamaica* (1929), gave empty, misleading and erroneous "evidence" that race mixing (miscegenation) caused cultural and biological degradation.

Robert Mearns Yerkes was a eugenicist who suggested that humanity "could benefit from intentional selective interbreeding." After the start of World War I, he helped the army develop a test supposedly designed to recognize recruits with low intelligence and recruits suited for special training and officers training schools.

Harry H. Laughlin was an Iowa-born teacher and principal who was influenced by Charles Davenport. He was a eugenicist who testified before Congress in favor of anti-immigration of southern and eastern Europeans who were supposed to have "excessive" insanity. Laughlin supported legislation that would have supported sterilization laws providing for mandatory sterilization of "unfit" members of the population.

Lothrop Stoddard, a native of Massachusetts and magna cum laude graduate of Harvard College, studied law and eventually earned a Ph.D. in History. Of his many racist books, his most famous was *The Rising Tide of Color Against White World Supremacy.* He also regarded Asians and Muslims as threats to white dominance. Madison Grant was his mentor, but he disagreed with Grant's Nordic theory and saw the world as being Black and white.

Stoddard's theories ushered in the theory of "Pan-Aryanism." He was appointed to the Board of Directors of the American Birth Control League, a forerunner to Planned Parenthood by Margaret Sanger, a prominent Eugenicist. More than 30 states adopted compulsory sterilization laws and more than 60,000 individuals were sterilized. North Carolina even had a Eugenics Board as part of its state government. Other prominent Eugenicists were Theodore Roosevelt, Alexander Graham Bell and John D. Rockefeller.

These names and their significance are mentioned so that the reader can see that what happened in the past and what is happening today are the same. It is a testament to the fact that enemies of humanity (many of whom allow themselves to be represented by flags of defeated and discredited philosophies) are relentless.

Solutions

Obviously, there are no easy fixes. The question of disparities is related to so many factors. Racial disparities in education, income, criminalization, and standards of living and health are all inter-related and due to the system of white supremacy, frequently called racism. The best way to eliminate disparities would be to eliminate racism/white supremacy, which would be a daunting task. To paraphrase the brilliant teacher, the late Dr. John Henrik Clarke, powerful people do not teach powerless people how to be powerful or how to take their power away.

The best way to start, however, is to admit the problem and perform an in-depth study of racism. The first step in curing any addiction is to recognize first that one is addicted. Racism can be considered as an addiction in that one has to recognize one's own addiction before anything can be done; the next step is to understand the addiction. As residents of America, exposed to the racist and white supremacist educational system, all Americans are potentially racist, even Americans of Afrikan origins.

Another way is to institutionalize "cultural competence," a course that should be required from preschool to professional school. True cultural competence should be a required proportion of all yearly CME for physicians. Evidence-based cultural competence is a worthy goal.

The granting of Reparations is another avenue to correct the problem. This does not mean to give money to individuals but to establish commissions and programs that are designated specifically to address the problem of disparities — not just health but education, economic, criminal justice and all other areas of disparities. Reparations could provide tuition-free educations, interest-free business loans (with options available for forgiveness) and tax-forgiveness for a set time period. The Association of Black Psychologists and the National Association of Black Social Workers could provide psychological counseling which would be arranged and mandatory. The Association for the Study of Classical African Civilizations could take the lead in providing appropriate history and culture-based content for Ausa.

The idea of affirmative action should be dealt with honestly. Affirmative action has been an American reality since the inception of this republic. In fact an examination of the entire history of America will show that affirmative action was a reality and favored white males, as previously mentioned, just as welfare can apply to big corporations who get tax breaks despite sending overseas what had been American jobs, even to foreign countries who have established strained or even adversarial relationships with America.

The culture of medicine should be re-examined and new paradigms explored. I am particularly concerned with the current attempts by drug companies, insurance companies, hospital systems and their governmental allies to objectify a subjective profession. Increasing the numbers of Afrikan American and other physicians of color is a worthy and necessary goal.

So, the discussion of racism is of utmost importance, despite the fact that so many people are rendered almost paralyzed and catatonic due to their extreme discomfort with the topic. As the discussion leads to real solutions, all people will see their lives optimized and their grandchildrens' grandchildrens' potential maximized.

Conclusion

On Sunday February 17, 2002, in *The State* newspaper in South Carolina, this writer was quoted in an article by Jaymi Frieden entitled "An Unhealthy Divide." The article dealt with what she called a "racial gap" in healthcare in South Carolina. I had given her information I had gathered from personal experience, discussions with patients and from research. Several days after the article was published with some of my comments included, I received a letter from a retired white physician in Columbia, taking me to task. He was "...curious as to your motivation for researching racism in medicine" and felt the article did "...a disservice to the physicians of Columbia and to the medical profession in South Carolina in general." He was convinced that "...our physicians' treatment of all our citizens was at that time entirely without racial bias" in the clinics with which he was familiar. In my reply, I thanked him for his interest in my interest in racism in medicine and sent him a five-page bibliography demonstrating that others had the same interest.

Memories of hospital segregation stimulated my answers to Ms. Freiden's questions. The single hospital in this writer's hometown of Hartsville, South Carolina, was segregated. However, this was not the only sore point. The "Colored" entrance of the "separate but equal" facilities in the hospital was located in the back. The unpaved parking lot was pock-marked with holes that were frequently filled with standing water after it rained. This entrance led into a large ward with many beds in one room. If they were supposed to be separated by curtains, they were not.

The smell was atrocious as might be expected with the diarrhea, vomiting and various infections from which the different patients in that one room were suffering. After inadvertently wandering into the "White" section, this writer was struck by the stark difference. The rooms had two beds; the floors and walls were shiny and spotlessly clean; the lighting was brighter, and the room had that clean, antiseptic odor frequently associated with hospitals. It *smelled* clean.

When I was five or six years old, I was admitted to that same hospital with pneumonia. My parents were afraid for my life because my mother's oldest sister had died from pneumonia during her adolescence. My main memories of that time center on the antibiotics I was given by deep injection into my buttocks four to six times a day. I do not remember which antibiotic, only that I was given too much and the injections hurt terribly; intravenous antibiotics would have been less traumatic. Perhaps this practice could be attributable to the fact that many physicians believed (and still believe) that Blacks do not experience pain the same and do not *feel* pain as intensely as whites.

Because Afrikan American physicians were unable to obtain privileges to admit patients in "mainstream" hospitals, patients requiring hospitalization had to be transferred to the "care" of a white physician and that was the rule. This went against the rule of "continuity of care" and potentially was detrimental to the patient in many ways.

My mother had a Black physician when she was pregnant with me. She experienced a complication requiring hospital admission and was referred to a white physician because Black physicians were not granted hospital privileges. Both physicians were general practitioners, having needed to complete only an internship for licensure at that time. Ironically, her Black physician had done an additional internship in OB-GYN and was probably more qualified to take care of the complication than the white physician. The outcome was successful in that, despite our severe, prolonged illness, both my mother and I survived; however, she was told she should not have any more children and I was an "only child."

I had suffered from recurrent tonsillitis for several years when, at eight years old, it was decided that I needed a tonsillectomy. My physician, who was Black, did not have privileges at the local hospital because of the color of his skin despite having been as well trained as any of the physicians who did have privileges. That Christmas, during a visit from my aunt and uncle from Newark, New Jersey, my physician and my uncle (who was also a physician) took out my tonsils on our kitchen table. My oldest cousin also assisted — he was about twelve or thirteen years old at the time — and later became a practicing Internist in Pittsburgh, Pennsylvania, until his death. I did quite well after the surgery and had no complications.

My uncle grew up in Orangeburg, South Carolina, during a time when Black men had so many restrictions on them that a simple trip to the grocery store could be potentially life threatening. Things have not changed much: Trayvon Martin, Tamir Rice, Michael Brown and Sandra Bland, Freddie Gray, Amadou Diallo, Sean Bell, Walter Scott, Stephon Clark, Oscar Grant, Evette Smith, Eric Garner, Armaud Arbury, Breonna Taylor and George Floyd are only the tip of the iceberg of the young Ausa women and men who have been killed unneccesarily, frequently by those who were supposed to be protecting and serving them. Like many Black men of his generation, my uncle left the South, settled in the Northeast and lived a materially and qualitatively better life than he would have had probably if he had remained in the South. He had hospital privileges in Newark, New Jersey, that included the ability to do minor surgical procedures such as cholecystectomy, hernia repair and, obviously, tonsillectomies.

During my adolescence, I worked summers as an orderly at the same hospital in which I was born. My experiences were varied and included bad as well as good things. I was called the "N" word on several occasions, mostly by patients and their families.

The absurdity of racism was illustrated by the case of a young exchange college student from Brazil, a few years older than I, who was admitted into the hospital in a coma after having had a motorcycle accident. His racial classification officially was given as "Dark White." His complexion was slightly darker than mine, his facial features were as Africoid as mine, and his hair only slightly less tightly curled than mine. Yet, he was the toast of my little hometown.

One of the physicians that I saw during my youth was one of the rudest, most racist individuals that I have ever met. His office had two waiting rooms, as was the custom at that time. The "colored" waiting room was reached only by walking to the back of the building. It was unpainted with bare walls and wooden or otherwise threadbare and very uncomfortable furniture. The "white" waiting room, which could be seen from the back Black waiting room, was a homey painted room with nice pictures on the walls and comfortable, plush furniture. Frequently, the Black patients had to wait until all the white patients were seen.

He was always gruff, hurried and rude when dealing with us but smiled and laughed with his white patients. He was so hateful to the hospital staff and his patients that, as an orderly, I found it difficult to understand how anyone could allow him to take care of them.

A final memory about a white colleague in Columbia shortly after I moved back home to South Carolina. Inside hospital walls, he would speak to me and was quite friendly. Outside the hospital, he studiously ignored me. The most glaring incident occurred one night when we were both in the doctor's parking lot. I was coming into the hospital, he was leaving, and we almost bumped into each other. I smiled and greeted him cheerfully. We made eye contact and he turned his head away and said nothing.

He was symbolic of several physicians with South Carolina ties or origins who have infamously distinguished themselves over the years. Josiah Nott, as previously noted, was a South Carolina native and one of the founders of the medical school at the University of Alabama. He published articles that supposedly proved the inferiority of Afrikans. In fact, he described his medical specialty as "Niggerology." J. Marion Sims, a South Carolina native who has a statue on the grounds of the South Carolina capital in Columbia, is celebrated as the "Father of Gynecology" after having developed a surgical procedure. Much of his experimentation was done on unanesthetized, enslaved Afrikan women. Of all the causes of racial health disparities, racism, especially the racism of health care providers, is the cause that creates the most discomfort and denial. As has been demonstrated, many experts consider racism to be a mental health or a public health problem and treatment cannot even be started until those affected are willing to admit, first, that it is a problem and second, that they have the problem. If racial disparities are to be eliminated, every cause should be given attention even, and perhaps especially, racism.

Racism is pervasive, insidious and seductive. It is my opinion that, to a greater or lesser degree, everyone who was born, socialized and/or educated in a Western nation is a racist. The list of the types of racism given in Tables 2-4 (see pages 114-116) is certainly quite inclusive. Many of today's racists are overt but this writer prefers to believe that many more are unconscious racists.

Although racism has a "power" component, Afrikans who were born, socialized and educated in the Western world are internalized racists. Most of us have absorbed and internalized the negative information and false history that has been taught in educational and religious institutions about us and our Ancestors and native homelands. Self-hatred frequently results in harmful and pathological actions against each other. This self-loathing is difficult to eliminate even though many of us are aware of its existence. But it is not impossible to eliminate. This explains why so many Ausa have profound self-hatred that manifests as scorn, distrust and disgust towards anything Afrikan. This also explains to some extent why so many Ausa do not take care of their health.

Despite the studies that indicate that Afrikans in America and Latinos prefer healthcare providers that look like them, there is a sizeable number that do not trust providers that do. These patients gravitate towards providers of other races, despite how these "other" providers treated them. Individuals in the Black community have told this writer that Black doctors are dumb and kill their patients.

Soon after this writer's family moved back to Columbia after medical school, specialty and subspecialty training, my wife had an experience that is quite illustrative of internalized racism. She was in a beauty parlor and a woman (we will call her Ms. Jones) was loudly disparaging African American physicians. She was saying things like, "They don't know what they are doing" and "You mess with them and they'll kill you." After this had gone on for a while, my wife quietly asked her what she did for a living. Ms. Jones smiled and replied proudly that she was a schoolteacher. My wife then stated very respectfully, "It's too bad that you are not as good a teacher as the white teachers that you work with." Ms. Jones' mouth opened with amazement, but her eyes revealed her frustration and anger. She realized that what she had just been told was indeed what she had been saying.

Ausa physicians have seen patients who were brought in by family members, frequently against their will, and several at death's door. They had been led to believe they were incurable, and they believed it. When appropriate treatment was given by the Ausa physician and they returned to their optimal health, many also returned to the same white doctors who had given up on them. Perhaps this is the basis of the paradoxical paranoia that many Black patients have regarding white physicians.

Despite the self-hatred, however, it has been repeatedly shown that a significant number of patients prefer physicians and other caretakers who share their race and ethnicity. This writer has been consulted many times for reasons that could only have been to help the white physician team to communicate with the Black patient and family. Although unorthodox, it did not represent a problem because teamwork was required and the patient and his/her family benefited from the collaboration.

The public, and especially healthcare workers, need to realize that many false truisms and stereotypes were created by individuals with racist agendas starting in the seventeenth century and are still occurring. One of the attempts was the publication of *The Bell Curve*, a book that all responsible and knowledgeable workers in that field agreed was based on pseudoscience. Unfortunately, the book made the best-seller list.

Even the most well-meaning of individuals can harbor subconscious beliefs in negative stereotypes. The result is that Ausa have traditionally had to work harder to achieve. It was a truism repeated by many in my generation, called the baby boomers, that Ausa had to be "twice as good" in order to achieve what average whites got ordinarily. It was repeated so frequently in segregated schools that the attainment of excellence was installed in most students. Films based on true stories like *Pride, Glory Road, The Tuskegee Airmen, Coach Carter, Glory, Remember the Titans, 10,000 Black Men Named George, Lean on Me* and others document a microcosm of the arenas in which Afrikan Americans have had to fight and the extraordinary battles required to achieve.

Many of these barriers are created by otherwise well-meaning people driven by subconscious stereotypes, implicit bias and unconscious racism. The same thing happens with physicians and patients. In early 2008, the American Medical Association issued an apology to Afrikan American physicians for the racism that had been demonstrated through the years.

In the CNN special, "Black in America," the point was made that Black college graduates have a harder time finding a job than white high school dropouts with criminal records. The fact that a Black man became president of the United States is not evidence of a "post racist America"; the fact is, the system of racism/white supremacy still exists and must continually be addressed. We must continue to use the social category of race to track our success and to prevent racist politicians and bureaucrats from undermining the health of America's minorities, as did John C. Calhoun of South Carolina in using the census of 1840 in an attempt to prove that freedom was harmful to the mental health of Afrikan Americans. Health data must be collected and reported by race, sex, ethnicity, disability, socioeconomic status and primary language until all indications confirm that racism and supremacy of any race has been proven to be abolished.

REFERENCES AND SUGGESTED READING

Agrawal, Sangeeta. "Colorectal Cancer in African Americans". *American Journal of Gastroenterology* 100:515-523, 2005.

Armstead, Cheryl A., Kathleen A. Lawler, Gloria Gorden, John Cross, Judith Gibbons. Relationship of Racial Stressors to Blood Pressure Responses and Anger Expression in Black College Students. *Health Psychology* 8:541-556, 1984.

Avery, Holly: How U.S. Laws and Social Policies Influence Chronic Stress and Health Disparities. Politics of Race, Culture and Health Symposium, Ithaca College, November 14, 2002.

Bediako, Shawn: Reducing and Eliminating Health Disparities: A Targeted Approach. *Journal of the National Medical Association*, January 1, 2005.

Bernal, Martin. *Black Athena: The Afroasiatic Roots of Classical Civilization.* London: Free Association Books, pp.189-223; chapter entitled "Hostilities to Egypt in the 18th Century," 1989.

Better, Shirley. *Institutional Racism: A Primer on Theory and Strategies for Social Change.* Lanham: Rowman and Littlefield Publishers, Inc., 2008.

Black, Isabella. Race and Unreason: Anti-Negro Opinion in Professional and Scientific Literature Since 1954. *Phylon: The Atlanta University Review of Race and Culture.* 36: 65-79, 1966.

Boutain, Doris M. and Cheryl Cooke. The Association Between Racism and High Blood Pressure Among African Americans. *Ethnicity and Disease* 11:793-799, 2001.

Bryant-Davis, Thelma and Carlota O'Campo. Racist Incident-Based Trauma. *The Counciling Psychologist* 33(4):479-500, 2005.

Byrd, W. Michael and Linda Clayton. The African-American Cancer Crisis, Part II: A Prescription. *Journal of Health Care for the Poor and Underserved* 2(2): 102-116, 1993.

Byrd, W. Michael and Linda A. Clayton: Racial and Ethnic Disparities in Healthcare: A Background and History. In: Smedly, B.D. et.al (Ed) : *Unequal Treatment: Confronting Racial and Ethnic Disparities in Healthcare.* The National Academies Press, Washington, DC, 2003.

Byrd, W. Michael and Linda A. Clayton. *An American Health Dilemma:*

Volume I: A Medical History of African Americans and the Problem of Race: Beginnings to 1900. NY: Routledge, 2000.

Byrd, W. Michael and Linda A. Clayton. *An American Health Dilemma: Volume II: Race, Medicine, and Health Care in the United States 1900-2000.* NY: Routledge, 2002.

Byrd, W. Michael and Linda A. Clayton: Racial and Ethnic Disparities in Healthcare: A Background and History. In: Smedly, B.D. et.al (Ed) : *Unequal Treatment: Confronting Racial and Ethnic Disparities in Healthcare.* The National Academies Press, Washington, DC, 2003.

Campbell, Christopher. *Race, Myth and the News.* Thousand Oaks: Sage Publications, 1995.

Carew, Jan. *Fulcrums of Change: African Presence in the Americas.* Trenton: Africa World Press, 1988.

Carruthers, Jacob H. *Intellectual Warfare.* Chicago: Third World Press, 1999.

Caughy, Margaret O'Brian, Patricia J. O'Campo and Carles Muntoner. Experiences of Racism Among African American Parents and the Mental Health of Their Preschool-Aged Children. American Journal of Public Health, 94:2118-2124, 2004.

Comer, James P. White Racism: Its Root, Form and Function. *The American Journal of Psychiatry* 126 (6): 70-73, 806, 1969.

Delany, Lloyd T. The Other Bodies in the River. In: *Black Psychology* (Third edition) Ed: Reginald L. Jones. Berkeley: Cobb and Henry Publishers, pp. 597-607, 1991.

Deutsch, Albert. The First U.S. Census of the Insane (1840) and Its Use as Pro-Slavery Propaganda. *Bulletin of the History of Medicine* 15:469-482, 1944.

Diop, Cheikh Anta. *The Cultural Unity of Black Africa.* Chicago: Third World Press, 1978.

Dressler, William W. Social Identity and Arterial Blood Pressure in The African-American Community. *Ethnicity and Disease* 6:176-189, 1996.

Dudley, William (Editor). *Racism in America: Opposing Viewpoints.* San Diego: Greenhaven Press, Inc., 1991.

Farley, John E. *Majority-Minority Relations.* NY: Pearson Publishing Co., 1982.

Fernandez, John P. The Impact of Racism on Whites in Corporate America. In: Bowser, Benjamin P. and Raymond G. Hunt (Editors): Impacts of Racism on White Americans. Thousand Oaks: Sage Publications, 1996.

Finch, Charles S. Race and Human Origins. In Echoes of the Old Darkland: Themes from The African Eden. Decatur: Khenti, Inc., 1991.

Finch, Charles S.: The African Background of Medical Science. In: Van Sertima, Ivan (Ed.): Blacks in Science: Ancient and Modern. New Brunswick: Transaction Books, 1983.

Friedan, Jaymi. An Unhealthy Divide: African-Americans Suffer More Illnesses But Physicians and Churches Aim to Close the Gap. The State. February 17, 2002.

Fuller, Kathleen E. Low Birth Weight Infants: The Continuing Ethnic Disparity and the Interaction of Biology and Environment. Ethnicity and Disease 10:432-445, 2000.

Gallman, Burnett W.: From Africa to South Carolina: A Brief Review of the Contributions of Africans and African-Americans to Medicine. Journal of the South Carolina Medical Association, May 1988, pp. 249-255.

Hacker, Andrew. Two Nations: Black and White, Separate, Hostile, Unequal. NY: Charles Scribner's Sons, 1992.

Haller, John S. Jr. The Physician Versus the Negro: Medical and Anthropological Concepts of Race in the Late Nineteenth Century. Bulletin of the History of Medicine 44: 154-167, 1970.

Haller, John S. Jr. Concepts of Race Inferiority in Nineteenth Century Anthropology. Journal of the History of Medicine 25: 40-51, 1970.

Haller, John S. Jr. The Negro and the Southern Physician: A Study of Medical and Racial Attitudes, 1800-1860. Medical History 16: 238-253, 1972.

Harrell, Camara Jules. Manichean Psychology: Racism and the Minds of People of African Descent. Washington, DC: Howard University Press, 1999.

Harrell, Jules P., Marcellus M. Merritt, Jimalee Kalu. Racism, Stress and Disease. In: African American Mental Health: Theory, Research and Intervention. Ed.: Reginald l. Jones. Hampton: Cobb and Henry Publishers, pp.247-280, 1998.

Hurley, Brian W. Race and Medical Publications. *Journal of the National Medical Association* 95(4): 307-308, 2003.

James, Sherman A. John Henryism and the Health of African Americans. *Culture, Medicine and Psychiatry,* 18:163-182, 1994.

Jones, Camara Phyllis. Levels of Racism: A Theoretic Framework and a Gardener's Tale. *The American Journal of Public Health* 90 (8):1212-1215, 2000.

Jones, James M. *Prejudice and Racism.* NY: McGraw Hill, 1972.

Jones, James M. and Robert T. Carter. In: Bowser, Benjamin P. and Raymond G. Hunt (Editors): *Impacts of Racism on White Americans.* Thousand Oaks: Sage Publications, 1996.

Kovel, Joel. *White Racism: A Psycho History.* NY: Vintage, 1970.

Krieger, Nancy. Shades of Difference: Theoretical Underpinnings of the Medical Controversy on Black/White Differences in the United States, 1830-1870. *International Journal of Health Services,* 17 (2): 259-278, 1987.

Kreiger, Nancy and Stephen Sidney. Racial Discrimination and Blood Pressure: The CARDIA Study of Young Black and White Adults. *American Journal of Public Health* 86:1370-1378, 1996.

Krieger, Nancy. Embodying Inequality: A Review of Concepts, Measures, and Methods for Studying Health Consequences of Discrimination. *International Journal of Health Services.* 29:295-352, 1999.

LaVeist, Thomas A. On the Study of Race, Racism, and Health: A Shift From Description to Explanation. *International Journal of Health Services.* 30:217-219, 2000.

Levine, Phillippa. *Eugenics: A Very Short Introduction.* NY: Oxford University Press, 2017.

Lombardo, Paul A. and Gregory M. Dorr. Eugenics, Medical Education, and the Public Health Service: Another Perspective on the Tuskegee Syphilis Experiment. *Bulletin of the History of Medicine* 80:291-316, 2006.

Malat, Jennifer and Michelle van Ryn. African-American Preference for Same-Race Healthcare Providers: The Role of Healthcare Discrimination. *Ethnicity and Disease* 15:740-747, 2005.

McIntosh, Peggy: White Privilege: Unpacking the Invisible Knapsack. In: Rothenberg, Paula S. (Editor): *White Privilege: Essential*

Readings on the Other Side of Racism. NY: Worth Publishers, 2005, pp.109-113.

Myers, Hector F., Norman B. Anderson, and Tony L. Strictland: Biobehavioral Perspective for Research on Stress and Hypertension in African American Adults: Theoretical and Empirical Issues. In: Reginald l. Jones. (Ed.): *African American Mental Health: Theory, Research and Intervention.* Cobb and Henry Publishers, Hampton, VA, pp. 209-245.

National Colloquium on African American Health. *Racism in Medicine and Health Parity for African Americans*: "The Slave Health Deficit." National Medical Association, 2002.

Newsome, Frederick. Black Contributions to the Early History of Western Medicine: Lack of Recognition as a Cause of Black Under-representation in U.S. Medical Schools. *Journal of the National Medical Association,* 71:189-193, 1979.

Pierce, Chester M. Offensive Mechanisms. In: *The Black Seventies.* Ed.: Floyd B. Barbour. NY: Porter Sargent Publications, pp. 265-282, 1970.

Pinderhughes, Charles A. The Origins of Racism. *International Journal of Psychiatry,* 8(6):934-41, 1969.

Rothenberg, Paula S. (Editor). *White Privilege: Essential Readings on The Other Side of Racism.* NY: Worth Publishers, 2005.

Satcher, David and Rubens J. Pamies: *Multicultural Medicine and Health Disparities.* NY: McGraw-Hill Medical Publishing Division, 2006.

Smedley, Brian D., Adrienne Y. Stith, Daniel J. Wooten, Thelma L. Cox, Sylvia I. Salazar (Editors): *Unequal Treatment: Confronting Racial and Ethnic Disparities in Health Care.* Washington, DC: The National Academies Press, 2003.

Tucker, William H. *The Science and Politics of Racial Research.* Chicago: University of Illinois, 1994.

United Nations International Convention on the Elimination of All Racial Discrimination. http://www.hri.org/docs/ICERD66.html NY, March 7, 1966.

Valls, Andrew (Editor). *Race and Racism in Modern Philosophy.* Ithaca: Cornell University Press, 2005.

Washington, Harriet A. *Medical Apartheid: The Dark History of Medical Experimentation on Black Americans From Colonial Times to the Present.* NY: Doubleday, 2006.

Welsing, Frances Cress. The Cress Theory of Color Confrontation and Racism (White Supremacy): A Psycho-genetic Theory and World Outlook. In: *The Isis Papers: Keys to the Colors.* Chicago: Third World Press, 1991.

Willliams, David R. and Harold Neighbors. Racism, Discrimination and Hypertension: Evidence and Needed Research. *Ethnicity and Disease* 11:800-816, 2001.

Williams, David R. The Concept of Race and Health Status in America. *Public Health Reports,* 108 (1):26-41, 1994.

Winant, Howard. Race and Race Theory. *Annual Review of Sociology* 26:169-185, 2000.

Wise, Tim. *White Like Me: Reflections on Race From a Privileged Son.* NY: Soft Skull Press, 2005.

Wright, Bobby E. *The Psychopathic Racial Personality and Other Essays.* Chicago: Third World Press, 1985.

Wright, Rosalind J., Mario Rodriguez, Sheldon Cohen. Review of Psychosocial Stress and Asthma: An Integrated Biopsychosocial Approach. *Thorax* 53:1066-1074, 1998.

Zuckerman, Marvin. Some Dubious Premises in Research and Theory on Racial Differences: Scientific, Social and Ethical Issues. *American Psychologist,*

CHAPTER 11

About Blackface

A resurgence of information has been flooding the media lately about blackface. Many prominent and otherwise well-educated white people have been implicated in indulging in these racist activities. The attention shown to this phenomenon is very beneficial because many Ausa are numb to these egregious displays of racism or are ignorant of the true meaning and history of these icons. We are in a very teachable moment, especially for our youth.

Blackface figures are caricatures, representations of people that exaggerate features or characteristics to create an impression of the person. This impression can be comical, grotesque or can render the person ridiculous. These caricatures can and often do create stereotypes that can also be comical or insulting. A stereotype is an overgeneralization about a person or group of people that frequently creates conscious and unconscious prejudice and erroneous impressions.

According to the National Museum of African American History and Culture, blackface images began with minstrel shows in the early nineteenth century. These images were created and perpetuated by working class whites who were positioned beneath and oppressed by upper class, land-owning whites and so they needed to express their assumed superiority over the enslaved and so-called "free" Blacks.

The "Father of Minstrelsy" was Thomas Dartmouth Rice who developed the first blackface character in 1830 whom he called "Jim Crow," which became a symbol of segregation. Jim Crow wore tattered, ragged clothing and moved with a slovenly, shuffling gait. Rice described his act as "Ethiopian delineation." It is interesting to note that minstrelsy started and became popular roughly at the same time as the start of the abolitionist movement.

Supposedly, Rice had observed an enslaved Afrikan dancing and imitated him. Rice's performances were tremendously successful, and Minstrelsy became the most popular form of entertainment for dozens of years and into the twentieth century. These minstrel shows characterized all Ausa (especially so-called "free" Blacks who were seeking equality) as lazy, stupid, hypersexual, superstitious brutes who were potential thieves and cowards. Taking these facts into consideration, it is telling, therefore, that all the early and most of the later Minstrel performers were white men. White America was bombarded with the image of happy and contented enslaved Afrikans.

These stereotypes served to reinforce the racist treatment of Ausa and uphold the belief in Ausa inferiority (as well as the myth of white superiority) and the necessity of maintaining the subjugation of Ausa. They also served to justify discrimination and racist behavior. In many areas of the country, minstrel shows were the only depiction of Ausa life that white audiences saw, further desensitizing them to the horrors of slavery.

Unfortunately, some experts believe that some Ausa internalized these stereotypes and came to believe, then and now, that there was/is truth in them, as in a self-fulfilling prophecy (a form of internalized racism).

Blackface caricatures became ubiquitous in American society. These were the blackface stereotypes before the end of slavery:

- **Mammy** was fat and loyal and happily defended slavery and her white "owners." She was obedient, docile, asexual and protective of "the big house." She was the "boss" of the enslaved family and was beloved by the slavemasters.
- **Sambo** was simple, docile, carefree, irresponsible and had to be controlled by Mammy.
- **Coon** was a dandy buffoon who tried to imitate whites.

- **Pickaninnys** were partially-clad Black children who were dirty, unkempt and uncivilized.
- **Jezebel** was an immoral, hypersexualized temptress readily available sexually to all who wanted her.

Other stereotypes included Uncle Tom, Buck, Auntie and Sapphire.

Interestingly, after the end of slavery the depictions of Ausa men changed. Black men were then portrayed as brutes and rapists who were a constant danger to the purity of "white womanhood." This was indicated in the book by Thomas Dixon, *The Clansman*, which was made into the movie *The Birth of a Nation* where white men in blackface portrayed Ausa men as savage rapists. This film was one of the first celebrated films in America. In fact, cartoons that were popular in the mid-twentieth century when this writer was growing up, as well as Tarzan books and movies and the Nancy Drew books were full of these negative stereotypes.

Several beloved white entertainers of the twentieth century earned popularity while performing in blackface. A list of these people includes Al Jolson, Shirley Temple, Judy Garland, and Mickey Rooney, all of whom were major stars. Unfortunately, there were some Ausa who were forced to perform in blackface or as stereotypes in order to make a living. Bert Williams, a talented, literate, dignified Ausa performer actually became a tragic figure during that era because of the indignities he had been forced to endure. Sammy Davis, Jr. performed in blackface as a child. Stepin Fetchit was a caricature of Sambo. The popular TV show of the 1950s, *Amos and Andy*, actually started out as a radio program by two whites who spoke in what they felt was a Black dialect. When the show transitioned to television, the stereotypes were depicted by Ausa actors but remained consistent.

To sum up, blackface is never harmless despite some white protestation that it is only neutral, harmless fun. They say that Ausa are being "oversensitive." The individuals who make that claim are either lying, ill-informed or delusional. The claim itself is a perfect example of white privilege. How dare they try to dictate how I should feel when they insult me?

References

Riggs, Marlon. *Ethnic Notions. http://newsreel.org/video/ETHNIC_NOTIONS*

Blackface: The Birth of an American Stereotype. https://nmaahc.si.edu/blog-post/blackface-birth-american-stereotype

Desmond-Harris, Jenee. *Don't Get What's Wrong with Blackface? Here's Why It's So Offensive. https://www.vox.com/2014/10/29/7089591/why-is-blackface-offensive-halloween-costume*

Kaur, Harmeet. *This is Why Blackface is Offensive .https://www.cnn.com/2019/02/02/us/racist-origins-of-blackface/index.html*

Boule, Jamelle. *Blackface is the Tip of the Iceberg. https://www.nytimes.com/2019/02/04/opinion/northam-blackface-racism.html*

Stereotype. *https://en.wikipedia.org/wiki/Stereotype*

CHAPTER 12

About Christopher Columbus

America celebrates Christopher Columbus, aka Cristobal Colon or Christophe Colombo. It is important that our children, their parents, grandparents, and adult "significant others" know that both the Columbus Day celebration and holiday are based on myth and lies.

Americans virtually ignored Columbus until after the War of 1812 when the need for non-British heroes caused the country to link with Washington Irving's book, *A History of the Life and Voyages of Christopher Columbus* in 1828. In it, Irving presented a false and romanticized version of the Columbus story. Since that time, hundreds of similarly untrue and romanticized works have been presented and have been accepted as fact. This chapter is an attempt to correct these inaccuracies. We are not rewriting history but we will correct untruths that have been written for whatever reason. The truth is the light of the world.

Columbus did NOT discover America!

In the first place, how can someone "discover" a place when they find people there already? It would mean grossly discounting the humanity of the kind and gentle people they encountered, who generally welcomed them with open arms. Secondly, Columbus never set foot on the mainland of either North or South America. Possibly, he was the first European to see the Caribbean islands. One cannot "discover" a place one has never been.

Columbus initiated one of the several world holocausts perpetuated by Europeans, usually upon non-Europeans.

More than 40 Caribbean islands were completely depopulated in less than 40 years. It is estimated that Columbus and his successors reduced the population of the Americas from approximately 80 million in 1500 to 10 million by 1550.

Columbus initiated the Atlantic Slave "Trade," our Maafa, at the suggestion of Father Bartolome de las Casas.

Father Bartolome de las Casas, a priest and historian who travelled to the Caribbean, felt sorry for the inhuman atrocities perpetrated against the Native Americans and wanted to spare them. So, he advocated enslaving Afrikans. Many "mainstream" authors deal with "slavery" in their work but few deal completely accurately with the true origins of this so-called "Trade." Many authors state that slavery was a "necessary evil" that occurred to make America rich and great. They almost invariably point out that many cultures had systems that included slavery, including Afrikan cultures, but conveniently neglect to mention the difference in concept and practice. They overlook the fact that the chattel slavery system of Europeans was a totally barbaric, dehumanizing and horrible institution compared to the Afrikan institution. In fact, they were so different that it is a stretch to even call them by the same name.

Columbus was a lying, cruel and immoral con man.

Our esteemed Ancestor, Dr. John Henrik Clarke, suggests that Columbus was aware that he was not in India but coerced his sailors and other men into signing an agreement stating that they would always say they had reached the coast of India. The ultraconservative "religious right" would be shocked to know that the very same Christopher Columbus that they frequently associate with "American values" not only fathered a child out of wedlock but also refused to marry the mother. On second thought, given the state of today's political climate, most conservative Christians would probably make excuses for him. Columbus was arrogantly materialistic, and he ruled the Caribbean islands so poorly, cruelly and ineptly that he was imprisoned in Spain.

Columbus' journey was financed at least in part by the riches the Moors had accumulated in Spain.

The Moors, who were Islamic Afrikans, controlled the Iberian Peninsula (Spain and Portugal) and Southern France from 711 A.D. to 1492 A.D. They were finally defeated by the joint forces of the Aragon and Castille families, united by the marriage of Ferdinand and Isabella. The Moors, whose educational, scientific, mathematical, agricultural, technical and academic superiority brought Europe out of the Dark Ages, had accumulated tremendous wealth as well as knowledge. These riches were claimed and stolen by the new Spanish rulers. Interestingly, the knowledge that the Moors possessed was probably taken from Kemet after the Arabs conquered Kemet in 642 A.D.

Columbus was not even the first European to come to the Americas and Afrikans also preceded him here by at least 2000 years. Much more could be written about Columbus and has been. Celebrating this man would be akin to celebrating Hitler.

References and Suggested Reading

Carew, Jan. *Fulcrums of Change: Origins of Racism in the Americas and Other Essays.* Trenton: Africa World Press, Inc., 1988.

Forbes, Jack D. *Black Africans and Native Americans.* NY: Basil Blackwell. 1988.

Koning, Hans. *Columbus, His Enterprise: Exploding the Myth.* NY: Monthly Review Press. 1991.

Sale, Kirkpatrick. *The Conquest of Paradise: Christopher Columbus and the Columbian Legacy.* NY: Alfred A. Knopf. 1990.

Todorov, Tzvetan. *The Conquest of America.* NY: Harper and Row Publishers, 1984.

Van Sertima, Ivan (Editor). *African Presence in Early America.* New Brunswick: Transaction Books, 1986.

Van Sertima, Ivan. *They Came Before Columbus: The African Presence in Ancient America.* NY: Random House, 1976.

Wiesenthal, Simon. *Sails of Hope: The Secret Mission of Christopher Columbus.* NY: MacMillan Publishers, Inc., 1973.

CHAPTER 13

The Myth of the Great Emancipator: The Real Abraham Lincoln

History has treated Abraham Lincoln well. He has received credit for doing things he did not do and did not believe in and we will discuss the two main myths associated with his life. This is not an attempt to discredit Lincoln; indeed, the facts and his words speak for themselves. Rather, it is an attempt to demonstrate to the Afrikan public in America that they need to question and think about what they have been asked to believe and accept.

Myth #1: *Lincoln freed the slaves with the Emancipation Proclamation.* The Emancipation Proclamation did not free anyone! The impact of the Emancipation Proclamation (E.P.) is in question. Just what was happening on January 1, 1863? Why was it necessary to create a document like the "E.P."? Did it really free the enslaved Afrikans?

We know that, as of January 1, 1863, the South was winning the Civil War and Lincoln was struggling to keep the border states — Kentucky, Maryland, Delaware and Missouri — happy. The border states were slave-owning states that fought on the Union side. West Virginia, which separated from Virginia because of the Civil War, was also considered to be a border state. Because of the tremendous racism in the North, at first Lincoln would not allow Afrikans to fight for their own freedom. From the Northern perspective, the initial intent of the Civil War was to save the Union, it was not to free the enslaved Afrikans. From the Southern perspective, however, the intent of the

Civil War was to continue the spread of slavery. The E.P. was a political and military maneuver that put slavery at the center of the war and freed no one. In a letter dated September 2, 1863 and addressed to Salmon P. Chase, his Secretary of the Treasury, Lincoln said, "The original proclamation has no constitutional or legal justification, except as a military measure."

To quote the wording of the Emancipation Proclamation:

> ...all persons held as slaves within any State, or designated part of a State, the people whereof shall then be in rebellion against the United States, shall be then, thenceforward, and forever free..."

What this really said was that those enslaved Afrikans in the border states were NOT freed by the Emancipation Proclamation. From a practical view, it did not free the enslaved Afrikans in the South, either, even though it was aimed at them, because the Confederacy was winning the war and Southerners could thumb their noses at anything Lincoln did or said. Quoting J. A. Rogers, "[The E.P.] was a gesture rather than a reality since it 'freed' only those slaves Lincoln had no power to free and kept in slavery those he had the power to free. "This fact has significance for those Afrikans who celebrate the Emancipation Proclamation in "Watchtower" sunrise services every January 1.

Another extremely important but overlooked fact is that the tide of the war did turn in favor of the Union after the E.P., not because of the E.P., but because Lincoln finally allowed Afrikans to fight for their own freedom. After the E.P., more than 186,000 Afrikans eventually fought for their own freedom in the Union army, not counting the more than 90,000 who fought for no pay before the E.P. and not counting the millions of Afrikans who worked behind the Union lines as laborers. It is also important to mention that after the E.P. Afrikans made up almost a third of the Union navy (about 30,000 sailors). Without the addition of Afrikans fighting for their own freedom, the Union might have lost the war; so we must not give false credit to someone else for freeing us when we contributed to our own freedom in a major way.

MYTH #2: *LINCOLN LOVED AFRIKAN PEOPLE AND BELIEVED IN THEIR EQUALITY.*

While it may seem obvious that Lincoln did hate the "Peculiar Institution" of slavery, we have to draw the line at stating that he loved Afrikan people. In his first debate on August 21,1858 with Stephen A. Douglas, his Democratic opponent in the presidential election of 1860, Lincoln said,

> I have no purpose to introduce political and social equality between the white and black races. There is a physical difference between the two, which in my judgment will probably forever forbid their living together upon the footing of perfect equality, and inasmuch as it becomes a necessity that there must be a difference, I, as well as Judge Douglass, am in favor of the race to which I belong, having the superior position.

In a letter dated August 22, 1862 to newspaper publisher and New York congressman Horace Greeley, Lincoln said:

> My paramount object in this struggle is to save the Union, and is not either to save or destroy slavery. If I could save the Union without freeing any slave I would do it, and if I could save it by freeing all the slaves I would do it; and if I could save it by freeing some and leaving others alone I would do that.

Abraham Lincoln was like many of the Abolitionists of his day. He disagreed with the institution of slavery for moral reasons or other reasons but believed strongly in white supremacy. We, as Afrikans, must never forget this simple fact. Many of the people whom we assume are friends are not really our friends.

Many see the Emancipation Proclamation as the forerunner of the Thirteenth, Fourteenth, and Fifteenth Amendments to the Constitution. But, can your freedom truly be legislated?

References and Suggested Reading

Amen-Ra, Jehuti El-Malik. *Shattering the Myth of the Man Who Freed the Slaves: A True Account of Abraham Lincoln's Failure to Free Enslaved Afrikans in America.* Silver Spring: IVth Dynasty Publishing Company, 1990.

O'Reilly, Kenneth. *Nixon's Piano: Presidents and Racial Politics from Washington to Clinton.* NY: The Free Press, 1995, pp. 42-49.

Puckrein, Gary A. (Editorial): African America's Magna Carta, *American Visions,* Volume 8, Number 1, February-March, 1993, p. 4.

Rogers, J. A. *Africa's Gift to America: The Afro-American in the Making and Saving of the United States.* St. Petersburg: Helga M. Rogers. 1961 pp. 134-167, 195-205.

CHAPTER 14

About Brazil

GENERAL

1. Located in South America, Brazil was colonized by Portugal, hence the official language of Brazil is Portuguese.
2. Brazil has the world's second largest population of people of Afrikan descent after Nigeria."

HISTORY

3. Enslavement lasted longer in Brazil than in the United States. It was ended in 1888 in Brazil and in 1865 in America.
4. Almost 50% of all kidnapped Afrikans were taken to Brazil to be enslaved while less than 5% were taken to the United States.
5. The first Afrikans in Brazil arrived about 1532.
6. Many of the Afrikans escaped and organized *quilombos*, which were communities of escaped fugitive enslaved Afrikans.
7. There were ten major quilombos in Brazil in the seventeenth and eighteenth centuries. Because they were such a threat to the plantations, offering a refuge for enslaved Afrikans, only three of the ten lasted more than two years. Several of these included the quilombo in Minas Gerias, which lasted from 1712 to 1719; the 'Carlota' of Mato Grosso, which lasted from 1770 to 1795; and Cumbe in Parhyba, which today is Fabrica Santa Rita.

8. The longest lasting quilombo was Palmares which lasted from before 1605 to 1697. Palmares was located in the Serra da Barriga mountains, which were difficult to penetrate and offered a natural defense against invasion. The population was estimated to be as high as 30,000 people. Its major occupation was agriculture although they raised chickens and other domesticated animals. They hunted and fished and some traded with gold and skins. The community included blacksmiths, weavers and potters and was located in what is today the state of Alagoas.
9. Members of the quilombos occasionally returned to the plantations and towns to encourage other enslaved Afrikans to join them. They burned plantations that they felt were too close to the quilombo.
10. The first king of Palmares was Ganga Zumbi but the most famous king of Palmares was Zumbi, believed to be the nephew of Ganga Zumbi who had the reputation of being a great warrior. Zumbi committed suicide rather than allow himself to be enslaved again.
11. In the quilombos, murder, adultery, stealing and desertion were punished by death.
12. Palmares was defeated by a siege initiated by 1000 archers and 200 gunmen, mostly Indians.
13. Afrikan religions were practiced in the quilombos. They were probably the forerunners of what today is called Candomble.

CHAPTER 15

About Kemet (Ancient Egypt)

GENERAL

1. Egypt is one of the oldest nations on Earth and some evidence suggests that it was a thriving and advanced civilization 30,000 years ago (perhaps the true Wakanda, referred to in the 2018 film, *Black Panther*).
2. Ancient Egypt's civilization was a major influence on what we now call Western Civilization and Christianity and other Western religions. Some Catholic academics have called Egypt the missing hyphen in the Judeo-Christian experience.
3. The people who founded ancient Egypt and created and sustained the civilization had dark skins, thick lips, tightly curled (or "kinky") hair and flat noses, which is not surprising since Egypt is in Afrika.
4. The ancient Egyptians did not call their country Egypt, they called it Kmt (Kemet), which translates to "Land of the Blacks."
5. The time periods in Kmt are measured in dynasties, the periods of time that one family ruled the nation. A dynasty ranged from a few years to as many as 300 years. There were more than 300 Pharaohs during the 30-plus dynasties that covered the more than 3000-year history of Kmt.
6. The first known Pharaoh was Narmer (also called Menes or Mena) who was a brilliant hydraulic engineer. It is said he came to power in 3100 B.C.E.

7. Imhotep of the Third Dynasty was a multi-genius. Not only has he been called the first known physician, he was also an architect who designed and built the world's first pyramid, the Step Pyramid at Saqqara, which is still standing. A priest, poet, scribe, sage, astronomer and magician, Imhotep was also the Prime Minister for the Pharaoh Djoser.
8. Kemetic architectural designs have been used and renamed by other cultures that took credit for their creation, such as Doric, Ionic and Corinthian architectural descriptions.
9. The first documented writing system was from this Afrikan people. They called the system *mdw ntr* (medew netcher); outsiders called it hieroglyphics.
10. The Arabs who now control Kmt have only been there since they invaded and forced the population to convert to Islam in 642 A.D. All of the inventions and discoveries known to Kmt were old by the time the Arabs invaded.

References

Akbar, Na'im. *Light From Ancient Afrika.* Tallahassee: Mind Productions & Associates, Inc., 1994.

Assman, Jan. *The Mind of Egypt: History and Meaning in the Time of the Pharoahs.* Cambridge: Harvard University Press, 2003.

Browder, Anthony T. *Exploding the Myths, Volume I: Nile Valley Contributions to Civilization.* Washington: The Institute of Karmic Guidance, 1992.

Carruthers, Jacob H. *Essays in Ancient Egyptian Studies.* Los Angeles: University of Sankore Press, 1984.

Diop, Cheikh Anta. *The African Origin of Civilization: Myth or Reality.* Westport: Lawrence Hill and Company, 1974.

Finch, Charles S. III. *Echoes of the Old Darkland: Themes From the African Eden.* Decatur: Khenti, Inc, 1991.

Hilliard, Asa G. III, Larry Williams, and Nia Damali. *The Teachings of Ptahhotep: The Oldest Book in the World.* Atlanta: Blackwood Press and Company, 1987.

James, George G. M. *Stolen Legacy.* San Francisco: Julian Richardson Associates Publishers, 1976.

Karenga, Maulana. *Selections from the Husia: Sacred Wisdom of Ancient Egypt.* Los Angeles: Kawaida Publications, 1984.

Obenga, Theophile. *Ancient Egypt and Black Africa: A Student's Handbook for the Study of Ancient Egypt In Philosophy, Linguistics, & Gender Relations.* Chicago: Karnak House, 1992.

Van Sertima, Ivan (Editor). *Nile Valley Civilizations.* New Brunswick: Transaction Books, 1984.

Van Sertima, Ivan (Editor). *Egypt Revisited.* New Brunswick: Transaction Books, 1989.

CHAPTER 16

The Red, Black and Green Flag

Red, Black and Green were adopted as the colors of the Black race in 1920 at the first International Convention of the Negro Peoples of the World. The Honorable Marcus Mosiah Garvey organized this convention which took place at a filled-to-overflowing Madison Square Garden in New York City.

The question of a flag for Black people had been an issue of concern for many Black people at that time. There was a popular song in America during that period entitled, "Every Race Has a Flag But the Coon," a song sung frequently by many whites in order to insult Afrikan people in America.

Bishop J. Lennox, of the African Methodist Church of Zion of Cleveland, Ohio, designed a flag shortly after 1912. A complicated flag, it was comprised of stars and bars in red, white (supposedly symbolic of the purity of the saints), blue (symbolic of the loyalty of Blacks to the United States) and purple (symbolic of Jesus' robe). Although 85,000 Afrikan people at a convention in Ontario, Canada, endorsed this flag, ultimately it was not a success.

On Garvey's flag, red symbolized the "color of the blood which men must shed for their redemption and liberty"; black symbolized "the color of the noble and distinguished race to which we belong"; and green symbolized "the luxuriant vegetation of our motherland." This flag has influenced several flags, including many flags of Afrikan nations. The gold, Black and green flag used by the African National

Congress (ANC) was directly influenced by Garvey. Its colors retained the same symbolic meaning, but the gold represented the mineral wealth Europeans exploited and removed from South Africa. The red, black and green flag with a shield, arrow and spear superimposed on it was used in Kenya in the 1950s by Jomo Kenyatta's Nationalist Kenya African Union.

All people of Afrikan ancestry owe the Hon. Marcus Garvey a great debt. He gave us a commonality and rallying point, regardless of our many nationalities and many languages, and this has been a tremendous gift. It is not an object of hate as is the Confederate flag but is a symbol of pride and unity for a great people.

Martin, Tony. *Race First: The Ideological and Organizational Struggle of Marcus Garvey and the Universal Negro Improvement Association.* Westport: Greenwood Press, 1976.

CHAPTER 17

No More Mentors

The discussion that follows has been taken from concepts and discussions that were initially mentioned by our Elder, Dr. Wade W. Nobles, and our esteemed Ancestor, Baba Hannibal Afrik, two of the brilliant thinkers and "role models" of our time.

The well-publicized plight of young Afrikan American men has stimulated many attempts at providing solutions for what the problems seem to be.

Individuals and organizations are a part of a growing movement to provide mentoring services for young people. This is especially frequent in men's organizations. Usually, young boys are exposed to older men who serve as positive role models. These men also provide tutoring and exposure to positive environments to let the boys understand the positive possibilities for life. Fortunately, because of the well-meaning nature of the relationship, some good is done, although, some would argue, only on a superficial level.

As Afrikans in America, it is becoming increasingly important to approach the world from our own particular point of view. Too often, we accept unthinkingly concepts and theories that have been handed down to us. We have been socialized to do this. It is necessary, however, to examine the concept of "Mentor"

Mentor was a character in Greek mythology who was a close friend of Odysseus. Odysseus wanted to fight in the Trojan War but was concerned about the welfare of his wife, Penelope, and his son, Telemachus. Because Greek culture was warlike and savage and had a very low regard and lack of respect for women, he had real fears that his home would be destroyed, his wife raped and possibly killed, and his son raped, demeaned, dominated, and also possibly killed. His friend, Mentor, volunteered to protect Odysseus' family and educate his son.

According to tradition, Mentor loyally and effectively protected Odysseus' household and educated little Telemachus. Because of this, those men who help in the positive development of other people's children have been called "mentors." Much of this story can be found in Homer's epic poem, *The Odyssey*.

What is implied but not stated is that Mentor probably had a homosexual and pedophilic relationship with Odysseus' young son. In his works *Symposium*, *Phaedrus*, *Lysis*, and *The Republic*, Plato and other Greek writers, such as Xenophane in his *Hiero* and Hesiod in *Works and Days*, assume that male homosexuality is the only form of "love" capable of satisfying a man's highest and noblest aspirations, while heterosexual love is merely a physical impulse to be used only for procreation.

The relationship between an older man and a boy was particularly desirable because it was felt that the man's teachings could prepare the boy for life. Therefore, Mentor was not only an "accomplice to rape, murder and destruction," he was, by today's standards, a sick, violent, perverted individual — a pedophile. So, it is important to place this idealistic story in its proper context and, to do this, a clear examination of Ancient Greece is necessary.

There was a lack of respect and even hatred for women in Ancient Greece. In his work, *Theogony*, the Greek poet Hesiod is the first to call a woman, Pandora, a bitch. In fact, this was the only society in the known history of mankind in which male homosexuality was the norm. It took two main forms. The first form involved two men who were lovers and soldiers. The theory was that "homosexual warriors" would fight even harder to protect their lovers. An example was the relationship between Achilles and Patroclus in *The Iliad*. The other form, which was probably practiced even more, was the attachment of a young boy with an older man. This relationship was considered an excellent way for the boy to learn about life. Frequently, a young boy's father would make arrangements with an older man on behalf of his son. This system is well documented in the writings of Plato, as stated above, and certainly gives another definition for the term, "platonic relationship."

This easily verified information places the idea of mentoring in another light. It could be surmised that Odysseus' decision had more to do with his either taking his "homosexual warrior" lover with him to war or procuring an older male lover for his young son in his absence. His fatherly instincts probably won out. Mentoring in that context today would border on child molestation.

*****

On Jegnoch

Our esteemed Ancestor, Dr. John Henrik Clarke, has taught us that we should never destroy something without having something to put in its place. This is the case now. Fortunately, when we go to the deep well of Afrikan culture, there is a concept that can work even better. *Jegna*, an Ethiopian word, is certainly appropriate in this situation. A Jegna is a special warrior who, according to Dr. Wade Nobles, has:

- *Been tested in struggle or battle.*
- *Extraordinary and unusual fearlessness.*
- *Determination and courage in protecting her/his people, land and culture.*
- *Shown diligence and dedication to our people in everything they do.*
- *Produced exceptionally high-quality work.*
- *Dedicated her/himself to the protection, nurturance and development of our young by advancing our people, place and culture.*

This is a powerful concept, much more powerful than mentoring. Inherently, it includes the necessity for a teacher to also be a Jegna. Of course, many Jegnoch (plural) exist in America today, but many "mentors" are not Jegnoch. This should stimulate those in responsible positions to aspire to become Jegnas.

People at almost any age can be Jegnoch. A major aspect of being a Jegna is knowledge of and loyalty to Afrikan people. This should be a part of all that we do. We should be raising and training Jegnas, not concentrating on mentoring. Although being a Jegna is a high accomplishment in Afrikan-centered philosophy, being an Elder is even more difficult to achieve. Eldership is what we all should aspire to become. Ideally, life is a series of challenges that help us successfully traverse the age-grades and reaching the level of Jegna and, ultimately, Elder.

ON ELDERSHIP

An Elder is much more than being fortunate enough to achieve an advanced age; it is proving oneself worthy of the respectful title of "Elder." An Elder is a Jegna who has achieved a certain age and who has also displayed moral character, which enables him/her to make a substantial contribution to the preservation and promotion of the community. Attributes of the moral character needed to become an Elder include:

- *Beneficence (self-sacrifice for the well-being of others).*
- *Forbearance (ability to survive dehumanizing conditions).*
- *Practical Wisdom (excellence of thought that guides good actions).*
- *Improvisation (unpredictable behavior).*
- *Forgiveness (through habitual exercises of kindness).*
- *Justice (civil law and common good, including the individuals' obligation to the community through social relationships and the community's obligation to its members and itself).*

ELDERS ALSO HAVE:

- *A collective Afrikan identity/consciousness (the collective Afrikan heritage) and he/she values the pursuit of self-knowledge.*
- *Recognition of Afrikan survival and affirmative development as a priority.*
- *Respect for and perpetuation of all things Afrikan, Afrikan life and cultural institutions.*
- *The maintenance of a standard of conduct of resolute and uncompromising resistance to all things "Anti-Afrikan."*

- *The ability to live life in the open without a private, secretive life and being prepared to confront and allow any situation to enter your life, at any time.*

For some, becoming a Jegna may be difficult, but it is special being and becoming an ELDER.

CHAPTER 18

THE AFRIKAN ORIGIN OF MEDICINE

For the past 200-300 years, the teaching of history and, indeed, historiography itself has gone through marked changes. The way Afrika has been portrayed has undergone tremendous changes, which Martin Bernal has documented in his book, *Black Athena.* However, generation after generation of scholars have continued perpetuating falsehoods about Afrika, which began in the 1700s, until these falsehoods have become institutionalized as truth. This state of affairs has progressed to the point that lies are not only accepted as truth, but scholars ignorant of the truth will fight ferociously to maintain the status quo. It might be added that some scholars who are not ignorant of the truth will also fight tooth and nail to maintain the lie.

The earliest system of medicine known to man comes from the Afrikan nation-state called KMT (The Black Land or Land of the Blacks), now known as Egypt. But, invaders now known as Greeks gave KMT that name towards the end of its history, after all the tremendous accomplishments of the native people had been achieved. This scenario has been played out repeatedly and, as a result, nations, places, people and things have been renamed as well as races of people.

One fact that has been distorted is that the ancient Kamites or Kamieu (we will call the original people of Egypt what they called themselves) were white. Images of Elizabeth Taylor and Charlton Heston have been given to provide a popular notion of the whiteness of the Kamites, but it has now been proven definitively that the

Kamites were dark-skinned, kinky-haired people with thick lips and wide noses. Dr. Cheikh Anta Diop's work has not only laid to rest whatever "controversy" existed but has made it much easier to prove the Blackness of the Kamites than it is to prove their whiteness. In fact, Herodotus, the so-called "Father of History," has described the Kamites as Black, kinky-haired, big-lipped people. It is interesting that Herodotus' books about Afrika are frequently not required reading for so-called "Classical" students. Many "scholars" have said frequently that the man celebrated as the "Father of History" really did not see what he was seeing, did not hear what he was hearing and did not know what he was writing.

The Kemetic historian, Manetho, stated that Aha-Mena (called Narmer by the Greeks), the Upper (Southern) Kemetic pharoah who is commonly credited with uniting the Two Lands of Upper and Lower (Northern) Egypt, had a son named Teta, called Athothis by the Greeks. He practiced medicine and wrote books on anatomy. Some evidence suggests that Teta was also the second or third pharoah of the First Dynastic period of KMT and possibly participated in the writing of the Edwin Smith Papyrus.

The original books have never been found but, if found, they would make him the earliest known physician because the founding of the First Dynasty is usually given as 3100 B.C.E., although it is probably much older. Charles Finch, M.D., who inspired me to research this topic, gives excellent evidence that the founding of the First Kemetic Dynasty was probably closer to 4236 B.C.E. (which was the first known calendar date).

Imhotep, the world's first known "Renaissance Man" or multi-genius was "the first figure of a physician to stand out clearly from the mists of antiquity" according to Dr. William Osler, a Canadian physician who co-founded Johns Hopkins Hospital and created the first residency program for the training of physicians. Imhotep was not only chief physician to the Pharoah Djoser of the Third Dynasty, he was also a sage, scribe, chief lector priest, astronomer, architect (he designed and built the first pyramid, the Step Pyramid, at Saqqara), and a poet. He is said to have originally used the phrase, "Eat, drink, and be merry for tomorrow we die."

The Greeks identified him later with their god of healing, Aesclepius. Imhotep was called "The Prince of Peace" and his name means, "He who cometh in peace." He was worshipped by many early Christians as one with Christ. He was also worshipped in KMT as a ntr (aspect of God) thousands of years after his death. The Hippocratic Oath, taken by all Western physicians upon graduation, is originally an oath to Aesclepius written by followers of Hippocrates and dedicated to Hippocrates; actually it is an oath to a Black man.

Hesy Ra was also a Third Dynasty physician who lived after Imhotep. A chief physician, scribe and scholar, he is considered also to be the first known dentist.

With the great deal of information that is known about Imhotep and Hesy Ra, it is difficult to understand how Hippocrates, who lived 2500 years later, could be called The Father of Medicine. Because of racism and the Western inability to understand how science and spirituality could be related, many writers have stated that the basis of Kemetic medicine was largely empirical and magical (read hocus-pocus). However, the extant medical papyri demonstrate that the medical knowledge of the Kamites, the physical, philosophical, spiritual, and intellectual ancestors of Afrikan people all over the world, was theoretical as well as empirical.

All the books in Kmt were usually rolls of papyrus with pages approximately 40 cm. (almost 16 inches) long and 32 cm. (about 12½ inches) wide and came in pieces eight meters long (a little more than 26 feet). The language in which they were written was a middle Egyptian language called *Hieratic*, which was read right to left. Titles, details about quantity and instructions for drug intake were written in red and everything else was written in black. These papyri, especially the so-called "Edwin Smith Papyrus," are probably "copies of medical papyri which date back to pre-pyramid times, to the very earliest historical dynasties."

Extant Medical Papyri

1. Edwin Smith Papyrus, named after the man who "discovered" or stole it, was written about 1700 B.C.E. and is kept at the New York Academy of Medicine. More than 15 feet long, it contains not only magical incantations and religion but is a very organized and systematic surgical textbook that reveals not only a detailed knowledge of surgery and surgical anatomy but also surgical techniques that are still used today in some form. Dr. Diop states that this papyrus speaks of 48 cases of surgery of the bone and of external pathology methodically arranged from the head and moving downwards. The back side has prescriptions including a diagnosis of a female disease and two beauty treatments. It is believed that this may be a copy of a "much more ancient treatise."
2. George Ebers Papyrus was written about 1500 B.C.E. and is the longest of the medical papyri, measuring more than 60 feet. It contains incantations and verbal charms as well as pharmacologic and mechanical means of therapy. It contains chapters on intestinal disease, Helminthiasis (worm infestation), ophthalmology, dermatology, gastroenterology and otolaryngology. There were more than 700 specific remedies in the *materia medica* of this papyrus. The precise record-keeping approach of the early Afrikan physicians of the properties of herbs and roots "was later to flower in the science of botany" according to Weatherwax. Of interest also is the fact that this knowledge is practiced by many so-called "root doctors" who have apprenticed and studied under older "root doctors" so that much of this knowledge has been passed on from generation to generation.

   Unfortunately, in Western culture two things have occurred to discredit these individuals. First, Western science does not recognize the validity of this method and it subjects practitioners to scorn and legal persecutions. Second, because of Western materialism, many frauds and con artists have used "root medicine" to take advantage of people, causing paranoia and suspicion to permeate this area too often and with good reason. This papyrus also describes the relationship of the heart and pulses; that is, it describes the circulatory system thousands of years before Harvey. It is kept in the library of the University of Leipzig in the German state of Saxony.

3. Kahun Papyrus deals with gynecology and obstetrics with a section on veterinary medicine. It is the oldest papyrus, written more than 3800 years ago. It is kept at the University College of London.
4. Chester Beatty Papyrus deals with headaches and treatment of diseases of the anus. It is the smallest of the medical papyri being 21 cm. wide and one meter long. It is believed to have been written in the nineteenth dynasty during the reign of Ramses II. It is kept in the British Museum in London.
5. Hearst Papyrus is believed to be a practical handbook rather than a textbook, much like *Cliff Notes.* It was written about 1550 B.C.E. and contains treatments for ailments of the skin, heart, bladder, chest, dental ailments, parasitic diseases, fractured limbs, bites and the loss and whitening of the hair. It is kept in the Bancroft Library at the University of California, Berkeley.
6. London Papyrus is believed to be a practical handbook rather than a textbook. It contains magical formulas for the treatment of diseases of the eyes, gynecological disorders and burns. It was written about 1350 B.C.E., is 17 cm. wide, 2 meters long and is kept at the British Museum in London.
7. Berlin Papyrus is also believed to be a practical handbook rather than a textbook and was written between 1350 and 1200 B.C.E. Actually, it is two papyri which were "discovered" near Saqqara. It is probably a book of Neonatology and Pediatrics since it deals with childbirth and children. It contains a urine test to diagnose pregnancy. Housed at the Aegyptisches Museum in Berlin, it is similar to the Ebers Papyrus (see medical papyrus #2).
8. The Carlesburg Papyrus contains a method designed to diagnose sterility in women which, according to Diop, Hippocrates copied

word for word. It contains mainly gynecological prescriptions and material concerning pregnancy and diseases of the eye. It is kept at the Egyptological Institute of the University of Copenhagen in Denmark.

9. Brooklyn Museum Papyrus is a treatise on herpetology and ophiology, describing different reptiles, the consequences of their bites and guidance for treatment. As the name implies, it is found in the Brooklyn Museum.
10. The Ramesseum Papyrus concerns ocular diseases, pediatrics, vascular disorders and women's diseases and is in the British Museum.
11. Magical Papyri of Leiden contains remedies and magical formulas against various conditions. It is a copy of an older text and is kept at the University Museum of Leiden in the Netherlands.
12. Insinger Papyrus is a wisdom text written in *demotic*, another Kmt script, which deals with the nature of God and human morality. It is kept at the Rijksmuseum van Oudheden in Leiden in the Netherlands.
13. The Louvre Papyrus in Paris, France, contains remedies for vascular disorders and worms.
14. Westcar Papyrus deals with childbirth and is in the Egyptian Museum of Berlin.
15. The Vatican Papyrus contains anatomical lists for the protection of parts of the human body and is housed in the Vatican Apostolic Library.
16. The Vienna Papyrus, aka the Crocodilopolus Medical Book, found in Vienna, contains a comprehensive pharmacopeia.
17. Brugsch Papyrus contains general medical cases and is similar to the Ebers Papyrus. It is said to have been used by Galen. It is found in the Berlin Museum.
18. The Erman Papyrus contains a list of anatomic names, magical formuli and is found in the Berlin Museum.
19. Papyrus Oxyrhynchus from the third century contains a fragment

of the Hippocratic Oath and treatments for hemorrhoids, hangovers and cataracts. This is part of many fragments, most of which are located at the Ashmolean Museum at Oxford University.

Specialization

As the earlier discussion suggests, the Kamites had a system of specialization not unlike that of today. Herodotus wrote, "Medicine with them (the Kamites) is distributed in the following way: every physician is for one disease and not for several and the whole country is full of physicians of the eyes, others of the head; others of the teeth; others of the belly; and others of obscure disease." The question arises as to what he meant by "obscure disease." It would be my guess that he was referring to illnesses of which he was unaware. If this is true, this could be interpreted as an admission his knowledge was less advanced than that of the Kamites. Several types of physicians were in Kmt:

- **Physicians** *had a system of specialization, not unlike today. Specialties included internal medicine, surgery and the treatment of diseases of the teeth and gums, today called dentistry. They had titles such as "Guardian of the Anus" and were also called "the knower of secret art." Doctors were ranked thus: average doctors, head of physicians, supervisor of physicians and head supervisor.*
- **Surgeons**: *Priests of the lion-headed ntr, Sekh-Met, were surgeons. Sekh-Met presided over war as well as healing and her priests provided care to those injured on the battlefield. These priests are considered by some to be the first organized medical association.*
- **Orthopedists** *were those who took care of broken bones and amputations. They were not considered to be physicians but artists.*
- **Obstetricians**. *Those who delivered babies were midwives and were not considered to be physicians.*

As above, significant specialization occurred in Kmt. Eye doctors were most distinguished, followed by those who dealt with the head, then dentists.

Herodotus called the Kamites, "The healthiest of all men." His opinion may be related to the fact that a type of socialized medicine was in force in KMT and all Kamites had access to medical care regardless of their station or economic circumstances. It was said that the government paid many of the physicians. Swnw (the Kemetic word for physicians) were held to a high standard. Patients and their families could stimulate investigations into physician performances. If the physician proved negligent, he or she could be punished.

Ancient Kamites, like all Afrikans, were traditionally a clean people. They paid a great deal of attention to the cleanliness of their bodies and their surroundings. They purged themselves and gave themselves regular enemas for a symbolic, internal cleansing. A remnant of this rite was passed on during the forced migrations to East and West Afrika during the decline of KMT and the waves of invasions. This custom survives today in many Ausa families even after our forced migration to this country. More specifically, many Ausa believe that a laxative or enema ought to be taken each week to "clean out the system." Unfortunately, this forms the beginning of a pattern of laxative abuse that results in the person needing stronger and more frequent laxatives because of a weakened and atonic colon (large intestine).

George G.M. James, in his seminal work, *Stolen Legacy*, teaches us that the Kemetic priests were the physicians, as were Imhotep and Hesy Ra. The Mystery System of KMT (the educational system) provided for specialized courses of study designed to produce priest-physicians. It would follow, then, the temples that had written over the portals the advice "Man, know thyself" were not only the first medical schools but were also hospitals. They also served as universities, libraries, clinics and seminaries. These structures were called "per ankh" or "house of life" and served also as astronomical observatories and music conservatories. Our honored Elder-Ancestor and brilliant scholar, Dr. John Henrik Clarke, has noted that the first temple of Imhotep was mankind's first hospital.

It is important to state that there were many female swnw (physicians) in KMT. There were no barriers to women becoming priests, scribes, or whatever they wanted to become, based on sexist prejudices.

Perhaps the best known of these was Peseshet, a Third or Fourth Dynasty physician whose title was "lady overseer of the female physicians." A Second Dynasty female swnw, Merit-ptah, was the chief physician of a pharoah's court.

As previously stated and demonstrated, Hippocrates copied many of the remedies from these Afrikans. Newsome states that, for Hippocrates, ancient medicine was Kemetic medicine. The belief is that Hippocrates also did an "internship" in KMT. It is also known that not only did Dioscorides, Galen, and Pliny use the remedies discovered by these Black people, but the medicine systems of the Hebrews, Syrians, Arabs and Persians benefitted greatly as well as has our system of medicine today. Galen continued to visit Kemetic temples and the library at Alexandria regularly in the early A.C.E. years in search of medical knowledge. A disciple of Hippocrates, Galen was repeating the teachings of his master when he wrote, "the invention of medicine was the experiences of the Egyptians."

Specific Treatments

A discovered jawbone from the Old Kingdom was noted to have had surgically created holes in it. This suggests that the holes were made to drain an abscess. The significance of this is that the Kamites were aware that antibiotics were insufficient to cure an abscess and that the appropriate way was surgical drainage. They were aware of many antibiotics, however, and used molds, rotten bread, myrrh, and honey all of which have antibiotic properties.

Copper was used to treat and prevent eye diseases. Because of the yearly Nile flood, the humidity was high on its banks at that time. The incidence of eye infections, especially with Chlamydia, was quite high. Because copper exerts an antibiotic action on that and on some other bacteria, copper was used around the eyes. Trachoma, the eye disease caused by Chlamydia and which can lead to blindness, is still common in Egypt. It is also still treated frequently by copper preparations; the bluish-green color of copper can be seen in Egypt around the eyes of many statues, mummies, and pictures. Dr. Charles S. Finch has suggested that this may have been the origin of make-up.

Night Blindness, which was caused by Vitamin A deficiency, was treated with ox liver which is rich in Vitamin A. Castor seeds were used as a purgative, much like we use castor oil now and scurvy, caused by Vitamin C deficiency, was treated with onions, which are rich in Vitamin C.

Angina Pectoris is chest pain that sometimes radiates down the left arm and is caused when the heart muscle does not get enough blood flow. The Ebers Papyrus states, "If thou examinest a man for illness in his cardia and he has pain in his arms, in his breast, and on one side of his cardia…it is death threatening him." A Stokes-Adams attack is fainting caused by an abnormal heart rhythm. The Kamites called it faintness due to a "dumb heart."

A stricture is an abnormal narrowing in a hollow organ that prevents the normal passage of body contents through the area. The Ebers Papyrus describes a "belly too narrow for food," suggesting a narrowing in the esophagus (food pipe) or stomach. Rectal problems like painful, bleeding, burning, thrombosed hemorrhoids were treated with several specific remedies given as suppositories, enemas, oral medications and local ointments. Obesity was mocked and frowned upon.

Colicky babies were treated with poppy extract, the active ingredient of which is opium. Until recently, paregoric was used for this purpose and the active ingredient is still opium.

Among the hundreds of substances the Kamites used as medication were antimony, salt, alum, carbon and iron. These substances were dispensed as pills, enemas, suppositories, infusions and elixers in accurate and standard doses.

There were descriptions of hundreds of diseases, including cardiovascular and neurological diseases, like polio. Surgery was performed frequently and was called "the knife treatment." This is believed to be related to the embalming practices, which acquainted the Kamites intimately with anatomy. Circumcision was performed on every man as a ritual and, in the ancient world, Afrikans were the only ones who performed circumcision, according to Herodotus.

They performed tracheotomies as evidenced in the Edwin Smith Papyrus, and they used fresh, raw meat (which contains clotting factors) to prevent hemorrhaging in surgical as well as battle wounds. Neurosurgical procedures were also performed. Trephine holes have been described in the papyri and seen on skulls found in KMT. Trephine holes are drilled through the skull to relieve elevated intracranial pressure, treat chronic headaches, drain blood clots, treat seizures, and to address other head/brain injuries.

Obstetrics is an area in which "modern" Western medicine is getting back to the ancient Afrikan way. Women gave birth in a birth seat while sitting upright utilizing gravity. This minimized traumatic injuries to the mother and to the child especially when compared to the supine method of giving birth used by Western methods. Nowadays, however, most obstetric suites have a birthing chair rather than a bed, using the wisdom of our ancient Afrikan ancestors, although they would probably deny the origin. The Kamites knew of uterine prolapse and treated it appropriately and they had knowledge of contraception and knew how to induce abortion.

Doctors who worked on bones were in a separate guild from the physicians and were also very skilled, as mentioned above. Not only did they use traction for broken bones, but they also used splints and did amputations when they felt it necessary.

Transmission of Knowledge

The flow of knowledge moved from KMT southward into West Afrika and East Afrika as a result of migrations induced by the wave of invasions that had plagued the Kamites in the final years of political KMT. These invasions moved knowledge northward into Eurasia also. It is interesting to note that there was no "Golden Age" of Greece until after they had invaded KMT and gained access to the libraries. Similarly, the Arabs and Moors had no science or advanced culture until after they conquered Egypt in 642 A.C.E. and gained access to the still-remaining literature.

The relationship of pharmacology, magic and spirituality was continued in Afrika, but the Europeans, who had no concept of spirituality, removed emphasis on religion and spirituality. There is now, however, a renewed emphasis on religion and healing in Western medical literature.

During the Golden Age of West Afrika, which was cut short by Arab and European slaving, the empires of Ghana, Mali, and Songhay continued the Afrikan reverence and respect for knowledge and science. It is very interesting that today's Black youth equate reverence for learning with other cultures rather than with their own, the result of ignorance of their own history.

According to Chancellor Williams (author of *Destruction of Black Civilization*) and John G. Jackson (author of *Introduction to African Civilizations*), the West Afrikan city Jenne, which Songhay finally conquered in about 1473 A.C.E., was at that time:

> "[the] home of advanced culture, being the seat of a noted university, which employed a staff of thousands of teachers who gave courses of lectures and conducted research on a variety of subjects. Their medical school trained physicians and surgeons of great skill. Among the difficult surgical operations performed successfully by doctors in Jenne was the removal of cataracts from the human eye."

In fact, Askia Mohammed, a great ruler of Songhay, made Songhay the home of high intellectual achievement. There were universities and other educational institutions with high caliber scholarship; medicine was only one of the courses offered.

At the University of Sankore at Timbuktu, there were not only students from all over West Afrika, but from countries outside of Afrika also. There were a large number of scientists and lawyers as well as doctors at Sankore in the fifteenth and sixteenth centuries. As an aside, Ahmed Baba, the last president of Sankore, wrote a series of biographies, 40 scholarly works on different subjects, as well as a comprehensive dictionary. He deserved the right to be considered the greatest scholar of the sixteenth century.

According to Dr. Chancellor Williams, "The first and most important fact is that the general enslavement of Africans (proclaimed to the world as savages) began during the very period and in the very West Africa, the center of which held one of the great universities of the world and other colleges." There was a high rate of literacy and education in that region at that time. It is easy to see that, frequently, the enslaved Afrikans were not only more intelligent than their kidnappers, enslavers, and oppressors, but frequently were also better educated.

While the empires of Ghana, Mali and Songhay were forming (about 300 A.C.E.), Europe's "Dark Ages" were beginning simultaneously. However, with the Moorish invasion of the Iberian Peninsula (Spain and Portugal) from Afrika in 711 A.C.E., they (the Moors) brought civilization and the light of knowledge to the European subcontinent. The Moors, who were Islamic Afrikans, had many medical colleges and graduates in medicine who were required to pass an examination given by the faculty before entering the practice of medicine.

Afrikans developed the concept of quarantine for contagious diseases for many years before Europeans understood the infectious basis of many diseases. The quarantine system for smallpox was called a "sick bush." All individuals with active smallpox were placed in a specific area and the only people who could approach that area were individuals who had already had smallpox, survived it and were immune. When the patients recovered the entire area was burned.

In fact, many enslaved Afrikans brought this knowledge with them from home. It was frequently misunderstood and deemed inferior by the narrow- minded, tunneled-visioned European colonists. The method of immunization that was called "buying the smallpox" is an excellent example of this. During one of the smallpox epidemics in 1721, Cotton Mather, a clergyman, noted that the enslaved Afrikan that he called his possession, never got smallpox. This man, who Mather renamed Onesimus (we don't know his real name or from where he was kidnapped explained that in his village in Afrika, whenever someone got smallpox, they were scratched with a sharp stick until they bled on the stick. This stick was then used to scratch previously unexposed persons and draw blood. They may have experienced a mild illness or no illness at all but were left with a scar and immunity from smallpox. Interestingly, after Mather made this information public, despite its proven efficacy, religious leaders opposed it because, they said, it was a heathen practice and Christians should not learn from heathens. This occurred before Edward Jenner's "discovery" of vaccination.

During the nineteenth century, Afrikan surgeons could remove part of a patient's lung to extract a penetrating arrowhead. They also operated successfully on a man who had had his belly ripped open by an elephant and had him back to work on a road gang in weeks.

In 1879, a European missionary doctor, R.W. Felkin, observed an elective Caesarean section in Uganda that was performed by an Afrikan surgeon which he reported in the *Edinburgh Medical Journal* (volume 20, pp. 922-930, April, 1884). The concepts used were the same as they are today: anesthesia (the patient was half intoxicated with banana wine); restraints (she was tied to the bed with bands of bark over her chest and thighs while an assistant surgeon held her down); sterilization of skin and utensils (the surgeon washed his hands with wine and water and put the knife in wine); and coagulation using heat (bleeding points in the abdominal wall were touched sparingly with red hot irons from a nearby fire). This procedure was a success and mother and child did well. The Europeans were quite amazed because, in 1879, Caesarean sections were performed in Europe only in desperate circumstances and then only to save the life of the infant or the mother but NEVER both. Saving both was unheard of in Europe.

Although there is much other information that is available, the above discussion represents a brief overview of the contributions Afrikan people have made to medical science. This information should be general knowledge because it could not only encourage young Afrikan Americans to seek a career in medicine but could also do wonders towards jerking our youth out of the apathy that rebellion and revolt without knowledge can cause.

Question to Ponder:

Why is Hippocrates called "The Father of Medicine" when we know about Teta, Imhotep, Hesi Ra and Peseshet who lived thousands of years earlier?

References and Suggested Reading

Bernal Martin. *Black Athena: The Afroasiatic Roots of Classical Civilization, Volume 1, The Fabrication of Ancient Greece, 1785-1885*, London: Free Association Books, 1987.

Byrd, Randolph C. Positive Therapeutic Effects of Intercessory Prayer in a Coronary Care Unit Population, *Southern Medical Journal* 81: 826-829, 1988.

Cobb, W. Montague: The Black American in Medicine, *Journal of the National Medical Association* 73: 1185-1244, 1981.

Diop, Cheikh Anta. Origin of the Ancient Egyptians In: *General History of Africa: Volume II, Ancient Civilizations of Africa*, Berkeley: UNESCO, 1990.

Diop, Cheikh Anta. *The African Origin of Civilization: Myth or Reality?* Westport:

Lawrence Hill and Company, 1974.

Diop, Cheikh Anta. *Civilization or Barbarism: An Authentic Anthropology.* Chicago: Lawrence Hill Books, 1991.

Finch, Charles S. *The African Background to Medical Science: Essays on African History, Science, and Civilizations*, London: Karnak House, 1990.

Finch, Charles S. *Echoes of the Old Darkland: Themes from the African Eden*, Decatur: Khenti, Inc., 1991.

Finch, Charles S. *Lecture at the University of South Carolina, 2/12/87.*

Finch, Charles S. III. Pharmacotherapy in Africa: From Antiquity to the Present, *Journal of the National Technical Association*, 65(4):34-36, 1992.

Gallman, Burnett W. From Africa To South Carolina: A Brief Review of the Contributions of Africans and African Americans To Medicine, *The Journal of the South Carolina Medical Association*, May, 1988, pp. 249-255.

Halioua, Bruno and Bernard Ziskind. *Medicine in the Days of the Pharoahs.* Cambridge: The Belknap Press of Harvard University Press, 2005.

Herodotus. *The History* (Translated by David Grene), Chicago: The University of Chicago Press, 1987.

Homer. *The Odyssey*, (Translated by W.H.D. Rouse), NY: A Mentor Book published by the New American Library, 1952.

Jackson, John G. *Introduction To African Civilizations.* NJ: The Citadel Press, 1970.

James, George G.M. *Stolen Legacy*, NY: Philosophical Library, 1954.

Khamit-Kush, Indus. *What They Never Told You In History Class*, NY: Luxorr Publishers, 1983.

Lyons, A.S. and Petrocelli, R.J. *Medicine: An Illustrated History.* NY: Harry Abrams, Inc. Publishers, 1978, pp. 76-103.

Newsome, Frederick. *An African American Philosophy of Medicine.* Charlotte: Conquering Books, LLC, 2005.

Newsome, Frederick. Black Contributions to the Early History of Western Medicine: Lack of Recognition as a Cause of Black Underrepresentation in U.S. Medical Schools. *Journal of the National Medical Association* 71: 189-193, 1979.

Nunn, John F. *Ancient Egyptian Medicine.* London: British Museum Press, 1996.

Osler, William. *Evolution of Modern Medicine.* Public Domain, 1919.

Rogers, J.A. *World's Great Men of Color, Volume I*, NY: Collier Books, Macmillan Publishing Co., 1972.

Sherrill, Kimberly A. Adult Burn Patients: The Role of Religion in Recovery, *Southern Medical Journal* 81: 821-825, 1988.

Stretter, Cornelius. *The Secret Medicine of the Pharoahs: Ancient Egyptian Healing.* Chicago: Edition Q, 1993.

Volney, C.F. *The Ruins, or Meditation on the Revolutions of Empires and The Laws of Nature*, NY: Peter Eckler, 35 Fulton Street, 1890.

Warrick, Sheridan. The Scar on the African's Arm, *Hippocrates*, March/April 1989, p. 20.

Weatherwax, John. *The African Contribution. San Francisco: Bolerium Books, 1968.*

Williams, Chancellor. *Destruction of Black Civilization: Great Issues of a Race From 4500 B.C. to 2000 A.D.* Chicago: Third World Press, 1976, p. 219.

Wilson, William P. Religion in Healing, *Southern Medical Journal* 81:819-820, 1988.

CHAPTER 19

Black Greeks? Or, Will Any Name Be Okay?

Introduction

The Black Greek Letter Organizations have played a very important part in the Black community in America. Their history is a noble one. Usually, they provided a way for like-minded, educated Afrikans to interact, express themselves among their peers, and plan and exert beneficial actions for the entire Ausa community, especially the communities surrounding college campuses. They were true to the early writings of one of the intellectual giants of the twentieth century, Dr. W.E.B. Du Bois. Designed to provide the "talented tenth" of our people with vehicles for what today we call mentoring and networking, these organizations became the proving grounds for our educated elite to learn community responsibility as well as to provide social outlets for members.

It is not surprising that these organizations were modeled after the society and organization of the early Greeks. Starting in Germany and since the seventeenth century, it was taught that the Greeks were the source of all things good, civilized, intelligent, beautiful and noble (see Chapter 4 in *Black Athena: The Afroasiatic Roots of Classical Civilization* by Martin Bernal). It was believed and taught that the Greeks "invented" philosophy, that the origin of the word *philosophy* was believed to be Greek. However, Theophile Obenga proves that the word and concept were Afrikan in origin in his *Ancient Egypt and Black Africa: A Student's*

Handbook for the Study of Ancient Egypt in Philosophy, Linguistics and Gender Relations. The belief in the Greek origin of philosophy has been so strong and fixated that even the highest attainable educational degree in most fields was called Doctor of Philosophy.

The truth of the matter is this: the basis of the brotherhood and sisterhood organizations had existed in Afrika for thousands of years before there was a place called Greece. When the Greeks became the first affirmative action students and were allowed to study in ancient Afrika approximately 2800 years ago, they were impressed with what they learned. None of them completed the course of study (which was 42 years); nonetheless, they took many Afrikan ideas and institutions back to their respective city-states (see George G.M. James' *Stolen Legacy*). Although they were "drop-outs" (Pythagoras stayed the longest at 23 years), they started schools that were based on incomplete knowledge.

At home, the Greeks did not respect the newly returned "philosophers"; all were persecuted and many were killed for teaching "foreign" disciplines. There was no such thing as a unified Greece then; the Greek city-states continuously fought each other and Persia, until Alexander unified them through conquest. Even then they remained barbaric until after their conquest of KMT. Only then, after learning about science, philosophy, medicine, religion, architecture and many other disciplines from our Kemetic Ancestors did they begin to approach the achievement of civilization. Only then, after the conquest of KMT, did the "Golden Age" of Greece begin.

When "classical education" was begun in eighteenth century Germany, the Greeks became the ideal of perfection for all of Europe and America. It is not surprising, therefore, that when the first fraternity was started at William and Mary College in Williamsburg, Virginia, in 1776, it was given a Greek name, Phi Beta Kappa. Because of excessive exclusivity and power over students that sometimes rivaled the faculty's power, many schools unsuccessfully tried to abolish fraternities. However, other such semi-secret social organizations soon followed. Because of white supremacy, enslavement, and American apartheid, Afrikans were barred from joining. Later, they started their own Greek letter organizations.

The names of these Afrikan Greek letter organizations, the titles of their officers, their mottos and much of what was important in these organizations were given Greek names. And why not?!! All the textbooks proclaimed (directly and indirectly) that the noble Greeks were worth emulating.

Initially, Ausa Greek letter organizations lived up to their promise. Indeed, most Ausa leaders in the twentieth century in science, law, politics, medicine, business, invention, so-called "civil rights" and all other fields of endeavor were members of one of the Black Greek letter organizations.

Eventually something went wrong. Too frequently the materialistic aspect of membership assumed primary importance to too many individuals. They began to emulate the snotty exclusiveness of the European organizations they had been organized to imitate. Achievement of the "American Dream" and its financial and social perks (and perceived power) became more important to some individuals than providing responsible leadership to our people. As an example, too many members of the Omega Psi Phi Fraternity (my fraternity) became more concerned with maintaining the "Que Dog" and "Nasty Dog" images than they did in respecting and elevating Black womanhood.

Many fraternity and sorority members ran to the suburbs at the first opportunity, not necessarily because our neighborhoods were decaying and not necessarily to avail ourselves of the "improvement" in lifestyle but to get away from our less fortunate brothers and sisters. Not all Afrikans who moved to the white suburbs were fleeing...but many were. These "fugitives from themselves" caused the Black Greek letter organizations to be further distanced from the masses of our people. A real elitism was begun that still exists today.

Many current members of the various organizations, especially the sororities, speak of a color line that still exists. They readily admit that it is not as bad as it had been but that it is still advantageous to be light-skinned.

This chapter is offered to start a dialog and is not intended to be the final word or the definitive cure. Although many people see Afrikan people as having many problems, it is my belief that we have one large problem with many symptoms. For an organized schema of these symptoms, see *The Isis Papers: The Keys to the Colors* by Dr. Frances Cress Welsing. We MUST have a clear understanding of the problem in order to come up with solutions.

Our main problem is one of racial and cultural amnesia with the imposition of alien worldviews, values, interests, principles and ethics. The symptoms include poverty (having an employee mentality); ignorance (we value belief more than knowledge and have become anti-intellectual); violence (rape, domestic violence, and fratricide); lack of self-respect; disrespect of elders; disrespect of women by men; disrespect of men by women; homosexuality, pedophilia, and other sexual deviations; child abuse and general irresponsibility. The answer to ALL these problems is a return to our classical Africanity, understanding what it means to be Afrikan. We do not attempt to romanticize Afrika. It is important, however, to be able to know enough about Afrika's history and culture that we can emulate its best and discard its proven worst. There are many solutions that must be addressed. This chapter simply offers one framework that can be investigated.

This chapter is intended to be a companion to James E. Brunson's excellent book, *Frat and Soror: The African Origin of Greek-Lettered Organizations.* Those interested in this topic are urged to study that book. Some members of the Black Greek letter organizations may be offended or even angered by this chapter; however, hopefully, that anger can be transformed into an honest re-appraisal of the Black Greek letter organizations. This is not intended to be destructively critical but to shed light on what the writer feels is wasted potential and possibly stimulate some constructive changes.

We will touch on various aspects of the Afrikan worldview as opposed to the European worldview. However, a complete analysis is beyond the scope of this chapter (see Chapter 7 on the Two Cradle Theory). Also, for an excellent, honest and complete analysis of the

European worldview and its effect on the world, we recommend strongly Marimba Ani's *Yurugu: An African-Centered Critique of European Cultural Thought and Behavior.*

Who and What Were the Greeks?

The Greek people were comprised of many racial elements. The image of the blond and blue-eyed Greek god and goddesses is wishful thinking, although some Greeks were blond and blue-eyed. Professor George Wells Parker's paper, *"The African Origin of the Grecian Civilization"* (published in the *Journal of Negro History,* Volume II, July, 1917) stated that two of the foremost Greek states were the Lacedaemonians (the Dorics or Pelasgic people) and the Athenians (the Ionics or Hellenes).

While the Hellenes were described as Aryans, the Pelasgians were described as "sunburnt Hamites" who were "strongly Negritic." Professor Parker used his knowledge of the Greek language to translate many old texts and found that the translations used in schools frequently were incorrect. He found several references to the Pelasgians (as well as the Egyptians, Assyrians and Etruscans) as "half-breed" and "mulattos."

Many of the day-to-day customs of the people called Greeks did come from the Aryans who had gradually migrated south into Greece after the Wurm Interglacial (Ice Age). Cheikh Anta Diop discussed many of these customs in his books *The Cultural Unity of Black Africa* and *Civilization or Barbarism: An Authentic Anthropology.* One significant custom is homosexuality.

Among Greek men, the bonds of homosexuality were believed to be the ideal of male relationships and strongly influenced fraternal organizations. Two particular works give more complete discussions on the topic of Greek homosexuality: an article, "Benyin-Besiaba: An Afrikan Centered Evaluation of Homosexuality" in *Innervisions: Rx For Survival For People of Afrikan Origin* by this writer, and the book *On Homosexuality: Lysis, Phaedrus and Symposium translated* by Benjamin Jowett. Mwalimu Baruti's *Homosexuality and the Effeminization of Afrikan Males* is also instructive. Suffice it to say that regardless of what the Greeks learned in Afrika — and it was not homosexuality — brotherhood and fraternity had a different meaning for them.

Many Afrikan men are very anxious to call themselves "Greek." They should, however, understand all the ramifications of that label.

Importance of Names

The importance of names and naming in Afrikan culture cannot be overstated. A person's name was felt to reflect the essence of the person and, more importantly, was identified not only with that person's soul but with the souls of his/her Ancestors. This fact was well known by our kidnappers, enslavers and oppressors so they always renamed places and people they conquered. A small example of this point is *The Roots* episode that showed the war of wills between Kunte Kinte and the enslaver/oppressor over the name "Toby."

A person who is separated from his/her Ancestors (history) is easily enslaved: body, mind and spirit; so, it should not be surprising that a major goal of our kidnappers, enslavers and oppressors was to separate us from our Ancestors. There has been significant success with this goal, so much so that they even have us honoring <u>their</u> ancestors.

This success has been incomplete, however, as shown by the fact that the debate still rages. In fact, the debate about what we are to be called has raged among people of Afrikan descent in America for the past 200 years. Initially, we were satisfied with being called Afrikans, then Afro-Americans, then Colored, then negro, then Negro, then Black, then Afro-American, then Afrikan American, and some of us prefer simply to be called "Afrikan" or "persons of color."

Because of the combination of several Afrikan ethnic groups in each of us, this writer prefers Ausa (Afrikan from the United States of America). Even a brief glance at these names suggests that there is a cyclical quality to the argument. Unfortunately, there are some people of Afrikan origin who feel we should be satisfied and proud of simply being called American. Obviously, they have not considered the question posed by Dr. Anderson Thompson of the Kemetic Institute of Chicago and paraphrased here: *"What do you think the*

Africans who arrived in chains fresh from Africa, your Ancestors, and found themselves in a strange and hostile place called America wanted?" What did they call themselves then? When did they stop wanting to go home and start wanting to be American? What prompted them to stop wanting to be what their Ancestors were and to want to be like the enslaver/oppressor?

Our Ancestors have said that to know a thing's real name is to know its power. Lorenzo Dow Turner, the eminent Afrikan American linguist, found when he lived among the Gullah people in the Sea Islands of South Carolina that "Africanisms" have persisted among our people in names and naming. In the Gullah culture, he discovered, each person had a secret personal name that was used only in private. It took Turner years before they revealed this to him; they never revealed this to white researchers. Turner documented this in his book, *Africanisms in the Gullah Dialect.*

Another factor in the debate is that the name "negro" was assigned to us and is etymologically related to an old European word that meant "dead." We know the variations of that word (especially nigra and nigger but also nigga). The designation "Colored" was inadequate for obvious reasons, although it was preferred by several prominent nineteenth century Nationalists. We must not answer to names assigned to us, especially by our enemies.

*****

Once again, we must see clearly that there has been a three-way struggle for supremacy in the world. Although the white race has been winning for the last 500 years, Afrikans have been in control of the world for most of man's existence on earth. Although not perfect, it was a more moral, ethical and spiritual world during those thousands of years. Contrary to popular belief, it was also a scientifically and technically advanced world. Now, the Asians are pressing hard for their "place in the sun." For Afrikans to ignore this history and aid other people in retaining dominance ("It's just a job"), especially when they are destroying us in so many ways, could be considered to be a form of treason.

The name "Black" is only symbolically descriptive because most of us are not physically Black. It describes a state of mind, Blackness. It is also instructive to understand the Western meanings of the word "Black." The film "X" illustrated a fact known by many, that the word Black, in English, has almost all negative connotations while the word white has almost all positive connotations. The dictionary supports this statement. These relationships (Black=bad, white=good) have been symbolized in the popular culture in ways that subconsciously reinforce self-hatred in Afrikan people and false superiority in European people.

It is important also to note that our Ancestors in KMT venerated the color Black and described themselves as Black. The use of the descriptive term "Black" did not begin in the 1960s. Despite all this, however, "Black" is still an incomplete way of describing a people. It describes the people symbolically and the psychology partially but does nothing as regards describing the history, culture, language or geographical place of origin.

There are few (if any) absolute arguments against the use of the term "Black" Most people who consider themselves Afrikan and/or Afrikan American also occasionally use the term "Black." It is also interesting to note that not very long ago, being called Black in America was an insult that frequently led to blows.

When one chooses a name that one is willing to answer to, that name should not only be descriptive but must place the person with a people, a history and a geographical place of origin. It should also be descriptive of a culture and reunite us with and keep us in communion with our Ancestors. A people become disoriented when they let their names go (see Asa Hilliard's introduction to Anthony Browder's book *From the Browder File*).

Malcolm X said if a cat gives birth in an oven, you don't call the newborns biscuits. Afrikan people born in America are still Afrikan.

Names and Afrikan Entities in the United States

The debate over names has other fronts. Many of our organizations and other entities have borne the name Afrikan or African. Some still do despite much opposition. On the other hand, many of our organizations, through their names, pay homage to the Ancestors of our kidnappers, enslavers and oppressors.

One of the best-known organizations with Afrika in the name is the African Methodist Episcopal Church. Unfortunately, most members of the A.M.E. Church do not realize the significance of the name or what it meant to the founder, Richard Allen. This writer grew up in that Christian protestant denomination and was a member of the youth organization, then called, "The Allen Christian Endeavor League." At least two prominent personalities in the A.M.E. Church could best be described as "Nationalists": Richard Allen and Henry McNeal Turner.

The African Methodist Episcopal Zion church is another organization that dates back to a time when our Ancestors were not ashamed of their Africanity.

Another well-known organization that had "Africa" in its name was the African Grand Lodge, which is known now as the Prince Hall Masons. However, the founder, Prince Hall, not only did not want the organization named after him, but he was also a "Nationalist." A newspaper that has been important over the years, especially in the South, is the *Afro-American*, which was started in Baltimore in 1892.

Even when we did not use "African" or "Afro" specifically, we were not afraid to point out our color in organizations. Examples include The National Association for the Advancement of Colored People (NAACP) and the Colored Methodist Episcopal Church (in 1954, the church body voted to change the name, so now C.M.E. means Christian Methodist Episcopal).

Finally, The African Heritage Studies Association and The Association for the Study of Classical African Civilizations (ASCAC) are modern organizations started by the philosophical descendants of Richard Allen and Prince Hall. Members of these organizations study and teach our Afrikan heritage to our people from an Afrikan perspective. They are not "feel-good" organizations; they stress accuracy, excellence and scholarship.

Suggested Organizational Framework

There are ten Black Greek letter organizations, either fraternities (brotherhoods) or sororities (sisterhoods):

- *Sigma Pi Phi (SPF) Graduate fraternity founded 5/15/1904 in Philadelphia, PA. Its members can be members of other Black Greek letter organizations.*
- *Alpha Phi Alpha (AFA) Undergraduate and graduate fraternity founded at Cornell University in Ithaca, NY on 12/4/1906*
- *Alpha Kappa Alpha (AKA) Undergraduate and graduate sorority founded at Howard University in Washington, D.C. on 1/16/1908*
- *Kappa Alpha Psi (KAY) Undergraduate and graduate fraternity founded at Indiana University in Terre Haute, IN on 1/5/1911*
- *Omega Psi Phi (WYF) Undergraduate and graduate fraternity founded at Howard University in Washington, D.C. on 11/17/1911*
- *Delta Sigma Theta (DSQ) Undergraduate and graduate sorority founded at Howard University in Washington, D.C. in 1913*
- *Phi Beta Sigma (FBS) Undergraduate and graduate fraternity founded at Howard University in Washington, D.C. on 1/9/1914*
- *Zeta Phi Beta (ZFB) Undergraduate and graduate sorority founded at Howard University in Washington, D.C. on 1/16/1920*
- *Sigma Gamma Rho (SGR) Undergraduate and graduate sorority founded 11/12/1922 in Indianapolis, IN; was granted a chapter at Butler University in Indianapolis on 12/30/29.*
- *Iota Phi Theta (Iotas) Undergraduate and graduate fraternity founded 1963 at Morgan State University in Baltimore, MD*

The undergraduate organizations are frequently referred to as "The Divine Nine." The membership of these ten organizations includes most of the Afrikans in America who hold positions of some power and responsibility in the general community and it includes those who have been fortunate enough to acquire an education, or mis-education according to your point of view.

Some degree of polarization exists among all the organizations, however. Although usually not violent these "friendly" rivalries can be profoundly damaging to Afrikan American people. Polarization tends to help some people in our communities but not others.

If these organizations formed a "collective" or large organization with common goals that are well planned, organized and discussed, the beneficial effects for Afrikan people would reverberate around the planet. I am not unaware of the so-called Pan-Hellenic Council; however, there has to be a basis for this "coming together," a commonality that is strong enough to bind these organizations together in a meaningful way. The one obvious commonality, the common Afrikan origin of the overwhelming majority of members of all nine organizations, is a logical starting point. Despite recent denials of a "monolithic" Afrikan American community, we need to investigate and evaluate that concept more carefully. Western society is not monolithic either except in one important area, the need to continue the practice of white dominion or supremacy.

We need to use every possible tool that would improve the condition of all our people. An alliance of the Black Greek letter organizations would be an excellent starting point and would be extremely effective in accomplishing that goal. The suggestions that follow are offered as "food for thought" in order to maximize the successful transition.

Afrikanize the Organizations

As mentioned in the Introduction, Greek letter organizations have their original theoretical and philosophical basis in Afrika. What this means is that any federation of Black Greek letter organizations should not be called Pan-Hellenic anything! Indeed, it seems odd (and perhaps a bit insane) that Afrikans would even want to be Pan-Hellenic more than Pan-Afrikan. It seems obvious that a major effort is needed to find out the details of what our Ancestors did that so fascinated and influenced the ancient Greeks that they copied and honored the Afrikans at every opportunity.

The first step in Afrikanizing the organizations would be in changing the names. This is not absolutely necessary as long as the philosophy and goals change. However, we suggest using an Afrikan symbol to reorganize according to the Nine Areas of Human Activity plus Health and Environment (see Chapter 8: Nine Areas of Human Activity).The symbols suggested are of Yoruba and Kemetic deities. Scholars and elders of Afrikan-centered organizations such as ASCAC, ABPsi and NABSW can take the lead in training.

Area of Activity	Greek Letter Organization	Afrikan Symbol
Economics	**Sigma Pi Phi**	**Obatala**

Note: Because the members of this organization are generally older and wiser, Obatala, the Elder is chosen.

Education	**Zeta Phi Beta**	**Aset (Isis)**

Note: Aset represented motherhood and the faithful wife. Teachers are extended mothers and fathers to their students.

Entertainment	**Phi Beta Sigma**	**Bes**

Note: Bes represented music and jollity and was integral for balance.

Labor	**Kappa Alpha Psi**	**Elegba**

Note: Elegba performed many tasks. He was a messenger, courier, policeman and guardian of the crossroads.

Law	**Delta Sigma Theta**	**Ma'at**

Note: Ma'at was the female wisdom principle that governed truth, justice, righteousness, harmony, balance, order, propriety and reciprocity.

Politics	**Alpha Phi Alpha**	**Shango**

Note: Shango personified stateliness, oratory, virility and masculinity.

Religion	**Alpha Kappa Alpha**	**Khephera**

Note: Khephera was the self-created aspect of God.

Area of Activity	Greek Letter Organization	Afrikan Symbol
Sex	**Sigma Gamma Rho**	**Oshun**

Note: Oshun personified sensuality, love, beauty, graciousness and gracefulness.

War	**Omega Psi Phi**	**Ogun**

Note: Ogun represented war, courage, strength, justice, force, security, protection and was the executioner.

Health	**Iota Phi Theta Fraternity**	**Sekhmet**

Note: Sekhmet was a warrior Goddess and the goddess of healing.

Economic Methodology

If all the Black Greek letter organizations would combine their local, district and national meetings for five years, yet still collect and save the money they would have spent, they would have almost enough money to build their own huge conference center. This center would be Black owned and could provide a meeting place for other organizations in the Afrikan community. It would also keep some of the 1.2 trillion-plus dollars that Afrikans spend yearly in the American economy. This is not only "do-able," but is necessary for our survival.

Many chapters of the various organizations are rightfully proud that they give scholarships to needy students and donate substantial sums to deserving organizations. It is suggested, though, that the economic and political consequences of owning our own conference center is so positive for all of us that a few sacrifices for a relatively short time would be worthwhile. It would provide jobs for many Afrikan people — construction companies and workers, financial planners and managerial and custodial companies, to name a few.

Ownership would be a prelude to other economic ventures that would be done on behalf of Afrikan people. Once this has taken root, attention can be given to the economic development of Ghana and other Afrikan nations in the Afrikan Union friendly to Ausa that have unlimited potential for Afrikan people worldwide.

A word of caution: If, and when, this becomes a real plan, we can expect TREMENDOUS opposition from non-Afrikan people many of us have believed were our friends and who had our best interests at heart. We can also expect people of Afrikan origin — people who look like us but have loyalties that are not related to us — to "come out of the woodwork" in an attempt to derail, co-opt and/or prevent us from achieving our goals. They are "skinfolk" but not "kinfolk."

Finally, it goes without saying that we would have to forego the many purely social functions that we spend lavishly on, unless they are purely fundraisers. Afrikan people do enjoy social functions but, again, sacrifices need to be made for the greater good of all Afrikan people.

Community Inclusiveness

The Afrikan community is a place of inclusiveness. Many capable and successful people in the Afrikan community have not attended or graduated from college and there are also individuals who have chosen not to pledge fraternities and sororities. These former Greek letter organizations should branch out and create community arms composed of these people. Together, they can be more effective and efficient. Like a finely-tuned car, the Afrikan community has to operate on all cylinders. We cannot afford to exclude any part of our community. We must not allow elitism or the appearance of elitism to splinter us. When this is done there would be a connectedness in the Afrikan community that has not been present since the era of enforced segregation or American Apartheid.

When these goals are met, then alliances with other organizations in the Afrikan community can be contemplated and pursued. Other organizations would include other fraternal and sororal organizations such as the Masons, Eastern Star, Elks, Groove Phi Groove, Links, Moles, Girlfriends, Carousels, Sophisticates, Guardsmen, NAACP, Urban League and others. These organizations can be included, as long as they accept the terms of Pan-Afrikan Nationalism that work for the good of Afrikan people all over the world. We must not fall victim to the idea that only Ausa, and not the greater Pan-Afrikan world can benefit from our efforts.

Youth Branches

Another logical extension of cooperation among these organizations would be youth branches organized in same-sex/age-grades until adolescence. At adolescence, the male and female age-grades would come together for cooperation and preparation for inclusion into society. A rites of passage program, with all organizations participating, would complete the transition from youth into adulthood after a suitable period. It is imperative that the opinions and input of the youth be encouraged, heard and respected.

To achieve all these things would not be difficult if an organized and concerted effort were put forth. No major changes in organizational structure or operations would be necessary, just changes primarily in self-perception, philosophy and emphasis. We must stop seeing ourselves as Greeks and stop honoring other peoples' ancestors for doing what our Ancestors did. It is important to encourage our youth to join these organizations, however. For any change to occur, it must start from within these organizations. In reality, little pressure can be exerted from <u>outside</u> that will make them change. This is a practical point and not an absolute statement. The very structures of these organizations insulate them a great deal from outside pressures, which is one of the points that make them so desirable as vehicles for liberation and sovereignty.

Many of the organizations' chapters have on-going "mentoring" programs with youth. It should be mentioned here that, for us, instead of mentoring, Jegna training is preferable as previously discussed. Unquestionably, this is desirable but, without knowledge of self (Afrikan principles, ethics and interests), many of these efforts are successful only at creating more confused negroes who perpetuate the values and interests of their kidnappers/enslavers/oppressors. It is suggested that a rite of passage program be provided for each member of the Black Greek letter organization <u>before</u> they embark upon any attempts to work with youth so the values they impart are consistent with the expressed goals of the Pan-Afrikan Organization.

Elders

Elders hold an important place in Afrikan culture. We cannot afford to miss out on the wisdom Elders possess. Each fraternity/sorority would have a Council of Elders from which three members would be represented, on a rotational basis, on a Supreme Council of Elders which would have oversight over the entire organization.

How to Start

Almost certainly, the movement will start on a local level and spread upwards. There is no reason not to consider the possibility of exposing regional and national leaders to these ideas, however. Members could compare membership in these Greek letter organizations, perhaps at a study group meeting or a meeting of other nationalist organizations. The plans could start now.

Among the general membership of the Greek letter organizations, there are individuals who, while not Afrikan centered in the classic definition, care deeply about the plight of Afrikan people. These individuals are the natural allies that we have in this endeavor. We will have to "walk the walk" as well as "talk the talk." Our people have been taken in by many smooth-talking people posing as religious, economic and cultural leaders. Because of that, we must demonstrate the principles of Ma'at in all that we say and do. We must earn the trust of our people and make sure that it is reciprocated.

A Note on Initiation

Afrikan initiation followed several general steps. The first step was to separate the initiates from the community to undergo a structured program designed to prepare them for successful functioning in the society. They had been socialized to be ready for the moment of initiation. Because all Greek letter organizations were based on the Afrikan model, initiation was not only required but was an integral part of the process.

One important part of initiation was hazing which was controlled and purposeful. Unfortunately, in recent times it has become sadistic and, too often, dangerous. The process of hazing has strayed away from its original purpose and has gained a life of its own. In order to *teach* self-control, we must *have* self-control. The more difficult an accomplishment is, the more it is appreciated. It should be difficult to achieve membership in a Greek letter organization or its community arm. It should not, however, involve brutality or senseless, meaningless or futile exercises.

The Pan Afrikan Council should design an initiation based on Afrikan models with the input of Afrikan-centered psychologists. This would eliminate the lawsuits and internal disciplinary actions that seem to be plaguing these organizations currently.

Synthesis

Many wise Elders have said that one reason Afrikans have been catching so much hell worldwide is that we have forgotten our Ancestors. We do not honor them like we did or still should. Traditionally, Afrikans have believed that the world is composed of the visible (material world) and the invisible (spiritual world, including the Ancestors). We knew the invisible is far greater than the visible.

Our kidnappers, enslavers and oppressors altered this belief. They had and still have control over most of our institutions, especially our (mis)-education, political life and other socialization processes. They do not have direct control over our churches or our fraternal and sororal organizations which is why we desperately need to make those organizations work for all our people and not just DuBois' "talented tenth."

We have been made to fear our Ancestors through ghost stories, "haint" stories and stories about evil mummies carrying out a curse. Using radio, motion pictures and especially television (which Afrikan people watch more than anyone), our beliefs were caricaturized and ridiculed and we were made to feel ashamed of them. The resulting reality is especially devastating. However, we can use those same methods to undo the damage.

Before we knew the truth about our Ancestors' teacher-student relationship with the Greeks, we did not know any better. But now we have no excuse; we have to decide what we are going to do with these rediscovered truths. Are we going to "ooh" and "ahh," intellectualize, say "That's interesting, I didn't know that" and continue to live in the same reality?

- *Are we going to continue to base our actions on these exposed falsehoods?*
- *Are we going to ignore the truth and take the easy way out —the lie?*
- *Are we going to question the veracity of these well-documented truths and participate in the attack on the scholar/messengers? OR,*
- *Are we going to have the courage not only to learn this important information but to make constructive use of it?*

The future of the world and the welfare of our grandchildren's grandchildren may rest on our decision. If we make the wrong decision, our progeny may not survive to curse and dishonor us as we have done our Ancestors.

To continue to deny our Ancestors the credit for their creations and the honor due them is not even the Christian thing to do. It goes against the Fifth Commandment (Exodus 20:12),"Honor thy father and thy mother...."

Time is running out. We must use the structures of these organizations for the direct good of ALL Afrikan people. We must stop fiddling like Nero while Pan-Europeanism and Pan-Asianism continue to make Europe/America and Japan/Korea/Hong Kong/Singapore/Taipan/China/India wealthy on the riches of Afrika while Afrikans negotiate, beg and imitate hoping the Europeans and Asians will "do the right thing," give their wealth, which is OUR wealth, back to us, or will make us honorary Europeans.

We must see the current Chinese incursions into Afrika as a new Scramble for Afrika and see Pan-Afrikanism as the way of survival. We must realize that the mainstream many of us have been taught to want to join is polluted. What sane person wants to dive into polluted water? By now, we should know we are not included as players in the "New World Order" except as pawns, entertainers, athletes, servants, pets or honorary Europeans (Afropeans or Afro-Saxons).

European Jews of pre-World War II Germany did not believe what happened to them would happen. We are hated more than the Jews and we need to stop fooling ourselves and look at the statistics. That we are doing so badly economically and health-wise is neither a coincidence nor an accident. Nobody wants to be poor and unhealthy.

It is getting late in the game. We have lost much of the last three generations of our children to the oppressors' thinking and the lure of the criminal life. We must move rapidly, accurately and decisively to prevent the loss of another generation to what will become an ongoing generational destruction of Afrikan people.

References and Suggested Reading

Ani, Marimba. *Yurugu: An African-Centered Critique of European Cultural Thought and Behavior.* Trenton: Africa World Press, 1994.

Benton, Joe, Derrick Jackson, Burnett Gallman. *Project Sankofa: A Rites of Passage Program: Philosophy, Theory & Overview.* Columbia: Our Community Organization, 1998.

ben-Jochannan, Yosef A.A. *Africa, Mother of Western Civilization.* Baltimore: Black Classic Press, 1988.

ben-Jochannan, Yosef A. A. *Black Man of the Nile and His Family,* Baltimore: Black Classic Press, 1990.

Browder, Anthony T. *From the Browder File: 22 Essays on the African American Experience.* Washington, DC: The Institute of Karmic Guidance, 1989 pp.1-2. (Chapter entitled "The Creation of the Negro")

Browder, Anthony T. *Nile Valley Contributions to Civilization: Exploding the Myths.* Washington, D.C.: The Institute of Karmic Guidance, 1992.

Brunson, James E. *Frat and Soror: The African Origin of Greek-Lettered Organizations.* A Cleage Group publication, 1990.

Carruthers, Jacob H. *Essays in Ancient Egyptian Studies.* Los Angeles: University of Sankore Press, 1984.

Carruthers, Jacob H. *African or American: A Question of Intellectual Allegiance.* Chicago: Kemetic Institute, 1994.

Diop, Cheikh Anta. *The African Origin of Civilization: Myth or Reality.* Westport: Lawrence Hill and Company, 1974.

Diop, Cheikh Anta. *Civilization or Barbarism: An Authentic Anthropology.* Chicago: Lawrence Hill Books, 1991.

Garner, Marcus K. *Black Greek Letter Organizations: What's Really Going On?* Upscale, September/October, p. 128, 1994.

Ghee, Kenneth L. The Psychological Importance of Self Definition and Labeling: Black Versus African American. The Journal of Black Psychology, Fall, Volume 17, Number 1, pp. 75-93, 1990.

Hilliard, Asa G. III. Pedagogy in Ancient Kemet. In *Kemet and the African Worldview: Research, Rescue, and Restoration.* Los Angeles: University of Sankore Press, 1984.

Hilliard, Asa G. III, Larry Williams, Nia Damali. *The Teachings of Ptahhotep: The Oldest Book in the World.* Atlanta: Blackwood Press and Company, Inc., 1987.

Hilliard, Asa G. III. *The Maroon Within Us: Selected Essays on African American Community Socialization.* Baltimore: Black Classic Press, 1995.

Holloway, Joseph E. *Africanisms in American Culture.* Bloomington: Indiana University Press, 2005.

James, George G. M. *Stolen Legacy.* San Francisco: Julian Richardson Associates, 1976.

Karenga, Maulana. *Selections From The Husia: Sacred Wisdom of Ancient Egypt.* Los Angeles: Kawaida Publications, 1984.

Karenga, Maulana. *The Book of Coming Forth By Day.* Los Angeles: University of Sankore Press, 1990.

Moore, Richard B. *The Name "Negro": Its Origin and Evil Use.* Baltimore: Black Classic Press, 1992.

Nobles. Wade W. *African Psychology: Towards Its Reclamation, Reascension, and Revitalization.* Oakland: A Black Family Institute Publication, 1986.

Obenga, Theophile. *Ancient Egypt and Black Africa: A Student's Handbook for the Study of Ancient Egypt in Philosophy, Linguistics and Gender Relations.* Chicago: Karnak House/Frontline International, 1992.

Stuart, Curtis. What is the Significance of the Name "African American"? *Action Newsletter: The Action Council for Cross Cultural Mental Health and Human Services,* First Quarter, Volume 1, Number 1, Columbia, SC, 1989.

Stuckey, Sterling. *Slave Culture: Nationalist Theory and the Foundations of Black America.* NY: Oxford University Press, 1987, pp. 193-244 (Chapter entitled "Identity and Ideology: The Names Controversy).

Van Sertima, Ivan (Editor). *Egypt Revisited.* New Brunswick: Transaction Publishers, (The Journal of African Civilizations, Volume10, Summer, 1989).

Van Sertima, Ivan (Editor): *Egypt: Child of Africa.* New Brunswick: Transaction Publishers, (The Journal of African Civilizations, Volume 12, Spring, 1994) Also includes Essays From Nile Valley Civilizations.

Welsing, Frances Cress. *The Isis Papers: The Keys to the Colors.* Chicago: Third World Press, 1991.

CHAPTER 20

Age-Grades and Education: A Suggested Model

Overview of Age-Grade Systems

Age-grade systems are social systems in which the society is organized according to age. They provide unity, security and order. Afrikan people are the oldest of the Creator's creations; therefore, we have had longer to learn about what works best and when and how. This makes us responsible for our own well-being and, more importantly, we are ultimately responsible for the future of the world.

Our knowledge and our wisdom are reflected in our culture. Unfortunately, many if not most of us — the Original People — have been disconnected from our culture through the intentional efforts of our immature and spoiled children, the interpreters and claimants of what is now called "Western culture." They kidnapped, enslaved, oppressed, tortured, and murdered us in a childish, tantrum-like orgy of cruelty. Consequently, our culture has been fragmented and we have lost the true meaning and significance of many things that we do and say every day.

The world changes frequently, although on a deeper level most things stay the same. We cannot go back to the culture of centuries ago and expect it to fit perfectly in today's world. We must be fluid and flexible enough to make yesterday work for today. We must relearn our history and culture so that we can restore the best parts and permanently discard the negative parts.

Afrikan people have been keen observers of nature for many thousands of years and have identified the cyclical nature of things natural. They/we recognized the profound significance of each stage of life and ritualized the passage from one stage to the other: Birth > Childhood > Adulthood > Eldership > Death. They felt that those who were born came from the same place that those who died went to: the place of the Ancestors. Hence, Those-Yet-To-Be-Born were also considered to be Ancestors, which probably explains, at least in part, why children were/are so revered and why Elders were so respected. Children are recently arrived Ancestors, frequently reincarnated from previous generations; Elders had the knowledge of years and the wisdom that socialization is far more important than education in that it provides for the continuation of a culture and gives a blueprint for survival in hostile environments. Both are critically important to the survival and well-being of a people.

Our traditional culture will be used as the template and background milieu for all our activities. We recognize that it would be inappropriate to thoughtlessly mimic what our traditional Afrikan Ancestors did or even what our Traditional Brothers and Sisters on the Mother Continent do today. As models, we are using what we consider to be the best and most appropriate aspects of Kemetic, Yoruba, Akan, Gikuyu and Congolese culture. Our Kemetic Ancestors are the prototype for most, if not all cultures today. Some cultures have strayed greatly from the original, for example, Western culture but others have kept many of the important features. We use Akan, Yoruba and Congolese culture as models also, because the majority of Afrikans in America, especially in South Carolina, have strong ancestral ties to the Akan and Congolese people. Gikuyu culture is an East Afrikan culture that further demonstrates the "cultural unity" of Afrika.

Tribe, as a concept, has been diminished by the Western world, but we recognize the totemic system that recognizes clans and tribes. Western culture paraphrases the concept of tribe and elevates the alternative term, "ethnic group." This is the reason why "tribal warfare" occurs in Afrika, but "ethnic conflict" occurs in Bosnia and Ireland. In the spirit of Kujichagulia, we have taken the liberty to paraphrase Dr. Wade W. Nobles and give ourselves (Afrikans from America) a tribal designation. We call ourselves Ausa (Ah-ooh-sah), which is Afrikans from the United States of America.

We have also formally raised a category above tribe (as many have done before). We call this category The People, Afrikans, The Race, or even Black People, which includes all tribes of Afrikan descent no matter where on the Mother Continent or in the Diaspora they may be found. This means that the ultimate secular allegiance is to the Race (Afrikan or Black People), then to the Tribe (Ausa), then to the Clan (whatever organization to which you belong) then to the Family (Extended and Nuclear).

Age-Grades will be institutionalized. A "Chain of Respect" must be formed that negates the petty jealousies, lack of cooperation and acts of sabotage so frequently seen in western culture. Members of each Age-Grade will respect and look up to all older Age-Grades and will be conscious of being role models and deserving of the respect of the younger Age-Grades. Although in some ways this is hierarchical, it is important to realize the emphasis is on the expectation of wisdom and the responsibility to be found in older people. This is not a hierarchy based on knowledge, position, office or title. It is a practice based on a demonstration of worthiness of respect. An Elder who does not act out her/his life in such a manner as to deserve respect will be afforded only the basic form of respect, that due to all strangers.

It is important to add that effective implementation will require much interaction, communication and cooperation between and among all interested and involved individuals. No one can truly operate in a separate void and be truly Afrikan. Optimal development of any individual requires the maximization of mental, physical and spiritual strengths.

Age-Grades provide lifelong relationships and reinforcements in meeting life's challenges. This is helpful in improving and increasing effectiveness and efficiency in learning and in creating close bonds of friendship in knowledge-based trust from familiarity and kinship.

Finally, Age-Grades perpetuate a system that trains all individuals to be followers to become leaders. Stated another way, Age-Grades create thoughtful, creative, effective leaders who have been followers. This will help clear up the "leadership void" in our communities. We have had far too many "leaders" who tried to be rulers and our community does not need rulers. Rulers create division, jealousy and destruction because of their attitudes and egos. Leaders remain in the ranks of the people and set examples for correctness in all things.

Suggested Age-Grades:

1. Children:	Age 5-11 years
	Junior level 5-8 years
	Senior level 9-11 years
2. Youth:	Ages 12-17 years
3. Asafo:	Ages 18-29 years
4. Jegna:	Ages 30-39 years
5. Linguist (Okyeame):	Ages 40-59 years
6. Elder:	Age 60 years or older

Each Age-Grade will develop an Advisory Group from within its ranks that will meet independently and provide input to the Council of Elders. This will ensure that the issues and concerns important to everyone will receive attention.

It is important to stress that despite the obvious progression of groups by age, training, achievement and responsibility, it is not hierarchical in the traditional way. No one group is more important. No one group has more power with the possible exception of the Elders, whose power derives from accumulated earned respect.

It is also important to stress that movement from one Age-Grade to another is earned, it is not automatic.

Purpose of Age-Grades

The purpose of Age-Grades is to present to participants the values, ideals and knowledge that it takes to be a true Afrikan in the idealistic sense, to develop true understanding and enlightenment about the world and to help re-stimulate the appetite to rediscover our culture. It will help build Afrikans who are conscious, competent, confident, committed and courageous. Above all, it will provide an appropriate socialization for our people using a multidisciplinary approach that includes (but is not limited to) history, culture, psychology, spirituality, and the realization of the use and importance of ritual and symbols.

Goals of Age-Grades

Our goal is to create a cohesive community of conscious, competent, courageous people who embody Ma'at (Truth, Justice, Righteousness, Harmony, Balance, Order, Propriety, Reciprocity) and the Cardinal Virtues (as taught to us by George G.M. James in *Stolen Legacy*):

1. Control of thought

   One should be disciplined and be able to analyze situations. To pro-act, act and not just react. Although the ability to effectively react is necessary in some situations, control of thought optimizes reaction and minimizes being reactionary.
2. Control of action

   This is a direct result of control of thought. With this control, one will always be able to do the right thing. It also enables one to be a positive role model.
3. Devotion of purpose

   Perseverance, steadfastness and consistency. Having the courage to do right, which usually is quite difficult.
4. Faith in the teacher's ability to teach the truth

   One must be able to trust someone with more advanced wisdom and knowledge to be an effective follower. This person should have demonstrated repeatedly their devotion and commitment to the advancement of Afrikan people.
5. Faith in one's ability to learn and use the truth

   One should be willing to learn and to change, based on what one has learned. Truth crushed to the earth will continue to rise. One must develop the confidence to learn despite the pain that might be associated with the truth. One must also develop the ability to use what has been learned in the best, most useful and most appropriate manner.

6. Freedom from resentment when wronged and persecuted
   This is, perhaps, the most difficult of all the virtues. It is merely human to resent wrongful treatment. However, one should be able to see through the actions to the motivations and reasons and use them to avoid negative emotions. Our Spiritual strength helps us greatly overtly and covertly.
7. Ability to tell right from wrong
   Absolute right is not relative. Western culture has developed highly sophisticated ways of disguising right. Some people will say right is relative. One must understand that, even if placed in a position to have to do wrong, one should not try to justify the wrongdoing.
8. Ability to tell the real from the unreal
   Reality in the Western world is an illusion. One must be able to distinguish between what is real and what others wish to impress upon you.

Detailed Discussion of Age-Grades

I. Children (2-11 years): Identity

A. Definition

This group will be made up of boys and girls from 2-11 years. The major emphasis of this group will be for them to identify themselves as part of a larger group.

1. It may be further subdivided to optimize learning since this age group contains so many different levels.
   a) ages 2-4
   b) ages 5-7
   c) ages 8-11

2. Names could be assigned to each group that symbolically would describe the function and goal, such as totemic names that represent desired qualities. These totemic names will stay with each person

for life and will be known only to their Age-Grade brothers and sisters and the Nanas (Elders).

3. This group may have occasional gender separations.

B. **Purpose**

To introduce boys and girls to Afrikan thought, culture and philosophy in order to begin the socialization process into Afrikanization (Identity). In short, the purpose of this Age-Grade is to introduce, strengthen and reinforce an Afrikan identity.

C. **Methods**

1. All other Age-Grades participate in the socialization process in overt and covert as well as formal and informal ways. The children are our future and we should not leave anything to chance. Although the primary responsibility will be with the Jegnoch, the Youth and Elders will play a large and important role in the socialization process.

2. This group's activities include participation in Saturday School, Sunday School and Vacation School.

   a. Frequent field trips and activities for instructional fun will be included.

   b. Storytelling of historical events will be done to teach about and model our great heroes and sheroes.

3. Rote memory is important for this age group. The younger children would be required to memorize things; older children will learn meanings and significance.

   a. Nguzo Saba

   b. Principles of Ma'at

c. Admonitions of Innocence

d. Their pledge

e. Afrikan countries, their capitals and eventually their leaders

f. The 50 states of the U.S. and their capitals

g. Specific information about South Carolina Afrikan history

h. Other information about Afrika and the Diaspora will be taught from the Afrikan perspective, both historical and contemporary.

i. Afrikan languages will be started (Mdw Ntr, Twi, Ki-Swahili and possibly Yoruba and Igbo).

j. Afrikan symbols will be emphasized (Adinkra and triliterals especially). This will lead to development of tee shirts, calendars and caps with Afrikan symbolic wisdom placed on them for use as possible fundraisers.

4. One prerequisite for promotion to the next Age-Grade will be understanding the meaning of Ma'at and the Nguzo Saba. The passage ritual might include the candidates' written and recitation of their interpretation of a principle(s).

   The last 2-3 years will consist of an intense preparation for the next stage. Achievement necessary for advancement will be discussed and decided on by the Council of Elders with input from Jegnoch and Okyeame. Minimum competency is required but maximum achievement is demanded.

5. It is suggested that the Youth, one or both parents/guardians and families participate in the passage ritual.

6. Self-defense training will be started, i.e. martial arts with an emphasis on discipline.

7. Contests will be held regularly, such as:
   a. Testing knowledge of the timetables
   b. Spelling bees
   c. History contests
   d. Essay contests

D. Duties

1. Study hard and learn all that is presented to them.
2. Small chores and errands to help them realize that they are an important part of something larger than they are.

II. Youth (12-17 years): Purpose

A. Definition

Because this is a difficult period, one that in Western culture is beset with confusion, peer pressure, rebellion and rage, this group will address itself to purpose, which will be taught exoterically as well as esoterically.

B. Purpose

To begin the development of leadership, the Youth will develop activities and programs for the Children. Each member of this group will serve as a role model for the Children. Each will be required to spend a specific amount of time with the Children as a group and with a specific child.

Cultural competence is of prime importance and the programs and activities should have this as the stated desired end result.

C. Methods

1. On or near each young person's twelfth birthday, she or he will be required to formally address a gathering at a time designated by the Council of Elders. The topic

will be the young person's choice. It is the duty of the Youth who help with the Children to alert the Council of coming birthdays at least 3-4 weeks in advance.

2. The Youth will have their own study group as part of a Saturday Shule and will study and master books like *The Teachings of Ptahhotep, The Bluest Eye, From the Browder File, Two Thousand Seasons, The Healers,* and *Destruction of Black Civilization.*

3. The Youth will do biographical research and study on the lives of important historical Continental and Diasporan Afrikans, e.g., Malcolm X, John Henrik Clarke, Maria Stewart, Nzinga, Yaa Asantewaa, Martin Delany, Henry Highland Garnet, Paul Robeson, Harriett Tubman, Kwame Nkrumah, Edward Wilmot Blyden, Ida B. Wells Barnett, Charshee McIntyre, Kobi Kambon, Nzinga Heru and Listervelt Middleton, to name a few.

4. The Youth will also conduct research on and interviews with important contemporary Afrikans, e.g., Marimba Ani, Adelaide Sanford, Wade Nobles, Anthony Browder and others.

5. Focus will be placed on the importance of family by doing family trees, going back at least three generations, and giving at least three facts about each person listed.

   a. If this exercise is successful, it will be very instructive in introducing the Young person to History, ethics and the practicalities of survival.

   b. If this exercise is unsuccessful or the information cannot be recovered, it will illustrate and highlight the damage that has been done to us as a people, especially in the separation of our families and loss of our family histories.

6. The Youth will be able to define and discuss the biological, cultural and spiritual functions of Manhood and Womanhood.

7. The Youth will conduct research and discussions to produce papers on topics such as economics (including budgeting, business ownership, stocks and bonds); economic systems (socialism, capitalism, and communism); politics and political systems; careers needed by a nation; the function of entertainment (including sports, TV and movies); the function of culture, sexuality, applied science. Example: How to run a household

8. The Youth will participate in activities, e.g., camping, survival, weapons training, as well as advanced martial arts.

9. There may need to be some gender separation in dealing with certain topics and issues so that the Youth can express themselves more comfortably.

10. The Youth will distinguish themselves as excellent students and respectful individuals in the "outside world."

11. The Youth will learn the principles of debate as well as political science and participate regularly in formal debate competitions.

III. The Asafo (18-29 years): Direction

A. Definition

The Asafo are warriors who are prepared to use whatever methods or degree of aggressiveness required to defend those institutions, organizations, persons, and ideas that are important to Afrikan people. This will be done by "walking the walk" as well as by "talking the talk" and "doing the do." The Asafo do battle mentally and psychologically as well as have the capability of physical warfare. They are the Clan's militia.

B. Purpose

1. To put into practice the principles and practices of leadership already learned.

2. To use efficiently the energy and idealism characteristic of this stage of life.

3. To crystallize the formation of a life direction.

4. To serve as a leader among their peers in the larger community and model positive behavior while battling negative behavior.

5. To serve as a defense body if necessary, militarily, culturally and intellectually.

6. To contribute to the thought processes of the Elders and Jegnoch.

C. Methods

1. Research techniques should be perfected.

   a. Biographies should be written of at least fifteen people, suitable for publishing.

   b. Research papers on at least five major topics in our history and culture should be researched and written about, e.g., Precolonial male-female relationships, Aspects of the Maafa, Nineteenth Century Nationalism, Pan-Africanism Movement, The Berlin Conference, The Civil War, Emigrationism, The Negro Convention Movement, the history of organizations (e.g., ASCAC, NABSW, and the NAACP), aspects of slavery, and the Asante Wars with the British.

2. Training in methods of advanced survival, weapons and martial arts.

3. Act as primary teachers of martial arts, weapons (handguns, rifles, swords, archery, shotguns, knife-throwing) and survival to younger age groups.

4. Learn military and war history and strategy, especially guerrilla warfare and including a study of *The Art of War* and other military and books on strategy.

5. Become representatives of the Afrikan-centered theory by being shining examples of excellence and positivity in the community.

6. Perfect principles of debate and political science.

D. Duties

1. Teach martial arts to the Children and Youth.

2. Serve as constant reference points and sounding boards for Children and Youth.

3. Be ready to provide whatever service is required of them for the Clan.

IV. Jegnoch (singular: Jegna; 30-39 years) Strategies

A. Definition

1. Jegnoch are those who: a. Have been tested in struggle or battle physically, mentally, spiritually and intellectually.

b. Have demonstrated extraordinary and unusual fearlessness.

c. Have determination and courage in protecting his/her people, land culture.

d. Show diligence and dedication to our people.

e. Produce exceptionally high-quality work.

f. Dedicate themselves to the protection, defense, nurturance and development of our young by advancing our people, place and culture.

2. To become a Jegna is the reward of being a successful Asafo.

B. **Purpose**

To provide living, breathing examples of excellence in all things.

C. **Methods**

1. Help reinforce the categories of Afrikan history and its subtopics.

2. Promote the Afrikan Worldview.

3. Continue martial arts training.

4. Continue research and publishing.

D. **Duties**

1. To assume primary responsibility for the training of the Children and the supervision of the Youth.

2. To devise and develop theory and programs to advance Ausa culture.

3. To be a public face of the Collective.

V. **Linguist (Okyeame) (40-59 years) Tactics**

A. **Definition**

These are individuals who have progressed successfully through all stages or who have completed requirements of all stages.

B. **Purpose**

1. Responsible for the "nuts and bolts" success of the entire program.

2. Serve as the "arms, legs and tongues" of the Elders.

3. Are actually "Elders-in-Training" or "Junior Elders."

C. **Methods**

1. Oversee the entire operation of the Collective.

2. Organize to have specific individuals responsible for specific areas of concern, which should include:

a. Interaction and relationship between all age groups.

b. Advising and meeting with the Elders about issues of concern.

D. Duties

Manage the cultural and other non-Spiritual affairs of the Clan.

VI. Elder (60 years and older)

A. Definition

An Elder is a person who has learned all that was necessary to be learned at all previous Age-Grades. She/he has observed the nature of the Western world through the lens of Afrikan culture and has become wise as well as knowledgeable.

B. Purpose

1. To actively teach and be available to teach all other Age-Grades, especially the Children and Youth.

2. To provide counsel and advice to all other Age-Grades, especially Jegnas and Okyeames (Junior Elders).

3. To provide a living example of the cyclical nature of life.

4. To be available for participation in the Mbongi (Council of Elders) which:

a. Oversees, wholistically, the entire organization.

b. Provides guidance as to the purpose and direction of the organization. All problems concerning organizational or practical issues are discussed first in the Mbongi (Council).

c. To process information provided by the Advisory Councils for presentation to the entire body with recommendations for actions (and reasons for those recommendations).

d. Interacts directly with representatives of the Jegnoch for strategy sessions.

e. Even if not yet 60 years old, the Priest is a member of the Council of Elders. If she/he is under 40 years of age, she/he will not vote but will be able to participate freely in discussions and potentially influence decisions.

f. Will operate on the model of Mbongi and make decisions based on consensus agreement in an atmosphere of positive spirit. Consensus will always be done in "good faith." If anyone feels an absence of "good faith" in themselves, Ma'at requires that they remove themselves from the decision-making process at that time. If one Council member senses an absence of "good faith" in another Council member, she or he is required to challenge that member so other Council members may observe and decide.

C. Methods

Once someone is eligible to be an Elder, they will undergo Eldership training. This will be arranged at regular intervals during the year until the Elders in the Clan are prepared and certified to do training.

D. Duties

1. Elders are responsible for the success or failure of the Collective. They are the final arbiters of every decision and are involved in every phase of the workings of the Collective, overtly and covertly.

2. All Elders are responsible for working with the Okyeame, both in a capacity as teacher and as co-worker. The Elders are responsible for the Okyeame, who serve as their representatives to the Collective.

VII. Master Teacher

A. Definition

A Master Teacher is an honorary position that confers great honor on the bearer. The bearers should come from the ranks of the Elders or the Okyeame. She or he is nominated from either the Council of Elders or the Council of Okyeame and needs a unanimous vote from both Councils. This is a purely honorary title and there are no specific responsibilities or duties. A high honor, not to be taken lightly, it is not bestowed according to popularity or withheld because you dislike someone. There are a few perks.

B. Perks

1. May attend Council of Elders Meetings and fully participate in the discussions (cannot vote unless he or she is a member of the Council of Elders).

2. May represent the organization in outside activities.

C. Qualifications/Requirements

1. Has performed important specific tasks to help the organization.

2. Has performed much general good to help the organization.

3. Has benefited the organization by their mere presence.

4. Has studied diligently and shows willingness and ability to share knowledge, information and wisdom with others.

References

Assimeng, Max. *Social Structure of Ghana: A Study in Persistence and Change.* Accra: Ghana Publishing Company, 1999.

Diop, Cheikh Anta. *The Cultural Unity of Black Africa: The Domains of Patriarchy and of Matriarchy in Classical Antiquity*, Chicago: Third World Press, 1990.

Fu-Kiau, K. Kia Bunseki. *Mbongi: An African Traditional Political Institution: A Eureka to the African Crisis*, Roxbury: Omenana, 1985.

Gyekye, Kwame. *African Cultural Values: An Introduction*, Philadelphia: Sankofa Publishing Company, 1996.

Kenyatta, Jomo. *Facing Mt. Kenya.* NY: Vintage Books, A Division of Random House, 1965.

Warren, Dennis. *The Akan of Ghana.* Accra: Pointer Limited, 1986.

CHAPTER 21

About Reparations

The topic of Reparations is being discussed more seriously now than it has ever been discussed before. In this chapter, we will attempt to expand the subject and explore aspects that may not be commonly known. But, first, we will deal with definitions.

DEFINITIONS

- **Reparations**: A making of amends; retribution and compensation; redress as for war damage; responses that seek atonement for the commission of an injustice. From *Webster's New World Dictionary and Thesaurus*
- **Maafa**: A ki-Swahili word that means "Great Disaster." It was first used by Dr. Marimba Ani to describe what many have called "The Black Holocaust." It is, however, more specific to Afrikan people and more comprehensive and, hence, more appropriate than the word, "holocaust." It refers to the 1380-year period (640-2020) of the Arab and European enslavement and oppression of Afrikan people. It refers to the 383-year period (1482-1865) of legal Euro-American enslavement of Afrikan people. It refers to the 89-year period (1865-1954) of legal American apartheid (segregation); and it refers to the 65-year period (1954-2020) of increasingly subtle discrimination against all people of Afrikan origin in all areas of human activity.

- Genocide: "The intent to destroy, in whole or in part, a national, ethnic, racial, or religious group by:
  (a) killing members of the group;
  (b) causing serious bodily or mental harm to members of the group;
  (c) deliberately inflicting on the group the conditions of life calculated to bring about its destruction in whole or in part;
  (d) imposing measures to prevent births within the group; or,
  (e) forcibly transferring children of the group to another group."
  From the 1948 Convention on the Prevention and Punishment of the Crime of Genocide It became enforceable in 1951.
- **Crimes Against Humanity:** "Murder, extermination, enslavement, deportation, and other inhumane acts committed against any civilian population before or during the war, or persecutions on political, racial, or religious grounds in execution of or in connection with any crime within the jurisdiction of the Tribunal, whether or not in violation of the domestic law of the country where perpetrated." From the Nuremberg Tribunal. May be applied retroactively.
- **Human Injustice:** "The United Nations shall promote...universal respect for, and observance of, human rights and fundamental freedoms for all without distinction as to race, sex, language, or religion." *Article 55 (c) of the United Nations Charter*

Requirements for Reparations:

(1) A human injustice must have been committed;

(2) It must be well documented;

(3) The victims must be identifiable as a distinct group;

(4) The current members of the group must continue to suffer harm; and

(5) Such harm must be causally connected to a past injustice.

Mari J. Matsuda (1987): "Looking to the Bottom: Critical Legal Studies and Reparations." In: *Harvard Civil Liberties-Civil Rights Law Review.* Volume 22, Number 323, pp. 362-397.

OVERVIEW

In order to fully understand the call for Reparations, one must understand what the Maafa was and what it was all about. The Maafa experienced by Afrikan people was not committed by just one group of people and has not been limited to just the time when we were enslaved by Europeans. As previously explained, our Maafa spans more than 1300 years, more than the "two thousand seasons" described by Ayi Kwei Armah in his book of the same name.

Although the Arabs enslaved us longer than the Europeans, we live in a world crafted by and controlled by Europeans and their Diaspora. It is they who have the power, wealth and influence which is directly related to their treatment of us. And, it is they who we concentrate on at this point.

When the Europeans arrived in Afrika after Islamic Afrikans brought them out of their "Dark Ages," they were, as our esteemed Ancestor Dr. John Henrik Clarke has said, "land poor, people poor, and resources poor." They saw the advanced standard of living and the material wealth of the Afrikans, wanted it for themselves and took it without paying for it. They had been welcomed into a society where visitors were well-treated and they took advantage of that very civilized custom.

First, they set up trade stations on the Afrikan coasts, dealing for gold, silver, salt and ivory, as well as for other things rare in Europe while they studied further the weaknesses of the Afrikans. Then, they brought the "twin destroyers": missionaries and teachers who used religion in an attempt to convert the adults to European "values" and used education to turn the children against their parent's culture, worldview and belief system. An honest evaluation of history shows they enjoyed remarkable success in this endeavor.

Next, they mated with Afrikan women. These unions produced children who were made to admire and emulate their fathers' people and have disdain for their mothers' people. The offspring ensured the success of the slave trade by participating as agents of the Europeans and using their familiarity with the terrain and local culture by serving as guides and interpreters.

Some Afrikans saw the schemes of the Europeans too late to do very much about it. By that time, the capture, kidnapping, warehousing, transport (Middle Passage), "slave breaking," auctioning, and selling of Afrikans was well established. When these kidnapped Afrikans arrived in the "New World," often it was believed to be more cost effective to work them to death and buy more Africans rather than try to feed and clothe them and keep them healthy.

In order for the enslaved Afrikans to be better, more controllable, they were stripped of cultural and historical memories and were taught to hate everything about themselves, from their appearances to their way of thinking and doing things to their way of seeing and appreciating The Creator. Often, they were convinced of their own inferiority. These enslaved Afrikans were taught to believe that Europeans were smarter, more beautiful, more spiritual, fairer and more God-like than they were. This was not an easy job and has not been totally successful, although our progress as Afrikan people has been severely retarded and our humanity damaged.

From Afrika to North and South America there were revolts and rebellions, many in South Carolina. Many Afrikans, called Maroons, escaped and created their own civilizations in the New World. Those of us who pursue and honor the true memories of our Afrikan Ancestors who suffered and died under the cruel yoke of a system that tried to make them "as beasts in the field" are, as Dr. Asa Hilliard has taught us, the new Maroons, noting that Maroons were Afrikans who refused to be enslaved.

Even after "freedom" came, the descendants of the kidnapped and enslaved Afrikans were oppressed tremendously. They were given the worst of everything and if they complained they were labeled troublemakers, persecuted further, and frequently killed. New enslavement methods were used in the mills and fields that, in essence, reduced the so-called free men and women to slavery in fact, if not in name. Sharecropping is only one of these methods. Criminalization, mass incarceration and chain gangs were another way of recreating slavery. We are owed for these crimes against humanity and attempts at genocide.

Results of the Maafa

The enslavement, colonization and oppression of Afrikan people by Europeans and European Americans over the past several hundred years has resulted in significant contemporary problems in people of Afrikan origin. These include on-going problems in health and mental health, education, political savvy and strength, economic position and unequal enforcement of laws.

Most importantly, none of these problems would be as serious if Afrikan culture had not been taken away. As if that were not enough, we were made to hate ourselves so much that we lost the desire to know who we are and were.

We will give an incomplete list of the enduring problems that result from the legacy of The Maafa:

1. Ausa families earn approximately $.60 for every dollar earned by white families.

2. Most hazardous and toxic waste dumps are located near communities of color. Approximately 60% of Ausa live in a community with at least one abandoned waste site and 75% of toxic waste dumps in America are located in the communities of people of color.

3. The Federal government fines polluters in white communities more than those in Ausa communities and moves 20% slower to clean up toxic contamination in communities of color.

4. The rate of suicide in Ausa, almost unheard of two generations ago, has increased steadily for almost all Ausa people, especially teenagers.

5. In 2018, almost 32% of Ausa children lived in poverty, while only 12.5% of white children lived in poverty.

6. Almost 70% of Ausa 4th graders watch 4 or more hours

of television daily while only about 40% of white 4th graders watch that much television daily.

7. Only 5% of newspaper reporters are of Afrikan descent and 45% of all newspapers have no non-white reporters.

8. Ausa are disproportionately convicted for the crimes they are arrested for, imprisoned more than whites for the same crimes and frequently given longer prison terms than whites convicted for the same crimes.

9. Racial profiling or "Driving While Black" (or even "breathing while Black") is a major problem.

10. Diabetes Mellitus is 33% more prevalent in Ausa communities and the death rate for Ausa is more than twice the white death rate.

11. The Black death rate from stroke is 80% higher in Ausa than in whites.

12. High blood pressure among Ausa men under the age of 45 years is more than 10 times the white rate and in Ausa women under 45 is more than 13 times the white rate.

13. The Ausa death rate for individuals under the age of 45 is twice the white rate.

14. Neonatal mortality in Afrikan Americans is 97% higher than the white rate.

15. Ausa men, women and children have been brutalized and murdered by law enforcement officers, without punishment, since the days of slavery.

Consequences of the Maafa

1. Historical misorientation. When a person loses her or his memory of themselves, the resulting pathological condition is called amnesia. When an entire group of people lose their collective memory of who they are, the illness is widespread collective amnesia. When this occurs, new information can be substituted for memory and slaves

can be created. The new information can even create a distaste for learning about oneself. This has happened to Afrikan people.

2. Cultural losses. Not only did we lose our culture, but we also lost the desire to know and relearn our culture. We were made to be ashamed of everything about us. We are so ignorant of our culture that we do not recognize it when it is claimed by other people. In essence, it was stolen before our very eyes.
3. Psychological damage. We have been made to hate the way we look as well as the way we do things. We spend billions of dollars on make-up, hair care products and other people's hair to look like something other than what the Creator made us to look like. Many of us use toxic skin lightening creams. We hate the things that make us unique and strive to be like our oppressors.
4. Economic depression. People of Afrikan origin are consistently at the bottom of every economic measurement. Although Afrika had created its own economic systems, we have been subject to the European systems of capitalism and communism in which there must always be a permanent underclass. People of color have always inhabited that underclass and have been trained to maintain that position. The disparity in wealth is a direct result of slavery and American Apartheid in which Afrikan people were the hardest working people in the country but their blood, sweat and tears benefitted and enriched people and industries other than the workers and their families. Because of the structure of society, Afrikans were unable to accumulate wealth and had nothing to pass on to their descendants.
5. Health disparities. Ausa lead the statistics in having the most serious and deadly illnesses. We are less healthy and die younger than many people in so-called "developing" countries. These health disparities arise from several sources, not the least is warfare through environmental racism.
6. Spiritual confusion. Without healthy skepticism, we have, eagerly accepted and adopted the religions of those who are/were

responsible for our Maafa, although it has been repeatedly proven that we were forced initially into those religions for the purpose of control. In many cases, we have become more defensive of these religions than the people who taught us.

7. Education deficits. Although we are a brilliant people, we lead the country in the statistics for poor educational achievement. Our schools, urban and rural, are underfunded. Our children are stigmatized and often believe that to achieve is other than being Afrikan.
8. Legal problems. We are subject to the criminal justice system in proportions that are much greater than our percentage of the population. Our young people are criminalized in proportions that do not make sense while Euro-Americans charged with the same offenses receive much lighter sentences, if they are sentenced at all.
9. Political ignorance. Our percentage of the population gives us the potential to be profoundly politically influential if we would just participate and vote. We must also hold our politicians to a higher standard than we presently do now and definitely to a higher standard than we hold politicians from outside our community.
10. Legislative impotence. Historically, Ausa have been the moral conscience of America. Yet, we have the lowest numbers of elected officials in the country and we do not hold them accountable.
11. Sexual confusion. Despite the fact that homosexuality was and is frowned upon in ancient and traditional Afrika, this alien practice has been adopted in increasing numbers by Ausa youth.

Anyone who accepts the above information without questioning the "why" is not using their God-given ability to think. Believing these problems are not intentional is not merely naïve but is an admission of surrender to the opinion that Afrikan people are inherently less intelligent, more violent and evil. We do know that we were not unscathed by the 300-plus years in the Hells of the Americas. Whether this sickness is called mental slavery, mentacide, or the post traumatic slave syndrome, if we are to be cured like addicts, we must realize first that we have been made to be very sick people.

We must understand that our minds and bodies were used to make America rich and powerful and we were paid only with negative physical and psychological bombardment. Non-Afrikans who say they or their ancestors never owned slaves are avoiding the fact that white privilege, which is a direct result of our Maafa, was and is experienced by every white person in America whether they want to admit it or not.

A Brief, Recent History of Reparations

As previously stated, the idea of Reparations is not new. One of the reasons Haiti is in the condition it is in currently is, after they revolted and won their freedom, they were forced to pay Reparations to France; they paid it off in 1947. Many so-called "Francophone" Afrikan countries are still paying France.

When Reparations for enslavement and American Apartheid are discussed, the hypocrisy is highlighted when considering Reparations paid to other people. In modern times, Reparations have been paid more than once. A chart listing many of these Reparations on N'COBRA's website is taken from a book by one of its past presidents, Dorothy Benton-Lewis, entitled *Black Reparations Now! Part 1, 40 Acres, $50.00 and a Mule.* An excellent book by Clarence J. Mumford, *Race and Reparations: A Black Perspective for the 21st Century,* also discusses past Reparations payments. Below are a few examples taken from those sources.

- 1952: Germany paid $822 million to Holocaust survivors.
- 1971: U.S.A. paid $1 billion plus 44 million acres of land to Alaska Natives.
- 1980: U.S.A. paid $81 million to the Klamaths of Oregon.
- 1985: U.S.A. paid $105 million to the Sioux of South Dakota.
- 1985: U.S.A. paid $12.3 million to the Seminoles of Florida.
- 1985: U.S.A. paid $31 million to the Chippewas of Wisconsin.
- 1986: U.S.A. paid $32 million to the Ottawas of Michigan to honor an 1836 treaty.
- 1988: Canada paid $230 million to Japanese Canadians.

- 1990: Austria paid $25 million to Holocaust survivors.
- 1990: U.S.A. paid $1.25 billion or $20,000 each to Japanese Americans who were incarcerated during the so-called World War II.
- 1994: The Florida legislature set aside $2 million to compensate the survivors and heirs of the Afrikan victims of white violence in Rosewood in 1923.
- 1994: Hungary and Slovakia agreed to give back land and other property to the heirs of Jews who were dispossessed during the period of the Holocaust and fascism.
- 2001: The Oklahoma Commission to Study the Tulsa Race Riot of 1921 recommended that the survivors and heirs of that Race Riot be paid Reparations and a scholarship fund be established for affected students. Also, they recommended establishment of an economic enterprise zone in the Greenwood District and a memorial for the reburial of the victims' remains from the Tulsa Race Riot.

There has been no greater crime against humanity than the crime perpetrated against Afrikan people that lasted hundreds of years, killed hundreds of millions of people, dispossessed people of hundreds of millions of acres of land, destroyed dozens of generations economically, and attempted to destroy a vibrant culture. Yet, even the mention of Reparations in this context causes severe negative reactions.

The Biblical Basis for Reparations

When the topic of Reparations for the oppressed descendants of kidnapped and enslaved Afrikans is raised, many so-called devout Christians object strongly to the very idea. Their objections are not biblically based, however, because the concept of Reparations is well supported in the Christian Bible. Since America calls itself a Christian nation, it would seem that Biblical ideas should rule, although the hypocrisy of American Christianity is so pervasive. The following verses are examples of Reparations in the Bible:

> **Exodus 12: 35-36**
> (35) The Israelites did as Moses had commanded: they asked the Egyptians for articles of silver and gold and for clothing. (36) The Lord indeed had made the Egyptians so well disposed toward the people that they let them have whatever they asked for. Thus did they despoil the Egyptians.

This passage suggests actions that occurred just after the first-born of Egypt had been killed by the God of the Israelites and suggests there was active participation in forcing their enemies to change their minds. Moses was proactive, not passive, in this "war." We must not be passive and wait for some outside hand to fight our fight for us. Now is the time. It is almost too late!

> **Numbers 5: 6-7**
> (6) "Tell the Israelites: If a man (or woman) commits a fault against his fellow man and wrongs him, thus breaking faith with the Lord, (7) he shall confess the wrong he has done, restore his ill-gotten goods in full, and in addition give one fifth of their value to the one he has wronged.

This is related more directly to the question, "Why Reparations?" What has been perpetrated against Afrikan people is the greatest single crime perpetrated by one human against another in the history of humanity. We have been wronged, but not only will the perpetrator not confess, he will not even acknowledge his wrongdoing.

The wealth and power of America and many (if not most) "old money" Americans and American institutions are directly or indirectly related to the enslavement of our Ancestors. Think about it: If you had access to a business run with little or no overhead expenses for at least sixteen generations, wouldn't your business and family become rich and powerful? Most people work hard for the sake of their children, so they can pass something along and their children will not have to endure what they did. Afrikan people have had nothing to pass on. Our Ancestors had nothing coming out of slavery and nothing during the era of American Apartheid called segregation. As a result, our children have been denied the birthright of the labor of their Ancestors. America's riches are, in great part, owed to us!!

Afrikan people have always been the conscience of the world. A confession and acknowledgment and, perhaps, an apology would not make any major difference to us, specifically, but might serve to help the overall situation. We must continually remind European Americans of their transgressions. We must also let them know that retribution is at hand.

> **Isaiah 58:12**
> *The ancient ruins shall be rebuilt for your sake, and the foundations from ages past you shall raise up, 'Repairer of the breach,' they shall call you, 'Restorer of ruined homesteads'.*

This speaks to what must be accomplished with any Reparations. We know if we were given 777 trillion dollars as a people, not only would most of it be back in the hands of the European American in one week, but a significant amount would be spent to maintain the status quo and to hold some of our people back. We are owed Reparations not only for our Ancestors' free labor during enslavement and not only for the unspeakable suffering they were forced to endure (even with "good," "compassionate" and "humane" masters), but also for the period of American Apartheid during which our Ancestors were unable to compete fairly in the marketplace and were denied fair compensation for their labor. We have a multiphasic complaint.

Any Reparations agreed upon must have a re-education and re-socialization process built into the process to combat the mental illness of anti-self that is so rampant/epidemic in the Ausa community. We must not fail our Ancestors.

Responses to Critics of Reparations

The idea of Reparations paid to oppressed Afrikan American descendants of kidnapped, enslaved and oppressed Afrikans apparently terrifies some people. They go into panic mode and try to reason or use logic to excuse themselves from responsibility. Or, they ridicule the idea.

It is interesting that, in a supposed Christian nation, there are people who forget the tenets Jesus taught in the Bible. Usually, they give pseudo-intellectual, supposedly logical and objective answers to the question of Reparations. This is most laughable because the emotional content is almost shrill in its desperation. What follows are some responses to some of the most frequent criticisms.

◊ **Neither me nor any of my ancestors ever owned slaves.**

The only way this statement has any significance at all is if the speaker or his/her ancestors actively fought against slavery and American Apartheid. The wealth of America, enjoyed more by whites than Afrikans, was created by the enslavement and debasement of Afrikan people. When one considers the concept, impact and prevalence of "white privilege" under white supremacy, it becomes obvious that whites could easily get benefits from slavery (then and now) without owning slaves. Reparations is not only demanded for slavery but for the period of American Apartheid that denied all people of Afrikan ancestry the opportunity to compete on a level playing field because of an established social system that favored white males exclusively.

◊ **My ancestors arrived in America after slavery was over.**

Again, this is ridiculous when the concept of white privilege under white supremacy is honestly considered. Whites who came to America after slavery benefited from the labor of Afrikans and benefited from white privilege as much as those already here. In fact, many of these immigrants were more virulently racist than the whites who enslaved the Afrikans.

◊ **Blacks are lucky they were taken away from Africa.**

Pure ignorance. At the time Afrikans were kidnapped and enslaved many of the West Afrikan empires were more advanced than the European in technology, culture and spirituality. Afrikan technology was not geared to warfare as was the Europeans' technology. Descriptions written by the earliest Europeans who went to Afrika speak of unfamiliar wonders. In fact, it took the predominately Afrikan Moors to bring Europe out of its "Dark Ages." At any rate, anyone who considers having no freedom; being raped and beaten at someone else's whim; worked brutally for the total benefit of someone else; separated from family and loved ones (including children); and being told constantly you are ugly, stupid and inferior as *lucky*, is stupid.

◊ Africans were sold by other Africans and are responsible for their plight.

Talk about blaming the victim. There were Afrikan slave traders and Afrikans in America who owned slaves. There are traitors and collaborators among all people. Jews collaborated with Nazis. Native Americans collaborated with whites who were saying, "The only good Indian is a dead Indian." A true look at what really happened in Afrika shows that many of the African collaborators were trusting people who became addicted to drugs and alcohol given to them by their white "friends." The out of wedlock children of the European slave traders and Afrikan women were trained to respect and idolize their white fathers' people and to be ashamed of their Blackx mothers' people. But, when they realized what was really happening, most Afrikans fought against slavery.

◊ Africans had slaves, so what's wrong with them being enslaved in America?

The institution called "slavery" in Afrika was so different from the Arab and European chattel slavery that it should not even be called slavery. In fact, many call it forced labor. Afrikan "slaves" were not chattelized and dehumanized. They could work for themselves, support their families, own land and possess other material goods, travel freely and could even marry into the families that "enslaved" them.

◊ African Americans today are not affected by slavery, the problems faced by Black Americans today have nothing to do with slavery.

One only has to understand what happened to us culturally and psychologically and look at health, education and economic statistics and this statement becomes profoundly silly. Ausa who have been materially and educationally fortunate are the exceptions rather than the rule.

◊ **Blacks need to stop playing victims.**

We are not playing! A definition of "victim" is "one who suffers some loss." The derisively negative concept of the word is an interesting ploy to evade responsibility and decrease the guilt in those ideological descendants of our kidnappers, enslavers and oppressors and to delay any healing. Effective treatment of alcohol addiction, drug addiction and many (if not most) psychiatric disorders involves the affected person coming to the realization that something is wrong, that is, developing insight.

The same is true of the problems of Afrikans in America. We must come to grips with what happened to us. We must relive the pain, processing it properly so we can move ahead healthily. We must understand that we have been victimized and get beyond that realization. It is not a proud thing to have been a victim; but, if you deny falsely that you have been a victim, you become an additional victimizer of yourself. In addition, the descendants of our kidnappers, enslavers and oppressors must also come to grips with what many call America's original sin.

◊ **Other immigrants have done well in America, why can't you Blacks pull yourselves up by your bootstraps?**

What bootstraps? Other immigrants came here voluntarily with intact cultures, which they respected and clung to; Afrikans came here by force. Their culture and history were taken from them and were disparaged and inferiorized so successfully that many Afrikans all over the world are ashamed of their culture, their history and their natural, unique features. An intact culture is the needed ingredient in the success of a people. In fact, as Dr. Asa Hilliard has told us, cultural destruction is a military tactic.

◊ **The white slave masters and Black slaves are long dead. Why bring it up now?**

The damage was done, is being done, and will continue to be done if nothing happens to break the cycle. Many people would like to believe that the violence in Ausa communities, so loudly proclaimed in the media, is due to some inherent violent tendencies in Afrikan people. They do not admit that historically and currently there is more violence in the non-Ausa communities, but it is not reported so loudly in the media. Besides, when you consider the relative absence of violence that existed in most continental Afrikan cultures (until they become confronted with and enamored of Western culture), it becomes obvious that something happened to their kidnapped, enslaved and oppressed brethren in the Diaspora to create whatever violence there is today. As mentioned, the fruit of the actions of the slavers and colonizers over centuries is still ripe and shows no sign of spoiling unless the enslaved and colonized understand what is being done and has been done.

◊ **Why not accept an apology and move on?**

People overestimate the power of an apology. While nice, it is merely symbolic and, in most cases, does nothing to undo the material damage that was done by the original action.

◊ **Any debt that may have been owed to Blacks has already been repaid by the 30 years of Affirmative Action, federal give-away programs, and HUD section eight vouchers.**

The mathematics of this statement is puzzling and the lack of command of facts is bizarre. Thirty years of any supposed remedy does not begin to eliminate the effects of more than 300 years of damage. Affirmative Action benefited other groups more than Ausa, especially white women. Many of the "give-away" programs have also benefited non-Ausa more so than Ausa. In fact, even though Ausa are stigmatized about being on "welfare," the truth is that there are far more non-Afrikans on welfare than Ausa. So, this statement is irrational and illogical.

◊ **You Blacks don't have anything in common with those Africans anyway.**

Coming from our enemies, this recurring theme aimed at Afrikan Diasporans should be underlined. We are an Afrikan people, more Afrikan that we realize and more Afrikan than our oppressors want us to realize. Powerful people have spent enormous amounts of time, money and energy to keep us from knowing who we truly are;

perhaps they know something about us that we do not but should know about ourselves. Dr. John Henrik Clarke told us powerful people don't teach powerless people how to be powerful and how to take their power from them. Not only have Ausa been told this lie but continental Afrikans have also been told they have nothing in common with Ausa.

◊ **If reparations are a good thing, why doesn't Egypt pay reparations to the Jews for 400 years of slavery?**

The total absence of historical knowledge in this statement is laughable. There is doubt that the Jews ever were enslaved in Afrika. Many Jewish scholars state that there was no Jewish enslavement in Egypt and no Exodus. The people involved in that story were not the people of today, anyway. In appearance, the Hebrews (or Habiru tribe) were Afrikan and the Egyptians (Kamites) were Afrikan.

◊ **People who demand reparations are racist.**

When the light shines on your faults, reverse the field and accuse the accuser. Racism is related to power and no Afrikan person in a world dominated by the doctrine of white supremacy has power. Therefore, it is impossible for Afrikan people to be racist in this world.

◊ **The demand for reparations is an admission of inferiority because we want whites to give us money.**

This is, at best, a short-sighted, tunnel-visioned, self-hating, and thoroughly unrealistic viewpoint. In fact, the demand for reparations is a call for justice. It has not been established what form reparations will take, but restitution, resolution and reparations are needed for healing. The few of us who have achieved materially in this society are the exception to the rule and have an obligation to provide help for others rather than indulging in name-calling. At the very least, engage in intelligent debate. Understand that 400 years of labor deserves 400 years of wages, especially if someone became rich and powerful because of your mental and physical labor while torturing and belittling you. We do not want each Ausa person to get a check; we want the elimination of all aspects of white supremacy combined with restitution for resolution and healing.

◊ **Whites were not the only people to benefit. Slavery put American Blacks in a position to make more money than most people in the world.**

This is a non-point. The appropriate response is, "so what." Anyone remotely familiar with history knows that West Afrika was more advanced than Europe materially, culturally, ethically and morally and is now poverty stricken, even though a huge proportion of the world's resources come from Afrika. Afrika is the richest continent in the world but has the poorest people. Overwhelmingly, whites benefited more from the kidnap, enslavement and oppression of Afrikan people. This statement dares to claim that the victim is a benefactor of his/her victimization.

Thoughts and Quotations on the Maafa and Reparations

"It is unfortunately forgotten that during slavery and colonialism Africa and its people suffered the greatest loss in population and cultural devastation of any people in history. There is no memorial calling attention to this event any place in all the world. The Africans in Africa have not properly memorialized their loss and the Africans outside of Africa, the major victims of slavery and colonialism, have erected no edifices or monument to remind their children that some of them survived the greatest protracted crime in history. I maintain that the people of the entire African world, both in Africa and abroad, are delinquent in their responsibility to their ancestors until some proper memorials are erected in every place in the world where there is an African population." *Dr. John Henrik Clarke (Christopher Columbus & the Afrikan Holocaust), p.101.*

"In the thinking of most white leaders and the white public, the actions of the founders and later political leaders that have benefited whites are given great weight and legitimacy. Such actions include the making of the Constitution and subsequent court decisions interpreting the Constitution in the interest of whites. However, according to the prevailing white view, the racially oppressive actions by the same white founders and later leaders should be forgiven and forgotten by those whose ancestors were victimized by their oppressive actions...Most whites have benefited from centuries of racist oppression and the transmission of many privileges and substantial amounts of ill-gotten wealth from that oppression to later generations...enslaved Africans and African Americans created much wealth and capital that to a significant degree spurred not only the economic development of the South but also the industrial revolution in the United States and Europe...The current prosperity, relatively long life expectancies, and relatively high living standards of whites as a group in the United States, as well as in the West generally, are ultimately rooted in the agony, exploitation, and impoverishment of those who were colonized and enslaved, as well as in the oppression and misery of their descendants...white Americans as individuals, families, and communities have done much damage to Black Americans. This damage is not just in the past, for Black Americans today suffer from the many psychological, economic, political, and social costs of past and present racism."

Joe R. Feagin (Racist America: Roots, Current Realities, and Future Reparations) p261-2.

References and Suggested Start-Up Reading on Reparations

There has been an explosion of information about the concept of Reparations. Although not new, this concept has become very popular. In order to fully understand Reparations, one must understand who we are and who we were as well as what happened to us and how it affects us today. The following brief list of books and articles will help to answer some of these questions. It is, by no means, a complete list, but is a good starting point for self-discovery.

Who We Were

Asante, Molefi K. *African American History: A Journey of Liberation.* Saddle Brook: The Peoples Publishing Group, Inc., 2001.

Browder, Anthony T. *Nile Valley Contributions to Civilization.* Washington: The Institute of Karmic Guidance, 1992.

Diop, Cheikh Anta. *The African Origin of Civilization: Myth or Reality.* Westport: Lawrence Hill and Company, 1991.

Jackson, John G. *Introduction to African Civilizations.* Secaucus: The Citadel Press, 1970.

James, George G.M. *Stolen Legacy.* San Francisco: Julian Richardson Associates, 1976.

Kunjufu, Jawanza. *Lessons from History: A Celebration in Blackness.* Chicago: African American Images, 1987.

Williams, Chancellor. *The Destruction of Black Civilization: Great Issues of a Race From 4500 B.C. to 2000 A.D.* Chicago: Third World Press, 1976.

On The Maafa

Anderson, S.E. *The Black Holocaust for Beginners.* NY: Writers and Readers Publishing, Inc., 1995.

Brent, Linda (pseudonym for Harriet Jacobs). *Incidents in the Life of a Slave Girl: An Authentic Historical Narrative Describing the Horrors of Slavery as Experienced by Black Women.* NY: A Harvest/HBJ Book, Harcourt Brace Jovanovich Publishers, 1873.

Carew, Jan. *Fulcrums of Change: Origins of Racism in the Americas and Other Essays.* Trenton: Africa World Press, Inc., 1988.

Clarke, John Henrik (Co-author and Editor). *Critical Lessons in Slavery and the Slavetrade: Essential Studies and Commentaries on Slavery, In General, and the African Slavetrade, In Particular.* Richmond: Native Sun Publishers, 1996.

Clarke, John Henrik. *Christopher Columbus and the African Holocaust.* Brooklyn: A & B Books, 1992.

Ginsburg, Ralph. *100 Years of Lynching.* Baltimore: Black Classic Press, 1988.

Harding, Vincent. *There is a River: The Black Struggle for Freedom in America.* NY: Vintage Books, 1983.

Jones, Del. *The Black Holocaust: Global Genocide.* Philadelphia: Hikeka Press, Inc., 1992.

Jones, Norece T. *Born a Child of Freedom, Yet a Slave: Mechanisms of Control and Strategies of Resistance in Antebellum South Carolina.* Hanover: University Press of New England, 1990.

McIntyre, Charshee C. *Criminalizing a Race: Free Blacks During Slavery.* Queens: Kayode Publications, Ltd., 1992.

UNESCO. *The African Slave Trade from the Fifteenth to the Nineteenth Century: Studies and Documents 2*, Paris: United Nations, 1978.

Williams, Eric. *Capitalism and Slavery*. London: Andre Deutsch, London, 1990 (First published in 1964).

On Health

Byrd, W. Michael, M.D. and Linda A. Clayton, M.D. (1992): An American Health Dilemma: A History of Blacks in the Health System. *Journal of the National Medical Association*, Vol. 84:189-200.

Byrd, W. Michael, MD, MPH & Linda A. Clayton, MD, MPH (1993): The African-American Cancer Crisis, Part II: A Prescription. *Journal of Health Care for the Poor and Underserved*, 4:102-116.

Clayton, Linda A., MD, MPH & W. Michael Byrd, MD, MPH (1993): The African-American Cancer Crisis, Part I: The Problem. *Journal of Health Care for the Poor and Underserved*, 1993, 4:83-101.

Harrell, Jules P., Marcellus M. Merritt and Jimalee Kalu. Racism, Stress and Disease, In: *African American Mental Health*, edited by Reginald L. Jones, Hampton: Cobb & Henry Publishers,1998.

Harrison, Dorothy D. (1988): An Anthropologist's Views of the Roots of Violence in the United States, *Journal of the National Medical Association*, 1988, 83:638-642.

On Psychological Damage

Akbar, Na'im, Ph.D. Mental Disorder Among African Americans. In: *Black Psychology* Edited by Reginald Jones. Hampton: Cobb & Henry Publishers, 1991.

Abdullah, Samella, Ph.D., Gimbu Kali, and Lloyd Sheppard (1994): Post Traumatic Stress Disorder. Chicago: Africa World Community Press, 1994.

Fanon, Frantz. *Black Skin, White Masks*. NY: Grove Press, Inc. 1967.

Kambon, Kobi K.K. (any of his books)

Wright, Bobby E., Ph.D.: Mentacide: The Ultimate Threat to the Black Race, 1979. (Unpublished Document)

On Spiritual Damage

Ani, Marimba. *Let the Circle Be Unbroken: The Implications of African Spirituality in the Diaspora*. NY: Nkonimfo Publications, 1997 .

Bennett, B. *Religion and the Rise of Jim Crow in New Orleans.* NJ: Princeton University Press, 2005.

Carruthers, Jacob. *MDW NTR: Divine Speech.* Lawrenceville, NJ: Red Sea Press, 1995.

Cone, J.H. *A Theology of Liberation.* Philadelphia: Lippincott, 1970.

Cone, J.H. *The Cross and the Lynching Tree.* Maryknoll, NY: Orbis Books, 2011.

Cooper-Lewter, Nicholas. *Black Grief, Soul Therapy.* Richmond: Harriett Tubman Press, 1999.

Crossan, J.D. *The Greatest Prayer: Rediscovering the Revolutionary Message of THE LORD'S PRAYER.* NY: HarperCollins, 2010.

Diop, C.A. *The Cultural Unity of Black Africa.* Chicago: Third World Press, 1959.

Felder, Cain H. *Troubling Biblical Waters: Race, Class, and Family.* NY: Orbis, 1989.

Flood, D. *Disarming Scripture: Cherry-Picking Liberals, Violence-Loving Conservatives, and Why We All Need to Learn to Read the Bible Like Jesus Did.* San Francisco: Metonia Books, 2014.

Jackson, John G. *Christianity Before Christ.* Texas: American Atheist Press, 1985.

Jackson, John G. *Man, God and Civilization.* NJ: Citadel Press, 1972.

Mitchell, H.H. and E. M. Thomas. *Preaching for Black Self-Esteem.* Tennessee: Abingdon Press, 1994.

On Economic Damage

Anderson, Claud, Ed.D. *Black Labor, White Wealth: The Search for Power and Economic Justice*, Edgewood: Duncan & Duncan, Inc., 1994.

Anderson, Claud, Ed.D. *PowerNomics:The National Plan to Empower Black America* Bethesda: PowerNomics Corporation of America, 2001.

Wilson, Amos N., Ph.D. *Blueprint For Black Power: A Moral, Political and Economic Imperative for the Twenty-First Century*, NY: Afrikan World InfoSystems, 1998.

On Educational Damage

Boutte, Gloria Swindler. *Educating African American Students: And How Are the Children?* NY: Routledge, 2015.

Freire, Paulo. *Pedagogy of the Oppressed.* NY: Continuum, 1992.

Gallman, Burnett W. The Importance of Africancentrism in Improving the Academic Performance of African Americans. From: *The State of Black South Carolina: An Action Agenda for the Future.* (Editor: Kenneth Campbell) Columbia: Columbia Urban League, 1991.

Hilliard, Asa G., III, Ed.D *The Maroon Within Us: Selected Essays on African American Community Socialization.* Baltimore: Black Classic Press, 1995.

Hilliard, Asa G., III, Ed.D *SBA: The Reawakening of the African Mind.* Gainesville: Makare Publishing Company, 1997.

Hilliard, Asa G., III, Lucretia Payton-Stewart, and Larry Obadele Williams. Infusion of African and African American Content in the School Curriculum: Proceedings of the First National Conference, October, 1989, Morristown: Aaron Press, 1990.

Hilliard, Asa G. III, Barbara Sizemore, et. al. *Saving the African American Child: A Report of the National Alliance of Black School Educators, Inc. Task Force on Black Academic and Cultural Excellence,* Washington, D.C., 1984.

Hilliard, Asa G. III. Pedagogy in Ancient Kemet. In: *Kemet and the African Worldview: Research, Rescue, and Restoration.* (Editors: Maulana Karenga and Jacob H. Carruthers) Los Angeles: University of Sankore Press, 1986.

Woodson, Carter G., Ph.D. *The Miseducation of the Negro.* Washington: The Associated Publishers, Inc., 1933.

On Racism/White Supremacy and White Privilege

Jensen, Robert William (query his name using keywords "white privilege")

McIntosh, Peggy: White Privilege: Unpacking the Invisible Knapsack. http://216.190.45.48/ccrr/packet/article.htm

Pierce, Chester: Offensive Mechanisms. In: *The Black Seventies,* Editor: Floyd Barbour, Porter Sargent Publications, 1970.

Reagin, Joe R. *Racist America: Roots, Current Realities, and Future Reparations,* NY: Routledge, 2000.

Rashidi, Runoko: Dangerous Liaisons: A Historical Survey of Black-White Interaction. *Image*, January, 1995, p. 15.

Rodriguez, Roberto. The Study of Whiteness. *Black Issues in Higher Education*, May, 13, 1999, pp.20-25.

Schedler, George. *Racist Symbols and Reparations: Philosophical Reflections on Vestiges of the American Civil War.* NY: Rowman & Littlefield Publishers, Inc., 1998.

Welsing, Frances Cress. *The Isis Papers: The Keys to the Colors.* Chicago: Third World Press, 1991.

Wise, Timothy: (Multiple Listings) On AlterNet.org and several books

Wright, Bobby E. *The Psychopathic Racial Personality and Other Essays.* Chicago: Third World Press, 1974, 1984.

On Reparations

Africa Reparations Movement Frequently Asked Questions (FAQs) (keywords: Africa Reparations Movement)

Afrik, Baba Hannibal. Forty Acres and a Mule: Fact or Fiction? (www.ncobra.com)

Araujo, Ana Lucia. *Reparations for Slavery and the Slave Trade: A Transnational and Comparative History.* NY: Bloomsbury Academic, 2018.

Barkan, Elaza. *The Guilt of Nations: Restitution and Negotiating Historical Injustices.* NY: W.W. Norton & Company, 2000.

Chinweizu, Prof. *Reparations and A New Global Order: A Comparative Overview.* 1993.

Laremont, Ricardo. Political versus Legal Strategies for the African Slavery Reparations Movements. *African Studies Quarterly*, Gainesville, FL: University of Florida.

Munford, Clarence J. *Race and Reparations: A Black Perspective for the 21st Century.* Trenton: Africa World Press, Inc., 1996.

Nixon, Ron. (2000). Peculiar Profits. www.findarticles.com/cf 0/m1329/4 25/63568373/print.jhtml

Obadele, Johnita Scott. Reparations: Linking Our Past, Present, and Future (www.ncobra.com)

Robinson, Randall. *The Debt: What America Owes to Blacks.* NY: A Dutton Book, 2000.

Robinson, Randall, John Conyers, Ronald Walters, Ph.D., Dr. Robert Westley, Eric K. Yamamoto, Dr. Ali A. Mazrui, Charles Ogletree, Jr., Adjoa Aiyetoro, Prof. Richard America, Prof. Mari Matsuda, Wade Henderson, Dr. Dorothy Height: The Case For Black Reparations — Transcript: Proceedings (key word: Transafrica)

Scobie, Prof. Edward: Reparations for the African Peoples, Department of Black Studies, The City College of New York, New York, NY 10031, 1993.

Thompson, Dudley. The Debt Has Not Been Paid, The Accounts Have Not Been Settled http://web.africa.ufl.edu/asq/v2/v2i4a4.htm

Winbush, Raymond A. *Belinda's Petition: A Concise History of Reparations for the Transatlantic Slave Trade.* Baltimore: XLibris Corporation, 2009.

Winbush, Raymond A. (Editor). *Should America Pay? Slavery and the Raging Debate on Reparations.* NY: Amistad/Harper Collins, 2003.

General

Chideya, Farai. *Don't Believe the Hype: Fighting Cultural Misinformation About African-Americans.* NY: A Plume Book, 1995.

CHAPTER 22

Asante Twi

A Brief Introduction to a Language of Ghana and Selected Aspects of Ghanaian History and Culture

NOTE: *Many thanks are due to Professor Kwame Osei-Wusu, a native Twi speaker, an esteemed Elder of Krst Universal Temple and my friend for his help in producing this chapter.*

Introduction

At the Berlin Conference of 1884-85, Europeans created what we know as the West Afrikan country of Ghana. Its borders were artificially drawn to fit the colonization schemes of the imperialistic European tribes. Originally, it was called the Gold Coast because large amounts of gold were found there.

The Gold Coast was the first Afrikan country south of the Sahara to gain it's independence. It broke from the colonial power, Great Britain, on March 6, 1957, and changed the name of the country to Ghana in honor of the first great empire of West Afrika's Golden Age, which flourished along the Upper Niger from the fourth century to the thirteenth century. The name Gold Coast is demonstrative of how materialistic the Europeans were and how they objectified our Afrikan Ancestors. This is made more obvious when one considers that Nigeria was once called the Slave Coast and Côte d'Ivoire is still the Ivory Coast. There was also a Windward Coast which is today's Guinea, Sierra Leone and Liberia.

Ghana is bordered by the Atlantic Ocean (the Gulf of Guinea) on the south, Togo on the east, Côte d'Ivoire (Ivory Coast) on the west and Burkina Faso (Upper Volta) on the north. Ghana has an area the size of Oregon, more than 92,000 square miles, and a population of more than thirty million people. Its coastline is almost 350 miles and mostly sandy beaches. Ghana is comprised of ten regions (their capitals are given in parentheses next to the names of the regions: Greater Accra (Accra), Ashanti (Kumasi), Eastern (Koforida), Central (Cape Coast), Volta (Ho), Western (Sekondi-Takoradi), Brong Ahafo (Sunyani), Northern (Tamale), Upper East (Bolgatanga) and Upper West (Wa).

The capital city of Ghana, Accra, has almost two million inhabitants and there are several other cities with more than 100,000 in population: Kumasi (almost two million); Sekondi-Takoradi (almost 500,000); and Sunyani (almost 250,000). Tamale, Cape Coast, Tema also have populations of greater than 100,000.

The four largest ethnic groups are the Akan, which is comprised of several sub-groups: Mossi, Ewe, and Ga-Adangme. Akan subgroups include the Asante (frequently and erroneously called Ashanti), Fante, Akim (properly written Akyim), Kwahu, Brong, Denkyira, Akuapim, Nkonya, Ahafo, Wassaw, Nzema, Agona, Abura, Bono, Ahanta, Sefwi, Chakosi and Ntchumuru.

Kwame Nkrumah was the first president of Ghana and an avid Pan-Afrikanist. The architect of independence, he stood on the shoulders of Joseph E. Casely Hayford, a Ghanaian journalist, activist, Pan-Afrikanist, as well as on those of others.

The Gold Coast was a frequent source of kidnapped Afrikans who were enslaved in the so-called New World. It was also a gathering point where Afrikans kidnapped from other parts of West Afrika were taken to await ships to begin the Middle Passage. A variety of Europeans, especially the Portuguese, Dutch, Danes and the British, had more than 40 forts/castles/dungeons on the coast from which they fought each other for stolen "spoils" and where they warehoused kidnapped Afrikans bound for the "New World."

The most famous and well preserved of these were Elmina (seen in the film, *Sankofa*) and Cape Coast. Others that can still be seen today are Fort St. Anthony in Axim, Fort St. Jago in Elmina, Fort St. Sebastian in Shama, Fort Orange in Secondi, Fort Amsterdam in Kormantin, Dixcove Fort in Dixcove, and the fort at Komenda.

Many Ghanaians call these structures castles, probably a result of their British education. However, when Afrikan Americans (Ausa) visit, smell the still-obvious musk in the walls and realize that their Ancestors were packed into these chambers awaiting ships to take them into the hells of North and South America and the Caribbean, the word *castle* doesn't come to mind. Instead, it conjures up images of a fairy tale place full of magic, chivalry and honor. To the Ausa descendants there is absolutely nothing magical, chivalrous or honorable about these structures. *As applied to us, they functioned as dungeons that is what we call them...dungeons!* Slave dungeons.

Many people argue that slavery was common in Afrika and that Afrikans sold their own people into slavery, an argument used most commonly as an excuse to get Europeans and Arabs off the hook. Although this is true to some extent, two points should be noted. First, there are traitors and people motivated by greed in every group of people. And, second, slavery in Afrika was a completely different institution and the enslaved persons were not considered chattel and were not dehumanized.

According to many published reports, no actual slave trade existed prior to the influence of the Arabs. People went into servitude when they owed a debt or to integrate into a foreign society, as with prisoners of war. Again, they were neither chattelized nor dehumanized. There were several categories of slaves among the Asante in Ghana:

- Akoa (plural nkoa) was voluntary servitude in which all Asante stood in relation to some other person or group, such as in being the "subject" of the Asantehene (king) who was, in turn, the akoa of the Ancestors.
- Awowa meant temporarily surrendering ownership of one's self in order to pay a debt (as in "pawning" oneself to pay a debt).
- Odonko is a person other than Asante (an enemy) purchased with the purpose of making a slave.
- Domun was a prisoner of war or tribute from a defeated/subjugated foreign power. A free Asante could fall to this state for repeated criminal behavior.

- Akyere were slaves held for sacrificial purposes at funerals. This occurred most frequently many years ago and was associated with the traditional religion. Interestingly, this type of slave, "slaves of the gods," was present also among other ethnic groups in other West Afrikan countries.

If this seems barbaric, keep in mind that, at the same time, Europeans and European Americans were burning alive women accused of being witches.

Despite the presence of servitude in Afrika, it cannot be compared with the inhuman, brutal and horrendous system of chattel slavery practiced by Arabs and Europeans. In Afrika, slaves enjoyed rights and privileges and were not considered to be property but were members of the families that they served. In many cases, slaves could hold political office and frequently married into the families that they served.

Ghana is a very special place for Ausa people as is demonstrated in the fact that Ausa tourism is a major industry in Ghana. In fact, Ausa visit Ghana more than any other people. Many Ausa have ancestral origins in Ghana and will see Ghanaian people who look just like their friends and relatives at home. Again, we use the term Ausa to describe the ethnic group of Afrikans in America. Most of us are mixtures of several different Afrikan ethnic groups (as well as Europeans and Native Americans). We can never become Asante, Ewe, Yoruba, Fante, Fon or Ga but we can be ourselves. We are a separate ethnic group of Afrikans living outside of Afrika. We are **A**frikans in the **U**nited **S**tates of **A**merica (AUSA).

This chapter is intended to help Ausa visitors to Ghana to understand a little of the language and culture, as well as make their stay easier and more pleasant. The Ghanaian people are extremely friendly and gracious and usually they are pleased and flattered that visitors have taken the time to learn a little of their language. This chapter does not attempt to be an authority on the language or culture. People who are serious about learning Ghanaian history, culture and the language, Twi, should purchase and study books listed in the reference list.

References and Suggested Reading

Agbo, Adolph H. *Values of Adinkra Symbols.* Kumasi: Ebony Designs and Publications, 1999.

Ajayi, J.F Ade and Ian Espie. *A Thousand Years of West African History.* Ontario: Ibadan University Press, 1981.

Assimeng, Max. *Social Structure of Ghana: A Study in Persistence and Change.* Accra: Ghana Publishing Corporation, 1999.

Boahen, Adu. *Topics in West African History.* London: Longman Group, Ltd., 1980.

Bureau of Ghana Languages. Language Guide *(Asante Version).* Accra: Bureau of Ghana Languages, 1987.

Der, Benedict G. *The Slave Trade in Northern Ghana.* Accra: Woeli Publishing Services, 1998.

Dolphyne, Florence Abena. *A Comprehensive Course in Twi (Asante).* Accra: Ghana Universities Press, 1996.

Ghana Information Services Department. *Ghana: A Brief Guide.* Accra: Ghana Information Services Department, 1991.

Sarpong, Peter. *Ghana In Retrospect: Some Aspects of Ghanaian Culture.* Accra-Tema: Ghana Publishing Corporation, 1974.

Tufour, Lawrence, Anthony Yeboah, Ebenezer Oteng-Preko. *Twi Language Course for Beginners.* Kumasi: Catholic Media Network, 1996.

Van Dantzig, Albert. *Forts and Castles of Ghana.* Accra: Sedco Publishing Limited, 1980.

Warren, Dennis M. *The Akan of Ghana: An Overview of the Ethnographic Literature.* Accra: Pointer Limited.

Willis, W. Bruce. *The Adinkra Dictionary: A Visual Primer on the Language of ADINKRA.* Washington: The Pyramid Complex, 1998.

The Language

English is Ghana's official language but other languages have official status, also. These other languages are Twi (frequently called Akan), Ewe, Dagbanli, Dagaare-Wali, Ga and Nzema. Although Hausa is not a Ghanaian language, it is an official language of Ghana also. Twi is Ghana's primary language and is the language of the Akan people who are the majority group. Twi is spoken as a first language by about

44% of Ghana's population. There are three written dialects of Twi: Asante Twi, Akuapim Twi and Fante Twi.

Pronunciation Code

The Twi alphabet is similar to the English alphabet except that Twi has 22 letters. There is no **c**, **j**, **q**, **v**, **x** or **z**, with one exception: Fante Twi does have a **z**. The main differences are in the vowels (which can be long or short):

a is usually pronounced **ah**;
e is usually pronounced **a** as in day;
i is usually pronounced **ee** as in tree;
o is usually pronounced **oh**; and
u is usually pronounced **ou** as in you.

Twi has two additional vowels:

ɛ (like a backwards 3) is pronounced **eh** and
ɔ (like a backwards c) is pronounced **aw**.

The consonants are the same as consonants in English except that the letter **g** is a hard g as in girl, rather than the soft g as in gerbil. Letter combinations called diagraphs are pronounced as such:

dw is pronounced **j** with rounded lips as in *jowon*, leaving out the first **o**, so the name Kwadwo is pronounced *Kwah-joe.*

gy is pronounced **geh**.
hw is pronounced as the **wh** in whew.
hy is pronounced **sh** as in shirt.
kw is pronounced as the **qu** in quick
ky is pronounced **ch** as in church.
nw is pronounced **nw** with rounded lips as in *nowon*, leaving out the first **o**.
ny is pronounced as a fast *knee-yah.*
tw is pronounced **chw** as in a fast *chee-wah.*

Twi is also a language in which word meanings can change with changes in tone and nasalizing sounds. These are beyond the scope of what this chapter is intended to do and will not be discussed at any great length. We will concentrate on spoken, rather than written, Twi.

There are differences between proper written Twi and everyday spoken Twi.

The following phrases and conversations will be useful to you in Ghana. English words or phrases usually will be written first followed by the corresponding Asante Twi word or phrase in parenthesis. A pronunciation guide follows the Twi word and is in bold type.

General Phrases and Greetings

May I come in? May I have your attention?—(Agoo) **ah-go**

Come in—(Amee) **ah-may**

Wait—(tw□n) **tchwane**

Hold it, hang on (don't come in right now)—gyina h□ **gin-a-haw**

Knocking (the sound of knocking)—kɔ k□□ k□ **kaw-kawww-kaw**

Come in—(bra mu) **brah moo**

Good morning, sir—(owura, makye) **oh-wu-rah, mah-chee** (owura is sir and makye is good morning)

Good afternoon, ma'am—(awuraa, maha) **ah-wu-raah mah-hah** (awuraa is ma'am)

Good evening, sir—(owura, madwo) **oh-wu-rah, mah-joe**

Yes, brother/sister (the response to the above)—(yaa onua) **yah onia**

How are you doing?—(Wo ho te sɛn) **who-hoe-the-sane**

I am fine—(me ho yɛ) **may-hoe-yeh**

How is everything at home?—(ofie te sɛn) **oh-fee-ay tay sane**

Everything is fine at home.—(ofie deɛ bɔkɔɔ) **oh-fee-ay day-eh baw-kaww)**

What is your name?—(Wo din de sɛn?) **wo den deh sane**

My name is (your name)—(Me din de [your name]) **may den day (your name)**

You have a beautiful name—(wo din yɛ me dɛ) **woe den yeh may deh**

My friend's name is Kwadwo—(m'adamfo din de Kwadwo) **mah-dahm-foe din day Kwa-joe**

What are you called? (Yefre wo sɛn?) **yeh-fray wo sane**

I am called (your name)—Yefre me (your name) **yeh-fray may (your name)**

Where are you from?—(Wofiri hene) **woe-fee-ree hay nay**

I am from America—(may fee-ree America) **may firi America**

I am pleased to meet you—(ɛyɛ me anigye sɛ mahyia woɔ) **eh-yeh may ahn-jay she mah-shee-ah woe-aw**

Why are you here? [Or] What is your mission?— (ɔkwanso?) aw-kwine-soe

The response is "no problem" or "it's cool"— ɔkwanso deɛ brɛɛoo **aw-kwine-soe day-eh breh-ooo** (**Note:** Some might leave the **ooo** off but either is correct.)

Yes—(aane) **ah-nee**

No—(dabi) **dah-bee**

Thanks—(meda ase) **meh-dah-see**

You're welcome or Don't mention it—(yɛnni adeda) **yeh-nee ah day dah**

Please (say this fast at the beginning of the sentence)—(Me pa wo kyew) **meh pah woe choe**

Welcome—(akwaaba) **ah-kwah-bah**

Goodbye (safe journey)—(nante yie) **nahn-tay yee-ay** (the response is yoo, which means "all right")

Goodnight—(da yiɛ) **dah-yee-eh** (the response is yoo, also)

I don't understand—(mente aseɛ) **men-tay ah-say-eh**

Leave me alone—(gyame haw) **gee-ah-may how**

I will go—(mɛkɔ) **meh kaw**

Don't go—(nkɔ) **en-kaw**

I don't want trouble—(mempɛ asɛm) **mem-peh ah-sehm**

Take your trouble away from here—Fa w'asɛm kɔdo) **Fah wah-sehm kaw-doe**

Common Ailments

I don't feel good—(me ho yɛ me basaa) **may-hoe-yeh may ba-saa**

My head hurts—(me tiri yɛ me ya) **meh tee-ree yeh may yah**

My tooth hurts—(me se yɛ me ya) **meh sen yeh-may-yah.** There is a line over the "e" in se that means that it is nasalized and the "e" is pronounced like sent (or it will have another meaning).

I have a toothache—(manya kaka) **mah-nyah kah-kah**

My stomach hurts—(me yafunu yɛ me ya) **meh yah-foo-noo yeh-may-yah**

My eye hurts—(m'ani yɛ me ya) **mah-nee yeh-may-yah**

My knee hurts—(me kotodwe yɛ me ya) **meh koe-toe-dway yeh-may-yah**

I have diarrhea—(me yɛm retu) **meh yehm ee-tu** The "r" in retu is silent. The literal translation is "my insides are freeflowing."

I am constipated—(me yɛm atim) **meh yehm ah-teem** Literal translation: "my insides are stuck."

I am nauseous—(me bo fono me) **may boe foe-no may**

I am vomiting—(merefe) **meh-eh feh** (the "r" is silent)

I am bleeding—(mmogya retu me) **em-moe-gah ray-too may**

I am feverish—(me ho ayɛ hye) **meh hoe ah-yeh shee**

I don't feel good/I'm out of sorts—(Me ho mmfa ne) **meh ho em-fah nay**

I am not feeling well—(mente apɔ) **main-tay ap-paw**

I'm going to see the doctor—(merekɔhunu ɔyaresafoɔ) **meh-reh-kaw-hoo-noo aw-yah ray-sah-foe-aw**

What ails you?—(ɛdeɛbɛn naɛha wo?) **eh-day-eh-behn nah eh-ha-woe**

Doctor or "the person who knows and practices medicine"—(oduyɛfoɔ) **oh-due-yeh-foe-aw**

Herbalist—(odunsini) **oh doon-see-nee**

Buying and Selling at the Marketplace

Please note that the format changes because of the dialog. The Twi phrase will come first, followed by the pronunciation, which will always be in parentheses and will still be in bold type. When shopping at the marketplace, ALWAYS bargain; NEVER pay what the venders ask for initially.

Seller: Wo pɛ? (wop eh)-Do you like it?

Buyer: ɛyɛ fɛ paa. (eh-yeh feh paah)—It is very beautiful.

B: Sɛn? (sane)—How much does it cost?

S: 10 thou cedi (ten tow see-dees)—ten thousand cedis.

NOTE: "Thou" is short for thousand and is pronounced without the "h" sound. It still rhymes with "tow."

B: Me sika sua (may see-kah swah)—My money is small.

B: Yɛnte so? (yentay so)—Is the price reducible?

S: Yɛteso (yeh-tay-so)—It is reducible.

B: Yɛteso sɛn? (yeh-tay-so sane)—How much do we reduce it?

S: Yɛteso 500. (yeh-tay-so 500)—It is reducible by 500.

B: Ne boɔ yɛ den! (Ne boy yeh dane)—The price is hard (It's expensive)!

S: Ne boɔ nnye den! (Ne boy nyeh dane)—The price is not expensive!

S: Wo bɛtua sɛn? (woe beh-tu-ah) sane)—How much will you pay?

B: Me tua 2 thou cedi (me tu-ah 2 tow see-dee)—I will pay 2 thousand cedis.

S: Dabi, mennye. (dahbee, men-yah)—No, I won't take it.

B: Wobɛ gye sɛn? (wo-beh gee sane)—How much would you take?

B: Wobɛ gye 3 thou? (wo-beh gee 3 tow)—Would you take 3 thousand?

S: Megye 5 thou. (meh-gee 5 tow)—I will take 5 thousand.

B: Mɛtua 4 thou. (meh tu-ah 4 tow)—I will pay 4 thousand.

S: Fa sika bra. (Fah seekah brah)—Let the money come.

B: Enie (ay-nia)—Here it is.

S: To So (toe so)—Add a "dash" (a tip)

NOTE: Numbers are usually in English. The author has tried this and it works!!

Tourist Catching a Cab

Tourist: Taxi!!! Service!!!

Driver: Worekɔ hene? (wo-e-kaw heh-neh)—Where are you going?

T: Merekɔ Afrikiko. (meh-reh kaw Afri-kee-koe)—I am going to Afrikiko (a restaurant in Accra).

T: Wobɛ gye sɛn? (woe-beh-gee sane) What is the fare?

Or

T: Sɛn na wobɛgye (sane nah wo-beh-gee-eh)—How much will you take?

D: Tena ase (ten-asi)—Sit down

D: Yɛgye 500 cedis dropping (yeh-gee 500 see-dees dropping)—We take 500 cedis dropping ("dropping" means alone with no other pickups).

T: Ma yɛn nkɔ (mah yehn kaw)—Let us go?

D: Afrikiko nie (Afri-kee-koe nee-ay)—This is Afrikiko.

T: Mepaakyɛw gyina ha (May-paa-shew gee-nah hah)—Please stop here.

T: Wo bɛtwen me? (woe beh-tchwane meh)—Will you wait for me?

Or

T: Twen (tchwane)—Wait

D: Aane mɛtwen wo (ah-nee meh tchwane woe)—Yes, I will wait for you

T: Wotwɛn me a ɛbɛyɛ sɛn? (woe-tchwane may ah eh-beh-yeh sane)—If you wait for me, how much will it cost?

D: Dɔnhwere baako biara yɛ 2 thou (Dawn-cherry bah-ko bee-ah-rah yeh 2 tow)—Every hour costs 2 thousand cedis.

Eating at a Restaurant

Customer: Awuraa, ɛdeɛbɛn nie? (ah-wu-raa eh-day-eh-behn nee-ah)—Ma'am, what is this?

Waitress: ɛyɛ nantwi ne ɛmoo (eh-yeh nahn-tchwee nay eh-moo)—This is steak and rice.

C: Metɔ bi (meh-taw bee)—I will buy some.

W: Wobɛ tɔ sɛn? (Woe-beh-taw sane?)— How much will you buy?

C: Mɛtɔ 2 thou. (meh-taw 2 tow) —I will buy two thousand worth.

W: Wobɛdi? (woe-beh-dee)—Will you eat?

C: Aani, mɛdi (ah-nee, meh-dee)—Yes I will eat or

C: Dabi, me,nni (dah-bee, meh nyee)—No, I will not eat.

C: Mepɛ akɔkɔ ne ɛmoo (May-peh a-kaw-kaw nay eh-moo)—I like chicken and rice. **NOTE:** "Mepɛ" can mean either like or want.

C: Mepɛ nantwi nam (me-peh nahn-tchwee nahm)—I like steak (cow meat, beef)

C: Mepɛ mmɔnkɔ (me-peh mmawn-kaw)—I like shrimp.

C: Mepɛ kɔtɔ (me-peh kaw-taw)—I like crab.

W: Wobɛnom ɛdeɛbɛn? (woe-beh-nom eh-day-eh-bane) What will you drink?

C: Dabi, me nnom biribi ara? (dah-bee, meh-nnyom bee-ree-bee ah-rah)—No, I will not drink anything.

C: Mɛnom nsuo. (meh nom en-sue-oh)—I will drink water.

C: Mɛnom toa mu nsuo. (meh-nom tchua mue en-sue-oh)—I drink bottled water.

C: Mepɛ abrɔbɛ. (meh-peh a-braw-beh)—I like pineapple.

C: Ma me asikyire (Mah may asi-cherry)—Give me sugar.

C: Ma me nkyene (Mah may en-chay-nee)—Give me salt.

C: Ma me mmako (Mah may m-mah-koe)—Give me pepper.

NOTE: hyew, pronounced "show," means "hot."

Common Food Names

Adua (ah-dwee-ah)—beans

Apatram (ah-pah-trahm)—lima beans (Served as a paste and not as an individual dish as in America.

Adwene (ah jeh-neh)—fish

Nyaadowa (nyah-ah-do-wah)—eggplant or garden eggs, as Ghanaians call them. **NOTE:** Served also as a paste rather than as an individual dish. Abomu (ah-boe-moo)—spinach casserole (also contains onions, peppers, tomato and sometimes corned beef).

ɛtɔ (Eh-taw)—mashed plantain or yam or potato or coco yam

apesie (ah-pay-see)—boiled yam, plantain, or coco yam

kɔkɔɔ a yɛakye (kaw-kaww ah yeh-ah-chay-eh)—ripe plantain which we have fried (or fried ripe plantain)

nkwan (en-kwine)—soup

nkruma kwan (en-kroo-mah kwine)—okra soup

abɛkwan (ooh-beh-kwine)—palm nut soup

nkate kwan (en-kah-tay kwine)—groundnut (peanut) soup

nkra kra (en-krah krah)—light soup (made of eggplant or lima beans)

ɛmoo (eh-moo)—rice

ɛmootua (eh-moo-too-oh)—balled rice (rice in a ball)

bayerɛ (bah-yay-reh)—yam

ma me apepa wo nsa (mah may ah-pay-pah woe en-sah)—Give me something to clean my hands.

ɛye dɛ (eh-eh-deh)—It tastes good or it is sweet.

ɛnnyɛ dɛ (eh-nnyeh deh)—It's not good.

Other Ghanaian foods are kenkey "dɔkono" (daw-koe-noe) which is a corn meal dish and palaver sauce. "Greens" in Ghana refers to coco yam leaves and is called "nkontomire" (en-cone-toe-mee-ray).

For Language Purists

Many people are able to understand languages better when they are able to conjugate verbs. I offer the conjugations below with great hopes that it will be of help. Usually, when two vowels meet (if the last letter of one word is a vowel and the first letter of the next word is a vowel), the second vowel negates and eliminates the first vowel, except in a name. Pronouns and verbs next to each other are combined to make one word, as are nouns and verbs. A pronoun and a verb continue to be two words.

Present

I go—(Me kɔ)	May-kaw	We go—(yɛ kɔ)	Yeh-kaw
You go—(wo kɔ)	Woe kaw	You go—(Mokɔ	Moe-kaw
He, she, it goes—(ɔkɔ)	Aw-kaw	They go—(wɔkɔ)	Won-kaw

Present continuous

I am going—merekɔ may-ray-kaw
You are going—Worekɔ
He, she it is going— ɔrekɔ Aw-ray-kaw

We are going—Yɛrekɔ
You are going—Morekɔ
They are going—Wɔrekɔ

Past

I went—(me kɔɔe) meh-koye
You went—Wo kɔɔe
He, she,it went— ɔkɔɔe

We went—Ye kɔɔe
You went—Mo kɔɔe
They went—Wo kɔɔe

Past perfect

I have gone—Ma kɔ
You have gone—Wakɔ
He, she, it has gone—Wakɔ

We have gone—Yakɔ
You have gone—Makɔ
They have gone—Wakɔ

Future

I will go—Mɛkɔ
You will go—Wobɛkɔ
He, she, it will go— ɔbɛkɔ

We will go—yɛbɛkɔ
You will go—Mobɛkɔ
They will go—wɔbɛkɔ

Future perfect

I will be going—Merebɛkɔ
You will be going—Worebɛkɔ
He, she, it will be going— ɔrebɛkɔ
I am—meyɛ
You are—woyɛ
He, she, it is— ɔyɛ

We will be going—yɛrebɛkɔ
You will be going—Morebɛkɔ
They will be going—Worebɛkɔ
We are—yɛyɛ
You are—Moyɛ
They are—wɔyɛ

I see—Mehunu	We see—yɛhunu
You see—wohunu	You see—mohunu
He, she, it sees— ɔhunu	They see—wɔhunu

My child—me ba	Our child—yɛnba
Your child—wo ba	Your child—mo ba
His, her, its child—ne ba	Their child—wɔn no bah

Important Cultural Points to Remember

1. Do not use your left hand to eat, shake hands, give or receive anything. In Ghana, that is a great insult. If for some reason, this is not possible, always say, "memma wo abenkum" (may-mah woe ah-benkum). This means, in essence, "Pardon my use of my left hand."
2. Do not laugh at people.
3. Do not give anything to people who are begging. You will only create more problems and attract more beggars. Giving to only one or a few children and not to all can upset adults. Begging is illegal in Ghana.
4. Do not take anyone's picture without permission.
5. In Ghana, just saying "hello" or "hi" is not enough. People usually ask about each other's health EXCEPT children do not ask about the health of adults.
6. Children are expected to be quiet and polite when around adults.
7. People usually shake hands when they meet each other. When there is a group, they shake hands in a counterclockwise direction (from right to left).
8. When you are shopping at the marketplace or at a street vendor, never pay what the vendor asks for, always bargain!! If you use some of the Twi that you learn in this book, you may get really good bargains. Sometimes, you can also bargain with a taxi driver. The price of goods in stores is fixed and bargaining is inappropriate. However, in small shops, one can ask for a discount or

reduction in price. The seller usually also begins his/her sentences with "Please."

9. If someone asks for a "dash" ("ntosoɔ or en-toe-so-aw), they are asking for a tip.
10. There is no word for cousin in the Twi language. The Akan call their cousins brothers and sisters, except the Fante who do recognize cousins.
11. Fruit and vegetable vendors usually add as a gift more of some of the items they are selling, especially if the customer buys a lot. This is also called a *dash.*
12. Afrikans respect age and seniority. The younger person in a dialog frequently addresses the older person as "Papa" or "Mama" even though they are not related.
13. All Akans have an extended family system in which the family (abusua or ah-boo-swia) consists of all maternal relatives. In a matrilineal system lineage is traced through the mother.
14. Do not point up either thumb (as with the "A-OK" sign). It is insulting, offensive and vulgar. It is equivalent to "flipping the bird" or giving the middle finger in America.
15. When in the presence of chiefs and elders, never cross your legs. It is a sign of disrespect.
16. Insults, especially public ones, are intolerable to Ghanaians. Abusiveness in public is a legitimate reason for *de-stooling* a chief (taking away his status as chief). In public, avoid words like *foolish, silly, stupid* and *dummy.* Referring to a Ghanaian as an animal, such as *beast* or *pig,* and referring to a part of the body are offensive. A woman calling a man a fool is seen as an invitation to fight physically. He cannot accept the invitation because he will be severely ostracized as "a woman fighter."

Days of the Week and Day Names

Almost every Akan person has a *Day Name,* which represents the day on which that person is born. The following is a list in which the days of the week are given followed by the female and then the male Day Names

Monday	ɛdwoada (eh-joe-ah-dah)
Tuesday	ɛbenada (eh-bin-ah-dah)
Wednesday	Wukuada (wu-kuwa-da)
Thursday	Yawoada (yah-woe-ah-dah)
Friday	ɛfiada (eh-fee-ah-dah)
Saturday	Memeneda (me-me-ne-dah)
Sunday	Kwasiada (kwak-see-ah-dah)

	Female Day Names	**Male Day Names**
Monday	Adwoa (ah-ju-ah)	Kwadwo (kwah-joe)
Tuesday	Abenaa (ah-been-ah)	Kwabena (kwah-been-ah)
Wednesday	Akua (ah-ku-ah)	Kwaku (kway-ku)
Thursday	Yaa (Yaah)	Yaw (yaw)
Friday	Afua (ah-fu-ah)	Kofi (koe-fee)
Saturday	Amma (ah-mah)	Kwame (kwa-mee)
Sunday	Akosua (ah-ku-su-ah)	Kwasi (kway-see)

Other Names

	Female	**Male**
Second-born child	Maanu	Manu
Third-born child	Mansa	Mensa

God's gift Nyamekye (Nyam-ay-chee) Usually a second name for males and females and comes after the day name.

Arrived with good fortune: Afriyie (Ah-free-yee-ay). Also, a second name for males or females after the day name

Born on Christmas Day	Buronya (Boo-ron-yah)
First child born to a chief or king	Ahenkan (Ah-hen-kine)

Limited Glossary/Word List

Actions/Activities

Sleep—Da (dah)
Dance—Sa (sah)
Marry—Ware (wah-ray)
Drink—Nom (nom)
Read—Kan (kahn)
Take—Fa (fah)
Get—Gye (gee)
Do—Yɛ (yeh)
Chew—Wesa (way-sah)

Eat—Di (dee)
Bend—Kontono (kohn-toe-no)
Say—Ka (kah)
Help—Boa (boe-ah)
Look—Hwɛ (sheh)
Come—Bra (brah)
Pull—Twe (ch-way)
Beat—Bo (boe)

Animals

Ant—Ntɛtea (en-the-tay-ah)
Dog— ɔkraman (aw-krah-mon)
Mosquito—Ntontom (en-than-tom)
Lizard— ɔketerɛ (aw-kay-tay-reh)
House fly—Nwansena (nwahn-say-nah)
Goat—Abirekyie (ah-bee-ray-chee-ay)

Common Items

Bed—Mpa (em-pah)
Chair—Akonnwa (ah-kone-wah)
Food—Aduane (ah-doo-ah-nay)
Umbrella—kyiniɛ (chee-neh)

Blanket—Kuntu (koon-too)
Clothes—Ntaade (en-taa-day)
Soap—Samina (sah-mee-nah)

People

Boy — Abarimaa (ah-bah-ree-maah)
Son — ɔbabarima (aw-bah-bah-ree-mah)
Girl — Abaayewa (ah-bah-ah-yay-wah)
Daughter — ɔbabaa (aw-bah-ah-ah)
Husband — Okunu (oh-koo-new)

Wife — ɔyere (aw-yay-ray)
Man — ɔbarima (aw-bah-ree-mah)
Woman — ɔbaa (aw-bah-ah
Baby/child — Abofra (ah-boe-frah)
Afrikan (Black people pleural) — Abibifoɔ (ah-bee-bee-foe-aw)
Black man, singular — Obibini (oh-bee-bee-nee)
White person, singular — Oburoni (oh-bu-roe-nee)
White people, plural — Abrofo (ah-broe-foe)

Places

Afrika—Abibirem (Ah-bee-bee-rame)
Home—Ofie (oh-fee-ay)

Speed/Direction

Left—Benkum (behn-koom)
Right—Nifa (nee-fah)
Quickly—Ntɛm so (en-tehm so)
Slowly—Brɛoo (breh-ooh)

Time/Duration

Day— ɛda (eh-dah)
Week—Dapɛn (Dah-pehn)
Year—Afe (Ah-fay)
Morning—Anɔpa (ah-naw-pah)
Night—Anadwo (ah-nah-joe)
Yesterday—ɛnnora (ehn-no-rah)
Tonight—Anadwo yi (ah-nah-joe yee)
Tonight—Anwumerɛ (ahn-woo-may-reh)
Tomorrow— ɔkyena (aw-chay-nah)
Always—Daa (Daah)
Never—Koraa (koe-raah)
Often—Mprɛ pii (em-preh pee)
Now—Seesei (say-say)
Sometimes— ɛtɔ da a (eh-taw dah ah)
Forever—Afebɔɔ (ah-fay-baw-aw)

Miscellaneous

Beautiful—fɛ or fɛ fɛ (feh or feh-feh)
Culture—Amamerɛ (ah-mah-may-reh)

Numbers

One—Baako (bah-koe)
Two—Mmienu (em-ee-a-nu)
Three—Mmiɛnsa (em-ee-ehn-sah)
Four— ɛnan (eh-nahn)
Five—enun (a-noon)
Six—nsia (en-see-ah)
Seven—nson (en-sohn)
Eight—nwɔtwe (nwaw-chway)
Nine—nkron (en-kron)
Ten—edu (a-doo)

Colors

Black—tuntun (toon-toon)
White—fufuo (foo-foo-oh)
Red—kɔkɔɔ (kaw-kawww)
Blue—hoa (hoe-ah)
Green—ahahan mmono (ah-ha-hine em-oh-noe)
Yellow—akokɔ saade (ah-hoe-kaw sah-ah-day-eh)
There are no specific words for orange, brown, pink, gray, purple and gold.

Things to See, Do and Buy

The following suggestions are not a complete listing of things to do but are mostly places that the author has visited and can speak about knowledgeably. Some of the places that the author has not visited are included because people who have visited them recommended them.

No trip to Ghana would be complete without seeing at least two of the slave dungeons: *Elmina* and *Cape Coast.* They are the best preserved of all the dungeons open to the public. As mentioned earlier, because Ghana has a British form of education, the local people were educated to call these structures castles. As suggested by Dr. Leonard Jeffries, we call them slave dungeons because our Ancestors were warehoused there to wait for ships named *Freedom, Hope, Liberty* and *Jesus* to take them to the New World, to chattel slavery, degradation, torture, dehumanization and death.

Entering the cells and smelling the musk still present from thousands of bodies that stayed there is an eerie experience, a spiritual experience and the Ancestors there still communicate with us. It is also an emotional experience; there are no dry eyes among visitors. These sites make the Maafa real so that we can always remain in contact with our Ancestors and never forget what they suffered.

The gift shops in these dungeons frequently have good bargains for souvenirs and books. Usually, they won't bargain as freely as the vendors at the marketplace but the prices are generally good. If you buy in quantity, usually they give some good deals.

Not far from Cape Coast is a town called *Assin Manso*, which is a must; the people there are wonderfully friendly. This Fante village is the home of several significant sites:

- The Slave Route Project. Assin Manso is at the end of a trail that slave traders frequently used to march the captured and soon-to-be-enslaved Afrikans from the interior of the country. It is preserved in a beautiful park.
- The Slave River is at the end of the trail that was said to have been the site of the last bath the captives took before entering the dungeon.
- Near these areas are two heavily guarded and well-kept tombs. They contain the remains of a man from the United States and a woman from Jamaica which were brought to Ghana and ceremonially entombed.

Near Cape Coast, about 38 miles, is the *Kakun National Forest.* A bridge walkway approximately 80 feet high and 240 feet long extends across the tops of the trees from which everything on the ground can be observed, including the animals. It is only one of three of its kind in the world.

In *Accra*, visit the George Padmore Library. Trinidad-born Padmore was one of the early twentieth century architects of Pan-Afrikanism and spent his last years in Ghana. The library is a reference library that collects books and documents on the Black experience in Afrika and the Diaspora. W.E.B. Du Bois's burial site is also in Accra. This tomb is surrounded by a museum and a center that preserve many of his possessions. It is well worth visiting.

Near the coast in Accra is the memorial to Kwame Nkrumah, the first president of Ghana who led the country to "independence" from

British rule. This memorial contains his tomb and a small museum. Statues of horn-blowers are icons of Ghanaian culture and folklore and the massive statue of Nkrumah and the building holding his tomb as well as some of the symbolic decorations are reminders of the relationship between West Afrika and Kemet.

Not far from the Nkrumah Memorial is the Arts and Crafts Marketplace. This is one of the main places to shop for clothing and souvenirs in Accra. Lessons learned earlier in this chapter will come in handy here. This writer enjoys the bargaining and vendors take delight in the fact that a visitor would take the time to learn some of his/her language. Almost anything can be found there.

The Makola Market is a section of town in which there are hundreds of stores. It is very crowded, and tourists should beware of pickpockets. Probably, it is best not to visit there without a Ghanaian to help translate and keep you safe. The National Museum is also an interesting place to go to view Ghana's history.

There are many things to be seen and to do in *Kumasi*, including visiting the Manhyia Palace Museum, shopping at the Kejetia Market, one of the largest markets in Afrika, and visiting the Okomfo Anokye Sword Site to learn the history of the Asante kingdom. Several villages outside of Kumasi always attract tourists also:

1. **Bonwire** (bon-weh-reh) is the place where most of the Kente cloth is made. Kente cloth is one of two ceremonial cloths made and used by the Akan people. Kente symbols are very popular all over the world and have inspired many clothing designs by Afrikan and non-Afrikan people, although most non-Afrikans would not admit the source of their inspiration. Kente is woven at looms, usually by men, and the symbols are mostly geometrical. All the patterns have meaning and some Kente was reserved for chiefs or the king. They are very colorful and are worn on joyful occasions.

2. **Ntonso** (En-than-so) is where Adinkra cloth is made. Adinkra symbols are stamped on cloth and each has profound symbolic significance. There are dozens of Adinkra symbols; usually, the cloth

is black or red. Black and red symbolize melancholy and death and Adinkra cloth is usually worn at Akan funerals.

3. **Ehwia** (eh-wee-ay) is frequently called the woodcarving village. All types of wood carvings can be purchased there, from stools and other pieces of furniture to dolls and walking canes.
4. **Ejisu** (Ay-jee-sue) is the home and burial place of Yaa Asantewa, a Queen Mother who inspired the last war against the arrogant British, a war which was named after her. She saved the Golden Stool from being taken by the British and a shrine in her honor is located there.

These are only a few of the attractions of Ghana. There are many, many more.

Enjoy your visit!!!!

A Word About Money

The cedi is the monetary unit used in Ghana. Its value fluctuates but, as of this writing, one American dollar equals approximately four cedis. The symbol for cedi is like a small "c" with a vertical line drawn through it.

You can change your dollars to cedis at government-owned changing "banks" called Fourex Bureaus, which are found all over the cities, at the airport and at most hotels. The rates at the hotels are usually not as good and their supply of cedis is limited sometimes. You will get better rates of exchange for cash than for travelers' checks. You will also get better rates of exchange with larger denominations of bills than with smaller ones (you will get more cedis per dollar exchanging $100 than if you exchange $50 or $20).

Most prices will be given in cedis and it is easy to know the approximate equivalent in dollars.

Approximate equivalencies:

$1.00= c4

$5.00= c20

Approximate equivalencies (continued):

$10.00= c40

$25.00= c100
$50.00= c200
$75.00= c300
$100.00= c400
$150.00= c600
$250.00= c1,000
$500.00= c2,000

Remember to always bargain!! If you feel that you have lowered the price too much, you can always give them a *dash.*

CHAPTER 23

Selected Biographies and Research Topics

As a physician and amateur historian, I have been engrossed in the history of medicine. When Dr. Charles Finch introduced me to the fact that the real "Father of Medicine" was an Afrikan, the next logical step was to research this fascinating man for myself and share my findings.

It is important that this information be made available to young people. It is important also to introduce little-known heroes and heroines who had contributed much to Ausa history but who had been ignored by mainstream historians. This chapter is the result of that research.

First, five heroes/heroines are introduced: Imhotep, Maria Stewart, Henry Highland Garnet, Martin Robison Delany and Dr. Matilda Arabelle Evans. Suggested references are provided for each individual. This chapter also includes lists of the names of men and women of honor that young people can use to pursue their own research into the lives and achievements of these remarkable individuals. And, for further study, the chapter includes a list of events, movements and organizations. At the end is a set of questions for individuals to consider and/or to prime a group discussion.

IMHOTEP

Imhotep's name should be a household word to all people of Afrikan origin. Imhotep was a multi-genius who excelled in many things. If he had been skilled in only one thing, he still would have been considered great. Imhotep lived in Kemet (ancient Egypt) in about 2980 B.C.E. (Before the Common Era), almost 5000 years ago. The name "Imhotep" means, "He who comes in Peace."

He was born in a suburb of the Kemetic city, Menefer (Memphis). His father, Kanofer, was a distinguished architect and his mother, Khereduankh, was a member of a prominent family. Imhotep's wife was Ronfrenofert.

He was a Sage, a person of great wisdom who was also an excellent teacher. His wise sayings have been quoted for thousands of years. One of his best-known quotes is, "Eat, drink, and be merry, for tomorrow we die."

Imhotep was a scribe and wrote and re-wrote many books. It is believed that he authored books on several topics, but these have been lost. He was a philosopher, a person who can think originally and evaluate the world without the influence of other people's opinions. This is not to say that Imhotep did not listen to or learn from others, he was able to evaluate their opinions on his own and not just take someone else's word for it.

He was also an astronomer and was familiar with the solar system. He knew that the world was round thousands of years ago and understood the relationship of the planets and constellations with the passage of time. He was an architect, following in his father's footsteps, and a master builder who designed and built the world's first pyramid, the Step Pyramid at Saqqara, which is still standing after more than 4000 years. This pyramid was also the first building ever built using limestone blocks.

Imhotep was Prime Minister or Vizier to the Third Dynasty Pharoah Djoser and is said to have advised his Pharoah wisely on many occasions. He was also a Chief Lector Priest. At that time, Priests were believed to have a special relationship with the *ntrs* (aspects of nature) that gave them some power over the forces of nature. Although now we call this magic, it had had significant meaning to ancient people.

Imhotep was also the world's first known physician, which does not mean he was the very first doctor, just the first one we know about. Even though the Greek, Hippocrates, is called the "Father of Medicine," Imhotep lived thousands of years before Hippocrates was born. Some evidence suggests that Hippocrates studied from some of the books Imhotep wrote. Imhotep was familiar with anatomy and pharmacology (chemicals used as medicines) as well as many diseases.

He was so famous as a healer that eventually he was worshipped as a god, mostly by the Greeks and Romans, and was called "The Son of Ptah," a Kemetic name for a specific aspect of God. He was also called "The Prince of Peace."

The Greek god of healing, Asclepios (Aesculapius), was modeled after Imhotep and was worshipped all over Greece and Rome. Early Christians worshipped Imhotep as one with Christ.

Photographs of statues of Imhotep show him to be a bald-headed, Black man with a wide nose, fleshy lips and dark Black skin.

References and Suggested Reading

Diop, Cheikh Anta. *Civilization or Barbarism: An Authentic Anthropology*, NY: Lawrence Hill Books, 1991, pp. 283-284.

Finch, Charles S. Imhotep the Physician: Archetype of the Great Man. In *Great Black Leaders: Ancient and Modern* (Editor: Ivan Van Sertima). Journal of African Civilizations, December 1987, Volume 9, pp.213-231.

Rogers, J. A. *World's Great Men of Color, Volume I,* Collier Books, NY: Macmillan Publishing Company, 1972, pp. 38-42.

Maria Stewart

Maria Miller Stewart, a renaissance woman, was born in 1803 in Hartford, Connecticut. She was a teacher, journalist, lecturer, essayist, abolitionist, women's rights activist and evangelist.

Her parents were "free" Afrikan Americans but they both died when she was five years old. She was sent to be a servant in the home of a white minister where she remained for ten years. Afterward, and for the next five years, she worked as a domestic and attended Sabbath School before church service on Sundays.

On August 10, 1826, at age 23, she married 44 year-old James W. Stewart in Boston. He died three years later and the white executors of his will cheated her out of her inheritance. She and her husband had no children, but she survived by living on his veteran's pension from the War of 1812 and by doing domestic work again.

She was positively influenced by David Walker, a leader in Boston's Black community and author of *David Walker's Appeal to the Colored Citizens of the World.* His book is still available and is a must-read for all people, especially for those of Afrikan origin. She was also influenced and supported by William Lloyd Garrison, a prominent white abolitionist and became a writer for his newspaper, *The Liberator.*

Maria Miller Stewart was the first:

- woman of any race to lecture in public on political issues;
- Ausa woman to lecture about black woman's health;
- Ausa to speak to a mixed audience of men and women, black and white;
- Ausa woman to make public anti-slavery speeches.

Later, she moved to New York where she published her collected works and taught school. Then she moved to Baltimore where she also taught school and, finally, she moved to Washington, D.C. where she taught school and became head matron of the Freedmen's Hospital and Asylum, the medical school of Howard University.

Maria Stewart died at the Freedmen"s Hospital on December 17, 1879, at the age of 76.

References and Suggested Reading

MacLean, Maggie. Maria Stewart. https://ehistory.osu.edu/biographies/maria-stewart

Maria W. Stewart. https://en.wikipedia.org/wiki/Maria_W._Stewart

Richardson, Marilyn (Editor). *Maria W. Stewart, America's First Black Woman Political Writer: Essays and Speeches.* Bloomington: Indiana University Press, 1987.

Stewart, Maria W. Miller 1803-1879. https://www.encyclopedia.com/people/history/historians-miscellaneous-biographies/maria-stewart

Henry Highland Garner

The life of Henry Highland Garnet is an example of extraordinary courage and undying commitment to Afrikan people. He was one of the greatest Afrikans to live during the 1800s. The study of his life can be very inspiring and educational, especially given the confusion

(much of it intentionally induced) exhibited in many of our young people today.

Reverend Garnet was born at New Market, Kent County, Maryland, on December 23, 1815. This third generation Afrikan born in America was always proud of his Afrikan heritage. He tried to make Afrikan Americans who lived during his lifetime remember that, both physically and culturally, they were Afrikan people. He was also a mortal enemy of the enslavement of Afrikan people.

His grandfather, whose slave name was Joseph Trusty, was a Mandinka chieftain. This is an important fact, especially if one realizes just who the Mandinka people were and what they had accomplished. The Mandinka came together to form the medieval West Afrikan country called Mali. Uncivilized white slave traders called them "Mandingo" but they were nothing like the people portrayed in the book and movie of that name. The Mandinka were successful traders, excellent farmers and courageous soldiers, and they valued education.

During the 1300s, Mali was about the same size as Western Europe and had a population of about ten million people. The Mandinka were also explorers and there is some evidence that they had visited America before Columbus and other Europeans had arrived here because they left writing on stone in Tennessee, Georgia, New Mexico and Nevada.

Mali was home to the famous University of Sankore in the city of Timbuktu. Most Mandinka people could read, and most could speak at least two languages and had some education. In understanding this history, it would be logical that the leaders had to be well educated.

Then, as a Mandinka chieftain, Reverend Garnet's grandfather had to have been both educated and intelligent and probably more so than the Europeans who kidnapped and bought him.

When Garnet was eight years old, his whole family escaped from slavery traveling on the Underground Railroad. His father, George, was the leader of this expedition. The family separated in Wilmington, Delaware; Henry's group, which included Henry's father and mother, two of his brothers, his sister and others — a total of eight — went to New Hope, Buck's County, Pennsylvania, where Henry attended school first. Eventually, they moved to New York City where they changed their name from Trusty to Garnet.

In New York, Henry attended The African Free School and was exposed to many Afrikan customs and native-born Afrikans. Henry was a good student, possibly because his grandfather had taught the family the value of an education. Even though it was against the law for enslaved Afrikans to be educated, most enslaved Afrikans realized the positive value of an education.

One significant incident in young Henry's life in New York occurred when some slave hunters from Maryland invaded their home and captured his sister. The fugitive slave laws allowed whites to kidnap escaped enslaved Afrikans anywhere they had fled and return them into slavery. Sometimes they kidnapped Afrikans who had never been enslaved and sold them into slavery (as per the book and film *12 Years a Slave*). Henry's parents barely escaped; his father had to jump from the roof of their two-story home into the yard of their next-door neighbors, the Crummells.

Although Henry was not at home when the incident occurred, he was so furious that he bought a knife and walked the streets hoping that the slave hunters would approach him. His sister was tried in a court of law as a "fugitive from labor" but was released when she convinced the court that she had actually been free in New York when she was supposed to have been a slave in Maryland!

In 1835, young Henry and two friends, Alexander Crummell, his neighbor from New York, and Thomas S. Sidney, went to the New Canaan Academy, an integrated school in New Hampshire. The 400-mile trip was difficult for the young men and especially for Henry who was partially crippled. The steamboat ride was tough because cabins were not rented to Afrikans and they had to ride outside in the elements for the entire time they were on the boat. Over land, they were allowed to ride on top (outside) of stagecoaches rather than inside with the other passengers. When the coach stopped, they had to seek shelter among the Afrikan people who lived in the area, sleep in barns, or sleep outside because hotels and inns refused them food and shelter.

After a week, a racist mob of local citizens, outraged that Afrikan students were being educated in their town, hitched 95 yoked oxen to the school building and dragged it to a swamp where they burned it. Then, they attacked the home where the young men were staying, but Henry fired a shotgun at the mob and they ran away. When the mob got their courage together and returned the next day with a cannon, the young men had to escape in a wagon, a good illustration that racism was and is not merely a Southern phenomenon. They completed their education at the Oneida Institute in Whiteboro, New York, under Beriah Green, a leading abolitionist and the first president of the American Anti-Slavery Society.

During this time, Garnet matured into a strong man with a majestic bearing and grew to be more than six feet tall. He was a brilliant and original student. When he married Julia Williams, a former classmate at the New Canaan Academy, people were amazed at the gentlemanly gallantry that he showed to her before and after the marriage.

By word and deed, Garnet's father had taught him that leadership was natural for Black men and from 1840-1860 he became a significant leader in the anti-slavery movement. Garnet had developed a Pan-Afrikan solution for change and the Black Nationalism in New York City during the 1800s helped him to mature in his political views. Initially, he believed slavery could be eliminated through the legislative process, but quickly he came to advocate armed revolt by the enslaved Afrikans as the answer to the slavery problem.

During the early and mid-1800s, "free" Afrikan American people would meet periodically at different places throughout the country for national conferences where they could discuss their views and opinions. This was The Negro Convention Movement. During the meeting in Buffalo, New York, in 1843, Reverend Garnet made an impassioned speech whose message Frederick Douglass opposed. It was voted down as the will of the body by one vote (the body voted on the position that the whole conference would adopt as its official position. Excerpts from that speech help us to understand Henry Highland Garnet:

> ...(B)ut you are a patient people. You act as though you were made for the special use of these devils. You act as though your daughters were born to pamper the lusts of your masters and overseers. And worse than all, you tamely submit while your lords tear your wives from your embraces and defile them before your eyes. In the name of God, we ask, are you men? Where is the blood of your fathers? Has it all run out of your veins?...Brethren arise, arise! Strike for your lives and liberties. Now is the day and the hour. Let every slave throughout the land do this, and the days of slavery are numbered. You cannot be more oppressed than you have been — you cannot suffer greater cruelties than you have already. Rather die freemen than live to be slaves. Remember that you are four millions.
>
> It is in your power so to torment the God-cursed slaveholders that they will be glad to let you go free. If the scale were turned, and Black men were the masters and white men the slaves, every destructive agent and element would be employed to lay the oppressor low. Danger and death would hang over their heads day and night...In the name of God, we ask, are you men? Where is the blood of your fathers? Has it run out of your veins? Awake, awake; millions of voices are calling you! Your dead fathers speak to you from their graves. Heaven, as with a voice of thunder, calls on you to arise from the dust. Let your motto be resistance! Resistance! Resistance! No oppressed people have ever secured their liberty without resistance. (author's emphasis). What kind of resistance you had better make you must decide by the circumstances that surround you, and according to the suggestion of expediency. Brethren, adieu! Trust in the living God. Labor for the peace of the human race, and remember that you are four millions!"

Frederick Douglass opposed Garnet because he (Douglass) felt that resistance ultimately would be crushed. It is also important to remember that at that time Douglass was under the influence and control of William Lloyd Garrison, a white abolitionist. Douglass' initial opposition was worded in a respectful manner but soon he began to use harsh and insulting language in responding to Garnet. However, several years later, Douglass said he would welcome knowledge of slave insurrection in the South. In fact, a famous quotation from an older and wiser Frederick Douglass states,

> If there is no struggle, there is no progress. Those who propose to favor freedom, and yet depreciate agitation, are men who want crops without plowing up the ground. They want rain without thunder and lightning. They want the ocean's majestic waves without the awesome roars of its waters.

Douglass continued to be a public and private adversary of Garnet's although, in the public eye, they were of equal status. Some people believe this speech marked the beginning of the end of Reverend Garnet's influence, which is not entirely accurate because Reverend Garnet's influence has lasted until today.

By the time Garnet discovered David Walker's *Appeal*, it was becoming lost. Garnet republished the third edition and now the *Appeal* is required reading for all who want to gauge the thoughts of nineteenth century Afrikan Americans.

During his later years, Reverend Garnet was under continuous attack by upper middle-class integrationist negroes. After the Civil War, he became saddened and disillusioned by these attacks. He was offered a position in Liberia, West Afrika and accepted it eagerly. He became so frustrated at being mistreated by the very people he had given his life for that he wanted to go to Afrika and die. Eloquently, he stated to his childhood friend, Alexander Crummell:

> What, would you have me linger here in an old age of neglect and want? Would you have me linger here in an old age of neglect and want? Would you have me tarry among men who have forgotten what I had done, and what I have suffered for them! To stay here and die among these ungrateful people? No, I go gladly to Afrika! Please the Lord I can only safely cross the ocean, land on the coast of Afrika, look around upon the green fields, tread the soil of my Ancestors, live if but a few weeks; Then I shall be glad to lie down and be buried beneath its sod!

He died February 1882, two months after arriving in Afrika and is buried there.

References and Suggested Reading

Adams, Russell A. Great Negroes: *Past and Present.* Chicago: Afro-Am Publishing Co., 1984 p. 52.

Brewer, W.M. (1928-1929): Henry Highland Garnet. *Journal of Negro History,* Volume 13-14, pp. 36-52.

Harding, Vincent. *There Is A River: The Black Struggle for Freedom In America.* NY: Vintage Books, A Division of Random House, 1983, pp. 133-136.

Hinks, Peter P. *To Awaken My Afflicted Brethren: David Walker and the Problem of Antebellum Slave Resistance.* University Park: The Pennsylvania State University Press, 2000.

Schiffrin, Steven H. The Rhetoric of Black Violence in the Antebellum Period: Henry Highland Garnet. Journal *of Black Studies,* September 1971, pp. 45-56.

Stuckey, Sterling. Slave Culture: *Nationalist Theory and the Foundations of Black America.* NY: Oxford University Press, 1987, pp. 138-192.

DR. MARTIN ROBISON DELANY

Martin Robison Delany is another example of a clear-thinking, proud Afrikan man who excelled in many areas. He could also be called a multi-genius, much like Imhotep.

He was born in Charles Town, Virginia (now Charleston, West Virginia), on May 6, 1812, the son of Samuel and Pati Peace Delany. Samuel was an enslaved carpenter and Pati was a "free" seamstress. Reportedly, Samuel could prove that his maternal and paternal grandfathers were chiefs of the Gullah and Mandinka people. He heard many proud stories from his maternal grandmother, Graci Peace. His family was said to have not been enslaved because of an unwritten law that no Afrikan of royal blood could be enslaved; however, some accounts relate that his mother was free and his father was enslaved.

He was a man of courage who started an organization in 1834 that he called the Philanthropic Society, believed by many to be the foundation of the Underground Railroad. In its first year of existence, 269 persons were helped to escape from enslavement to Canada and elsewhere. Delany even traveled through Mississippi, Louisiana, Arkansas, and Texas to witness "slavery" firsthand. During that era, when European-Americans violently expressed their fear and hatred of Afrikans, it was very, very courageous for an educated Afrikan to travel among these barbarians, as documented by Solomon Northrup in his 1853 book, *Twelve Years A Slave.*

Also, during this period he married Catherine Richards. They had seven children, all of whom they named after great Afrikans in history. Three of his children were named Toussaint L'Ouverture, Alexander Dumas and Ethiopia Hallie.

Delany wanted to share his experiences and observations with other people. To do this, he wrote many articles but found he could not get them published without being forced to make changes that really altered the views that he expressed in his articles. So, in 1843, he started his own newspaper, *The Mystery.* It was very successful and he only stopped its publication when Frederick Douglass persuaded him to help in starting another newspaper, *The North Star.* He and Douglass disagreed on many tactics in the struggle and, after three years, he dissolved his interest in the paper.

Delany then turned to the practice of medicine. Later on, he received several offers to start another paper but instead advised those who made him the offers to support *The North Star.* Besides his loyalty and honesty, he felt that to get the best results all efforts should be concentrated in one direction. Delany was a much sought-after speaker and traveled extensively to Abolitionist meetings throughout the East and Midwest. Most of this time he was in danger and, on at least one occasion, barely escaped lynching.

During that era, most physicians were educated and trained by the process of apprenticeship. This meant they would work for older, more experienced physicians to learn from them and then they would open their own offices. Martin Delany studied medicine under not one but three well-known and respected abolitionist Pittsburgh physicians: A.N. McDowell, J.P. Gazzan, and F.J. Lemoyne. Because of their recommendations, Delany was accepted into Harvard Medical School in 1850.

He left Harvard before graduating, however, because he and the other Afrikan medical students were asked to listen to lectures from the hall outside the lecture room. Apparently, the white southern students objected to sitting in the same room with the Afrikan students. Delany refused to lower himself to that level and returned to Pittsburgh where he distinguished himself as a caring and able physician during the cholera epidemic of 1854.

He was extremely proud of his Blackness and of his very dark complexion. It was said that he would become envious when he saw someone with a darker complexion than he had. His friend Frederick Douglass said, *"I thank God for making me a man simply; but Delany always thanks Him for making him a Black man."*

Delany participated in several of the National Negro Conventions. He was distressed when he felt that, after white abolitionists had been allowed to attend the Convention, the Afrikans became complacent and docile and waited for the whites to take the lead.

His love for his people and his interest in race led him to write two books, *The Condition, Elevation, Emigration and Destiny of the Colored People of the United States Politically Considered* in 1852 and *Principia of Ethnology: The Origin of Races and Color* in 1879. As a result of these studies, he was called an Ethnologist.

He is also called the Father of Black Nationalism:

> *Every people should be the originators of their own designs, the projectors of their own schemes, and creators of the events that lead to their destiny—the consummation of their desires...We have native hearts and virtues, just as other nations; which in their pristine purity are noble, potent, and worthy of example. We are a nation within a nation; as the Poles in Russia, the Hungarians in Austria, the Welsh, Irish and Scotch in the British dominions... The claims of no people, according to established policy and usage, are respected by any nation, until they are presented in a national capacity.*

Delany's first book elaborated on the proud history of Afrika and Afrikan people and demonstrated that any claim of the inferiority of Afrikan people was without merit. It also dealt with the different economic developmental methods between the European-dominated government and the Afrikans. A major focus of his attention was the growth of Black mutual aid societies all over the country. Indeed, Dr. John Henrik Clarke called him an "African socialist thinker and theoretician" who was a contemporary of Karl Marx but addressed his concerns to Afrikan people in an Afrikan manner.

Delany lectured frequently all over the world on abolitionist topics. Initially, he believed that Afrikans in America deserved equal rights in their native land. However, in the 1850s he completely changed his attitude (possibly because of his experiences at Harvard). He began to believe that Afrikans in America would never gain equal rights with whites regardless of ability and began to favor emigration.

He organized three National Emigration Conventions after the publication of his 1852 book. It is important to remember that emigration was one of the major issues being debated by Afrikan American leaders of that day. At first, Delany favored Afrikans in America emigrating to Central America — he attempted to set up a Black state in Nicaragua — and South America but eventually changed and favored Afrika as the destination. He clashed with older leaders who believed white Americans eventually would do the right thing out of moral and religious benevolence. He said, "...the colored people today are not the colored people of a quarter of a century ago, require very different means and measures to satisfy their wants and demands, and to effect their advancement." Delany felt military, political, and economic strength and independence were necessary for Afrikans to gain true respect.

The first Emigration Convention was held in Cleveland, Ohio, in August 1854. Delany delivered a tremendous speech that is still an extremely impressive literary work. Some excerpts from that speech are offered here:

> "Can we be satisfied in this enlightened age of the world, amid the advantages which now present themselves to us, with the degradation and servility inherited from our fathers in this country? God forbid."
>
> Half a century brings about a mighty change in the reality of existing things and events of the world's history.

> Fifty years ago our fathers lived. For the most part they were sorely oppressed, debased, ignorant, and incapable of comprehending the political relations of mankind. They lived amidst a continual cloud of moral obscurity; a fog of bewilderment and delusion. They were content with privileges; we will be satisfied with nothing less than rights. They considered themselves favored to live by sufferance; we regard it as a degradation. A subordinate position was all they asked for; we claim entire equality or nothing. They admitted themselves to be inferiors; we barely acknowledge the whites as equal.
>
> There is but one question which presents itself for our serious consideration, upon which we must give a decisive reply: Will we transmit, as an inheritance to our children, the blessings of unrestricted civil liberty, or shall we entail upon them, as our own political legacy, the degradation and oppression left us by our fathers?"

Delany believed that if logic and politics were looked at realistically, and considerations of morality and right taken from the argument, Afrikan Americans had no relationship to the rights and privileges of America. He pointed to the fact that Afrikans had not only built America but that Southern white men depended on the labor of Blacks to sustain them. He saw this as evidence that, no matter how hard working and industrious Afrikans were, they would never share in the benefits of America. Is this still true today?

Delany was critical of established Black leaders who urged their people to work hard while waiting for God to set them free. He felt, as did other emigrationists, that it was possible for Afrikans to get equality in America but only if they were willing to lose their Afrikan identities and assimilate into white society. Is this argument being made still? He wanted Afrikans *as a people* to maintain their identities and achieve greatness. He said, as many Nationalists have said since, Afrikans were (are) not the same as Europeans, should not try to be, and the sooner they realized this the better off we would be as a people.

During the first Emigration Convention. three points of view emerged: Delany wanted to go to the Niger Valley in West Afrika;

another group led by James M. Whitfield of New York wanted to go to Central America; and the third, led by Theodore Holly of Canada, wanted to go to Haiti. It is important to mention that only those individuals interested in emigration were invited to the convention, a fact which irritated Frederick Douglass tremendously; he was very much against emigration.

The Second Emigration Convention was held in Chatham, Canada, in 1856 where Delany himself had emigrated. From this meeting he was sent to West Afrika to look for lands that Afrikans in America could go back to and was accompanied by the Jamaican, Robert Campbell. Dr. John Henrik Clarke lauds Campbell's report, *Pilgrimage to My Motherland*, as worthwhile reading. *Search For A Place* is the name given to Delany's report plus Campbell's report.

Delany started in Liberia, then Lagos, Nigeria, where he signed a treaty with the Alake (King) of the Egbe people, who gave them permission to establish a settlement. Then, Delany explored the region to study the illnesses endemic to the area as well as its sanitary conditions. Eventually, he signed agreements with eight kings. Before the move could be completed, however, the Civil War broke out.

In 1860, he read a scientific paper before the Royal Geographic Society and the International Statistical Conference in London. When a respected British scientist, Lord Brougham, commented favorably on Delany, several delegates from the American South withdrew.

Delany was a novelist as well as a journalist, lecturer, abolitionist, physician, author and scientist. His novel *Blake, or the Huts of America* was not a literary or commercial success, but it was an important and timely statement. The book *Uncle Tom's Cabin* by the white female abolitionist, Harriett Beecher Stowe, had as its hero an elderly, docile, and religious enslaved Afrikan man. Delany's hero was a religious leader who spread seeds of revolution and insurrection throughout the South. He felt that religion as practiced hypocritically by whites and taught to enslaved Afrikans by these same whites was counterproductive to the enslaved Afrikans' pursuit of freedom. Delany's work pointed out that religion was used as an opiate to control the enslaved Afrikans but that religion should be used as justification for revolution. He argued that Christianity and slavery were incompatible concepts but that religion and revolution were very compatible. Religion, as practiced, he felt was the major obstacle that prevented a successful "slave revolt" and not fear because of the psychologically enslaving influence of religion, as practiced.

At the end of the Civil War, he attempted to persuade President Abraham Lincoln to create an army of Afrikans commanded by Afrikans but was unsuccessful in achieving this goal. He was one of the first officers of Afrikan ancestry to serve in the Union army and the first to reach the rank of Major. He served as a medical officer with Company K of the 104th Regiment and was one of approximately 75 officers of Afrikan ancestry who served during the Civil War.

After the war, Delany worked with the Freedman's Bureau for three years, and then he became a customs inspector in Charleston, South Carolina. He went on to become a trial justice in Charleston and fought political corruption in that capacity. His political career was erratic while he was in South Carolina because he endorsed Wade Hampton for Governor. Hampton was a former Confederate officer and one of the biggest enslavers before the Civil War.

Martin R. Delany died on January 24, 1885 in Xenia, Ohio, home of Wilberforce University.

References and Suggested Reading

Adams, Russell L. *Great Negroes Past and Present.* Chicago: Afro-Am Publishing Company, 1984, p. 66.

Bennett Jr., Lerone. *Before the Mayflower: A History of Black America.* NY: Penguin Books. 1985.

Clarke, John Henrik. *Notes for An African World Revolution: Africans at the Crossroads.* Trenton: Africa World Press. 1991.

Delany, Martin R. *The Condition Elevation Emigration and Destiny of the Colored People of the United States.* Baltimore: Black Classic Press, 1993 (First published in 1852).

Dick, Robert C. *Black Protest: Issues and Tactics.* Westport: Greenwood Press, 1974.

Green, Richard L. (Editor). *A Salute to Historic Black Abolitionists.* Chicago: Empak Publishing Company, 1988.

Levine, Robert S. (Editor). *Martin R. Delany.* Chapel Hill: The University of North Carolina Press, 2003.

Levine, Robert S. *Martin Delany, Frederick Douglass and the Politics of Representative Identity.* Chapel Hill: The University of North Carolina Press, 1997.

Sterling, Dorothy. *The Making of an Afro-American: Martin Robison Delany: African Explorer, Civil War Major, and Father of Black Nationalism.* NY: DaCapo Press, 1996.

Woodson, Carter G. *The Negro in Our History.* Washington, D.C.: The Associated Publishers, 1927.

Dr. Matilda Arabella Evans
A Life Well Lived

Follow in the footsteps of your ancestors, for the mind is trained through knowledge. Behold, their words endure in books. Open and read them and follow their wise counsel. For one who is taught becomes skilled. Do not be evil for kindness is good. Make the memory of you last through love of you. Multiply the people whom the city shelters, then God will be praised for your donations. And the people will...give thanks for your goodness and pray for your health.

The Book of Kheti, Axiom 2, The Husia

Introduction

Certain rules are learned during a traditional "old school" Ausa upbringing. Many of these same rules are also traditionally learned during and after medical specialty training. Uppermost of these rules is that we should respect and learn from Elders who are willing to teach us. We also venerate the accomplishments and contributions of those who came before us, our Ancestors. Perhaps this bit of knowledge originated with the first known physician, Imhotep, the African who was also the world's first known multi-genius. We know that medical knowledge during his time was both empirical and scientific and the educational system (frequently called the Mystery System) called for respect for the teacher. The exoteric and esoteric methods that were used extolled the virtues of learning from the honored Elders.

Any study of the life of Dr. Matilda Arabella Evans is very instructive because it contains many lessons that are part and parcel of an Afrikan-centered perspective as well as the history and health of the Ausa people in America. She had a "...consuming zeal to render service rather than to accumulate money or to acquire popularity..." John Wilson wrote in a Black Columbia, South Carolina, newspaper. For a woman, and especially an Afrikan American woman, to achieve what she did during the time period that she did it is remarkable, considering the prevailing racism, sexism and scientific racism. She lived and practiced during a pernicious period in American history in which scientific racism and eugenics were popular and frequently looked upon as the norm.

It is remarkable also that many lesser known and less educated Afrikan American women and men were doing many of the things that she was doing at the same time: working and striving for the good of all humanity and especially for Afrikan people. These include people like Dr. Rebecca Lee, Dr. Lucy Hughes, Dr. James McCune Smith, Rev. Hosea Easton, Dr. Daniel Hale Williams, Professor Booker T. Washington, and Dr. George Cleveland Hall, to name a few. Their lives were and are still teaching tools in courage, strength, perseverance, morals and ethics.

Dr. Evans is a shining example of Afrikan potential in action, noble Afrikan womanhood, and the Ma'atian principles of ancient Afrika (truth, justice, righteousness, harmony, balance, order, propriety, and reciprocity). Her life is a great medium for studying several issues that have been problematic in today's America as well as in her era. Frequently, these issues were forces swirling like tornadoes, moving and manipulating thought, actions, attitudes and decisions. The individuals driving these forces were often completely opposed to each other in worldview and personal philosophy; yet, they all had a part in influencing the person Dr. Evans would become. The discussion of racial health disparities, scientific racism (which still exists) and reparations are enlightened by considerations of her life, interests and accomplishments.

A Remarkable Woman

Matilda Arabella Evans was born in Aiken County, South Carolina in 1870 or 1875 during the presidency of Ulysses S. Grant, who "gave white supremacy free reign" supposedly to avoid a race war. Her parents were Andrew and Harriett Corley Evans. Her maternal grandmother was Edith Corley, the daughter of Henry and Julia Willis who had left Pennsylvania in the early 1800s as "free Blacks" but were captured and ended up in a group of enslaved Afrikans. How this happened is not known but we do know that many so-called "free Blacks" were kidnapped and sold into slavery. Nothing is known of the reasons why they were moving South or what happened to them subsequently. What we do know is that Henry and Julia became the parents of Edith who married a Corley and gave birth to Harriett, who married Andrew Evans. Andrew and Harriett had three children, Matilda Arabella (the oldest), Andrew (Andy), and Aurora.

In order to help her family make money, Matilda mowed hay for the Schofield family who were Quakers. The Schofields were Abolitionists who evidently practiced what they preached. A significant number of abolitionists hated human slavery but believed in white supremacy. Abraham Lincoln, America's sixteenth president, may have disagreed with the institution of slavery but believed strongly in white supremacy and had no love for the enslaved Afrikans (see Chapter 13 on Lincoln).

Matilda's positive qualities caught the eye of Martha Schofield who became one of her major lifelong supporters. Martha had started the Schofield Normal and Industrial School for the formerly enslaved Afrikans in Aiken in 1870. Frequently, she was harassed and threatened by racist, small-minded whites. After Matilda completed the course of study at Schofield, Martha encouraged young Matilda to continue her education at Oberlin College in Ohio. Oberlin was the first coeducational college in the United States, the first to award a college degree to a woman (in 1841) and, from the time it was founded in 1833, it was Oberlin's policy to admit students regardless of race, which was against the political grain of the nineteenth century. Because of that era's political and social need to justify slavery and racism, many attempts were made to support scientifically the inferiority of Afrikans and to validate slavery and discrimination.

Since her early childhood, it had been young Matilda's desire to go to Afrika as a missionary; but, to achieve this goal, she needed an education.

According to some accounts, she went to Philadelphia first to earn money for college. These accounts state that, ultimately, she arrived at Oberlin with $65 and quickly ran out of money. All accounts relate that she earned money by waiting tables and, soon after, earned a full scholarship. Some accounts also relate that she taught for one year after graduation in Augusta, Georgia with Lucy Laney, an Ausa educator who founded the first school for Ausa children in Augusta. Matilda taught a second year at Schofield before going to medical school.

Early Training

Evans gained entrance into the Women's Medical College of Pennsylvania in 1893, partially financed by a scholarship from a Mr. Alfred Jones of Philadelphia and as evidenced by a letter she wrote thanking him and asking him to help one of her younger friends. That letter is in the Drexel University library. Apparently, she made lasting friends although she was the only Afrikan in a class of 25 women. Her application for admission to examinations and subsequent admission sheet, dated April 1897, listed the following subjects as her areas of concentration: Surgery, Obstetrics, Gynecology, Paediatrics and Hygiene. Evans graduated in 1897 and had to decide whether to follow her dream of going to Africa or do something else. Fortunately for South Carolina, she decided to return to her home state where she became the first native South Carolina Afrikan female to be licensed to practice medicine in the state.

After she graduated from medical school in 1897, she moved to Columbia, South Carolina, where she opened a practice from her home that same year. She did so well that her practice soon outgrew the facilities. Some sources have said she was the first female physician of any race to practice in Columbia. Her fees were very modest by today's standards and ranged from $.50 to $1.50 for an office visit. Like most Afrikan physicians then and many now, she practiced charity and served the needs of her patients frequently and willingly whether they could pay her or not. When she made house calls, as all physicians of that era did, she traveled by bicycle, horseback, horse and wagon, and horse and buggy. She bought her first car, a white Buick, around 1912.

Life as a Physician

In traditional Afrikan culture, all girls are socialized from birth to become good mothers and wives (just as boys are socialized to become good fathers and husbands). If a woman was unable to become pregnant, the culture frequently dictated that she was still a mother in the eyes of the community. All the children of a community were considered to be the children of all the adults of the community and could be rewarded and punished as was felt justified by any adult. Also, many women who were unable to become pregnant were given children by relatives and close friends to rear so that they could indeed know the joys of parenthood, a practice that continued among Afrikans in America.

In America, these same cultural norms were practiced by the Afrikans who had been made to forget their origin. In this matter, also, Dr. Evans was a mother. Upon the deaths of her siblings (her sister died in 1914 but we do not know the death dates of her other siblings), she took their small children to raise. According to the niece she raised, Mrs. Jessie Trottie Hill, Dr. Evans raised a total of eleven children, several of whom were her patients' children. Because of her heavy schedule, she employed a "house lady" to help with them. All the children got along like blood brothers and sisters and all had the opportunity to get a college education. Dr. Evans traveled as much as she could and would take all her children with her on trips, such as to the National Medical Association's national conferences.

All her children and some others of their friends were given music lessons. Dr. Evans played the piano and on Sunday afternoons they would have their own music concerts that would include not just the household but neighbors as well.

She owned and operated a twenty-acre farm, Lindenwood Farm, which was located off Two Notch Road near where Beltline Boulevard is now located in Columbia. She raised chickens, cows, ducks, hogs, pigeons, vegetables and fruit trees. That farm was also called "The Dr. Evans Park and Swimming Pool." Food from this farm helped to feed her family, her unfortunate patients, the nursing students, and patients hospitalized in her hospitals.

The farm also provided recreation for young people. She offered the grounds for community use for picnics and games. Besides crops and livestock, the grounds contained a dwelling house, a pavilion, bathhouses and a swimming pool.

Of particular interest is an anecdote that gives some insight into the strength, intelligence, and perseverance of this amazing lady. She was unable to swim. After she had opened the swimming pool to the public, she found an article written by an old sea captain and studied it so zealously that she not only learned to swim but eventually gave lessons and taught hundreds of people, especially children, to swim. She had little leisure time but found time to indulge in hobbies, crocheting and knitting. She made a rug that she gave to the Women's Medical College and which was exhibited proudly, according to her niece, Jessie Hill.

Evans was a devoted member of the St. Luke's Episcopal Church in Columbia and served her church in many capacities. It was said, however, that Second Calvary Baptist Church had "a claim on her."

Some sources state that in 1897 she opened the first hospital for Afrikans in South Carolina at 1019 Lady Street in Columbia. At any rate, in 1901, she established the Taylor Lane Hospital and Training School for Nurses which was located at what was then the intersection of Taylor and Heidt Streets near what is now a Church's Chicken. She is also credited with establishing clinics that were located at 502 Sumter Street and at 1326 The Frederick Building.

She nurtured the Taylor Lane Hospital and Training School for Nurses to the extent that she gave up her private practice to assume the duties of Superintendent. All available documents that discuss this topic state that she had the support of "all" the white physicians in Columbia. In fact, many of them admitted their Ausa patients to this hospital since the Columbia Hospital, later called Richland Memorial Hospital, then called Palmetto Health Richland and now called Prisma Health Richland, refused admission to Afrikan patients and refused admitting/practicing privileges to Ausa physicians. The politicians had consistently refused to organize a hospital for the city's taxpaying Afrikan "citizens."

During this era of American apartheid many, if not most, of her patients were white. Some members of her family have stated to this writer that, at many periods of her career, most of her patients were white. Some written histories state that these were mostly white women of some wealth who, to a great extent, subsidized her charitable activities. One article described her "clientele" as majority "Nordic." This is very interesting in light of the fact that one of the leaders of scientific racism, Georges Vacher de Lapouge, classified Europeans in three groups of which "Nordic" was the highest and most superior. Lapouge's writing was popular during Dr. Evans' career.

White physicians who supported her were men mostly, and many new to Columbia, who performed surgery at Taylor Lane as well as provided fiscal support. Dr. LeGrand Guerry, a prominent Columbia surgeon, served as chief surgeon. A female physician, Dr. Jane Bruce Guignard, a later graduate of Women's Medical College, also lent considerable support.

The nurse graduates of Taylor Lane Hospital and Training School for Nurses apparently never had to look long for work. The training school's reputation was so good that prospective employers waited outside during graduation to secure the services of these young women. Many whites preferred Afrikan females as nurses during that time. On November 19, 1926, as a result of her contributions to nursing, the nurses of the Waverly Hospital, another of Columbia's Black hospitals, organized a club in her honor called the M.A. Evans Club.

Taylor Lane Hospital and Training School for nurses was chartered by South Carolina in 1902 but was destroyed by fire several years later. By the time it was destroyed, however, it had about 30 beds and had provided a site for more than 500 surgical operations in two years.

Dr. Evans opened St. Luke's Hospital that was located at 1019 Lady Street, the site of her previous hospital. Again, she soon outgrew this site (perhaps it was just a stopgap measure) and moved St. Luke's Hospital to 502 Sumter Street, where she had fourteen rooms and twenty beds and used modern/state of the art equipment.

Public Health Career

In 1914, Booker T. Washington, the most influential Ausa of his time, became interested in the health of the "Negro." He wrote many articles about these concerns because he saw the disparity between white and Black health, healthcare and life expectancy as obstacles to the economic advancement of the Negro. Later that year he started a national movement that he called Health Improvement Week. When Washington died the following year, his movement was renamed National Negro Health Week (NNHW) and was celebrated during the first week of April, Washington's birth week.

Local, regional and national civic organizations, businesses, churches, hospitals and healthcare providers of African origin celebrated Negro Health Week nationally. Ironically, the president during this era was Woodrow Wilson, a Southern racist who used false promises of racial fairness to deceive W.E.B. Du Bois, William Monroe Trotter, an AME Bishop, and others into endorsing his candidacy.

In 1920, NNHW became a program of the United States Public Health Service. Because of these efforts, there was a significant improvement in Black life expectancy. The Public Health Service ended its support in 1950 when Dr. Montague Cobb, an influential Afrikan American Washington, DC, physician, anthropologist and integrationist insisted that no special effort was needed for "Negro" health. A staunch integrationist, he felt there needed to be efforts to improve the health of all Americans.

Perhaps because of Booker T. Washington's efforts, Dr. Evans was extremely interested in public health and sanitation issues among the Afrikan people of South Carolina. She noted that there were "deplorable" disparities in mortality between the races and felt that those disparities could be improved. In 1916, she started a short-lived medical journal, *The Negro Health Journal.* In this regard, she was probably the first or one of the first South Carolinians to be truly concerned with public health.

Also, in 1916, and to this end, she organized and had chartered by the South Carolina Secretary of State The Negro Health Association of South Carolina, later called the South Carolina Good Health Association. This organization tried to place trained nurses and special welfare workers into each South Carolina county to educate the people and stimulate an interest in health. It was a volunteer organization that depended solely on donations. Unfortunately, it did not survive. Reportedly, Dr. Evans never gave up the dream of restarting the organization. She published a book that year also, *Martha Schofield, Pioneer Negro Educator,* in honor of her lifelong supporter.

In 1918, Dr. Evans became a registered volunteer in the Medical Services Corps of the United States. She closed St. Luke's Hospital to perform this duty but continued to practice medicine and located her office at 1501 1/2 Taylor Street.

*****

In May 1930, Dr. Evans was elected to the board of trustees of Haines College in Augusta, Georgia. Haines was an accredited Junior College founded by Miss Lucy Laney, who also served as its president. Haines College (or Institute) eventually became Lucy Laney High School.

Dr. Evans achieved what was perhaps her greatest professional accomplishment also in 1930. In late May and early June, she invited to her home the "movers and shakers" of Columbia's Ausa community. After meeting separately with the women and the men, and after organizing clubs to help in the sponsoring of a children's clinic in Columbia, a girl's club was organized which sponsored a popularity contest to raise money for the children's clinic.

Collectively, these clubs called themselves the Columbia Clinic Association. The Clinic started meeting in the basement of the Zion Baptist Church, which was partitioned to assure at least a minimum amount of privacy. According to her niece, the Clinic was moved to 1200 Harden Street in Columbia. Volunteers used the door-to-door method to gather preliminary information concerning need. When the information gathering was completed, word was spread to the public about the plans to vaccinate schoolchildren for free through the churches.

After all the preliminary work had been done, the plans made, and the date set, there was worry as to how successful the effort would be. It was hoped that 150-200 children would come. As it turned out, it was successful beyond their wildest expectations. On the first day they saw more than 700 children. To say they were overwhelmed would be a gross understatement. They secured more volunteers and more organization for the next day and saw even more children. On the third day the crowd was so large that traffic backed up causing the police to have to check out the cause of the traffic jam. When "the smoke cleared," they had seen more than 3,000 children during the first several days of clinics, had immunized all and examined many — all free of charge.

Understandably, Dr. Evans was exhausted following this success. The Association persuaded her to take a vacation and she visited New York, Philadelphia and Durham while investigating ways of making the Clinic more effective. She was tremendously impressed with Durham. While she was away, the Columbia Clinic Association arranged for a permanent "headquarters" for the Clinic, located in a two-story building at the corner of Harden and Lady Streets. Its many benefactors paid the rent frequently and donated much of the furniture and equipment.

It should be noted that Dr. Evans did not just become complacent and wait for the children to come to her; she still traveled to areas surrounding Columbia and gave service. In October 1930, she dismissed her patients and went to Eastover where she saw more than 200 children and vaccinated all that needed it without charge.

On July 27, 1931, the Secretary of State of South Carolina incorporated the Evans Clinic Association of Columbia, South Carolina, *In perpetuity*. In addition to Dr. Evans, the officers of the Association were as follows: W.C. Johnson, Rev. J.P. Reeder, Dr. J.J. Starks, Dr. D.H. Sims, C.A. Johnson, R.L. Peguese, H.W. Baumgardner, A.W. Simkins, Dr. N.A. Jenkins, Dr. S.R. Greene, Albertha Simons, N.J. Frederick, R.W. Mance and Henry Marshall.

For the next several years, the Evans Clinic continued its services. Renovations were initiated in May 1932, so the specialty work that had been started earlier could be completed more effectively and efficiently. A Dental Clinic was held four days a week by Dr. H.H. Cooper; and a Dr. Green conducted a twice-weekly Eye, Ear, Nose, and Throat Clinic. Dr. Evans taught a weekly course on mental hygiene and a weekly course to expectant mothers and fathers. There was also a Kindergarten Department for young toddlers.

Dr. Matilda Arabella Evans died at her home November 17, 1935 and is buried in Palmetto Cemetery on Fairfield Road in Columbia. As might be expected, a great many people mourned her death. St. Luke's Episcopal Church was filled to overflowing. Her pallbearers included many distinguished members of the Palmetto and Congaree Medical,

Dental and Pharmaceutical Associations, several college presidents, prominent clergy, and respected citizens from around the Southeast United States.

Summary

Dr. Evans never married but hardly allowed that fact to create a void in her life. Love for her people and for the children she raised gave her life fullness and meaning that can always be seen in her legacy. Her life is truly a beacon for all young people today who find it difficult to maneuver through life's twists and turns. Her life is also a constant reminder to those of us who are older to stay the course and not seek the easy or most convenient way out.

Remembering and honoring our ancestors insures their immortality. If these memories are kept fresh in the minds of our children, they can pass these memories to their children — The Ones Not Yet Born. This memory will contain a legacy that will not only challenge unborn generations to aspire to greatness but will provide a model and roadmap towards the achievement of that aspiration. If we let that memory dissipate, it is murder, we have killed our Ancestor. But, if unborn generations are made to keep the memory fresh and realize the importance of the memory (history), our Ancestors will never die.

So it is with Dr. Matilda Arabella Evans. Her strength of spirit, the love and respect she inspired during her lifetime and her dynamic legacy will, and should, cause her to live forever in the memories of the countless spirits that she touched directly and indirectly and as an ancestor, she will never die.

References and Suggested Reading

Amen-Ra, Jehuti El-Malik (1990): *Shattering the Myth of the Man Who Freed the Slaves: A True Account of Abraham Lincoln's Failure to Free Enslaved Afrikans in America.* IVth Dynasty Publishing Company, 8401 Colesville Road, Suite 208A, Silver Spring, Maryland, 20910.

Bodie, Idella. *South Carolina Women.* Orangeburg: Sandlapper Publishing, Inc., 1991, pp.56-58.

Caldwell, A.B. (Editor). *History of the American Negro: South Carolina Edition.* Atlanta: A.B. Caldwell Publishing Co., 1919, pp.393-396.

T*he Charlotte Observer*, Charlotte, N.C.:Maintains Home for Recreation: Operates Evans Clinic in Columbia, S.C., Recognized As Leader of Her Group. November 20, 1932.

Davis, Marianna W. (Editor). *Contributions of Black Women to America, Volume II*, Kenday Press, Inc., 1982, pp.378-379.

Department of the Interior, Bureau of Education. *Negro Education: A Study of the Private and Higher Schools for Colored People in the. United States. Volume I*, Government Printing Office, Washington, DC, 1917, p.176.

En.wikipedia.org/wiki/Georges_Vacher_de_Lapouge

Evans, M.A. *The Fourth Annual Report of the Taylor Lane Hospital and Training School For Nurses.* Aiken: Schofield School Press,1906.

Gallman, Burnett W.: From Africa To South Carolina: A Brief Review of the Contributions of Africans and African-Americans To Medicine. T*he Journal of the South Carolina Medical Association*, May, 1988, pp.249-254.

Haller, John S. (1972): The Negro and the Southern Physician: Medical and Racial Attitudes 1800-1860. *Medical History, Vol. 16*, 1972, pp. 238-253.

Haller, John S. Jr. (1970): The Physician Versus The Negro: Medical and Anthropological Concepts of Race in the Late Nineteenth Century. *Bulletin of the History of Medicine.* Vol. 49, pp.154-167.

Hennig, Helen Kohn (Editor): *Columbia: Capital City of South Carolina, 1786-1936.* Published by The Columbia Sesqui-Centennial Commission, The R.L. Bryan Company Printers, Columbia, pp.313-314, 1936.

Hill, Jessie T.: Unpublished Biographical manuscripts

Hine, Darlene Clark: The Corporeal and Ocular Veil: Dr. Matilda A. Evans (1872-1935) and the Complexity of Southern History. *The Journal of Southern History* LXX (1): 3-34, 2004.

Interview with Dr. Matilda Evans' niece and nephew, Mrs. Jessie T. Hill and Mr. Sidney Trottie

Jerrido, Margaret J.: Early Black Women Physicians. *Women and Health*, Volume 5(3), Fall 1980.

Jerrido, Margaret J.: Early Black Women Physicians. *Women and Health,* Volume 5(3), Fall 1980.

Johnson, Thomas L. and Dunn, Philip C. *A True Likeness: The Black South of Richard Samuel Roberts, 1920-1936.* Bruccoli Clark, Columbia, S.C. and Algonquin Books of Chapel Hill, Chapel Hill, N.C., 1986.

Krieger, Nancy: Shades of Difference: Theoretical Underpinnings of the Medical Controversy on Black/White Differences in the United States, 1830-1870. *International Journal of Health Services,* Vol. 17, Number 2, pp. 259-278, 1987.

Letter from Dr. Evans in Columbia to Mr. Alfred Jones of Philadelphia dated 3/13/1907.

Lott, CCE: Waverly Hospital News. *Palmetto Leader,* December 24, 1926.

Moore, John Hammond. *Columbia and Richland County: A South Carolina Community, 1740-1990.* Columbia: University of South Carolina Press,1993, pp.372, 377, 381.

Oberlin Alumni Magazine, April 1930.

O'Reilly, Kenneth. *Nixon's Piano: Presidents and Racial Politics from Washington to Clinton.* NY: The Free Press, 1995, pp. 42-49.

Palmetto Leader, (September 13, 1930) The Columbia Clinic Now Functions In Its Permanent Headquarters Columbia, S.C.

Palmetto Leader, Columbia, S.C.: September 20, 1930: The Columbia Clinic Association: This Institution Offers Medical Inspection and Free Vaccination to All Negro Children of this City.

Palmetto Leader, Columbia, S.C.: September 20, 1930: Dr. Matilda Evans Interviewed

Palmetto Leader, Columbia, S.C.: October 18, 1930: The Columbia Clinic Preparing to Meet All Demands

Palmetto Leader, Columbia, S.C.: November 8, 1930: The Columbia Clinic Enlarges Its Scope of Its Endeavor

Palmetto Leader, Columbia, S.C.: November 15, 1930: The Columbia Clinic Association (editorial)

Palmetto Leader, Columbia, S.C.: October 31, 1931: Evans Clinic News and Announcement Extraordinary

Palmetto Leader, Columbia, S.C.: February 27, 1932: Evans Clinic Notes

Palmetto Leader, Columbia, S.C.: May 7, 1932: Evans Clinic to Be Renovated

Palmetto Leader, Columbia, S.C.: March 9, 1935 Dr. Matilda A. Evans Given Testimonial Banquet

Palmetto Leader, Columbia, S.C.: Dec 11, 1926, Rev Richard Carroll. Some Outstanding Characters

Palmetto Leader, Cola, S.C.: March 22, 1930, John R. Wilson: Dr. Matilda A. Evans, Noted Physicians and Surgeon, Humanitarian, Outstanding Citizen of Columbia

Palmetto Leader Apr. 2, 1932, Dr. M.A. Evans Tells About Florida

Palmetto Leader, Columbia, S.C.: November 23, 1935: Dr. Matilda Evans Passes: Noted Succumbs After More Than 37 Years of Notable Service

The State (Columbia, SC) March 13, 1994, Michael Sponhour: Black doctor gave hope, health to Columbians in depression.

State of South Carolina, Executive Department Certificate of Incorporation by the Secretary of State. Evans Clinic Association of Columbia, S.C., July 27, 1931.

Szasz, Thomas S. (1971): The Sane Slave: An Historical Note on the Use of Medical Diagnosis as Justificatory Rhetoric. *American Journal of Psychotherapy*. Vol. XXV, Number 2, pp. 228-239.

The State, Columbia, S.C.: Clinic Doing Good Work Among Negroes of City: Institution on Harden Street Comes Into Being When Need Made Evident by Great Outpouring of Children-Doctor Evans Moving Spirit in Venture, October 29, 1931.

The State, March 24, 1998, Profile: Women's History Month, Matilda Arabella Evans

Trapp, Willie M. *Dr. Matilda Arabelle Evans*. (Unpublished document), April 25, 1975.

Wilson, John R. (May 24, 1930). Dr. M.A. Evans, Columbia's Noted Physician, Elected Trustee of The Haines College in Augusta, Georgia *The Palmetto Leader*, Columbia, S.C.

Wilson, John R. (June 21, 1930): Will Have Clinics For Colored Columbians *The Palmetto Leader*, Columbia, S.C.

Wilson, John R. (August 16, 1930): The Columbia Clinic: An Effective

Reality: Has Temporary Quarters in the Basement of Zion Baptist Church — A Number of Children Treated. *The Palmetto Leader*, Columbia, S.C.

Wilson, John R. (August 23, 1930): The Columbia Clinic Justifies Expectations. *The Palmetto Leader*, Columbia, S.C.

Men of Honor

The list that follows includes men who have contributed positively to Afrikan people in one way or another. Young people can use this list as a foundation for researching and writing papers, as well as for studying their work and accomplishments.

Cheikh Anta Diop	Carter G. Woodson
W.E.B. Du Bois	Imhotep
Amiri Baraka (LeRoi Jones)	Martin R. Delany
Arturo Schomburg	Percy L. Julian
Kwame Ture (Stokely Carmichael)	Zumbi Dos Palmares
Paul Robeson	Antenor Firmin
Benjamin Banneker	Marcus Garvey
George Washington Carver	Alain Locke
Frederick Douglass	Frantz Fanon
Kwame Nkrumah	Ahmed Baba
Ernest Everett Just	Alexander Crummell
Henry Highland Garnet	Steven Biko
Kelly Miller	Malcolm X
Martin Luther King, Jr.	Adam Clayton Powell
Jean-Jacques Dessalines	Garrett A. Morgan
Robert Smalls	Charles Drew
John Henrik Clarke	Denmark Vesey
Elijah McCoy	Prince Hall
Chaka Zulu	Hannibal of Carthage
Booker T. Washington	David Walker
Paul Cuffe	Richard Allen
Josef ben-Jochannon	John G. Jackson

Chancellor Williams
Henry McNeal Turner
William Monroe Trotter
Edward Wilmot Blyden
Narmer
Akhenaten
Nat Turner
Toussaint L'Ouverture
Joe Louis
Asa G. Hilliard, III
Thurgood Marshall
Bob Marley
Huey P. Newton
James Baldwin
John Horse
Medgar Evers
Patrice Lumumba
C.L.R. James
Henry Sylvester-Wiliams

Benjamin E. Mays
Askia the Great
Cetewayo
John A. Russwurm
Daniel Hale Williams
Walter Rodney
Gabriel Prosser
Jackie Robinson
Spike Lee
Jomo Kenyatta
Barack Obama
Dick Gregory
Ivan Van Sertima
Jean Baptiste Pointe DuSable
Matthew Henson
Muhammad Ali
Amos Wilson
George Padmore

Women of Honor

The list that follows includes women who have contributed positively to Afrikan people in one way or another. Young people can use this list as a foundation for researching and writing papers, as well as for studying their work and accomplishments.

Nzinga
Tiye
Maggie L. Walker
Madame C.J. Walker
Mary Church Terrell
Gwendolyn Brooks
Nannie Helen Burroughs
Winnie Mandela

Sojourner Truth
Hatshepsut
Harriet Ross Tubman
Ida B. Wells Barnett
Mary McLeod Bethune
Zora Neale Hurston
Dorothy Height
Wilma Rudolph

Frances Cress Welsing
Dona Marimba Richards
Candace of Ethiopia
Toni Morrison
Sonia Sanchez
Audley (Queen Mother) Moore
Modjeska Monteith Simkins
Anna Julia Cooper
Amy Jaques Garvey
Audre Lorde
Maria Stewart
Mary Ellen Pleasant
Marjorie Joyner
Ruane Jeter
Coretta Scott King
Ella Baker
Bessie Coleman
Sister Rosetta Tharpe
Hattie McDaniel
Marian Anderson
Queen of Sheba
Amanitenas
Amy Ashwood Garvey
Carlota Lukumi
Deolinda Rodriguez de Almeida
Henrietta Lacks
Laura Adorkor Kofi
Nanny
Assata Shakur
Diane Nash
Oprah Winfrey

Charshee McIntyre
Lorraine Hansberry
Yaa Asantewa
Charlotte Forten
Rosa Parks
Septima Clark
Nehanda
Daisy Bates
Makeda
Fannie Lou Hamer
Shirley Chisholm
Mae C. Jemison
Mary Kenner
Ellen Johnson-Sirleaf
Josephine Baker
Maya Angelou
Cathy Hughes
Angela Davis
Ruby Bridges
Bessie Coleman
The Dahomey Warriors
Amina, Queen of Zaria
Matilda A. Evans
Carol Mosely Braun
Fannie Jackson Coppin
Josina Muthemba Machel
Miriam Makeba
Phillis Wheatley
Elaine Brown
Vanessa Williams
Althea Gibson

Events, Movements and Organizations to Study

Events

- Who built the pyramids?
- Maafa
- The Red Summer of 1919
- Birmingham Church Bombing
- Nat Turner's Revolt
- Stono Rebellion
- Haitian Revolution
- Tuskegee Experiment
- The Scramble for Afrika/Berlin Conference
- 1884 Orangeburg Massacre
- Slave revolts
- Middle Passage
- Bloody Sunday 1965
- Freedom Summer 1964
- Million Man March
- John Brown's Raid
- Gabriel Prosser Conspiracy
- Lynching

Movements

- The Negro Convention Movement
- Mau Mau Revolution
- The sit-ins
- Black Power Movement
- The Underground Railroad
- Montgomery Bus Boycott
- Student Non-Violent Coordinating Committee (SNCC)
- Niagara Movement

Organizations

- The Negro Academy
- National Urban League
- Congress of Racial Equality (CORE)
- NAACP
- Universal Negro Improvement Association
- Black Panthers
- National Negro Business League
- Institute of the Black World
- The Association for the Study of Classical African Civilizations (ASCAC)

The Association for the Study of Afro-American Life and History
Afrikan Heritage Studies Association
National Association of Black Social Workers

Cultural Expressions

Freedom's Journal
The North Star
Frederick Douglass' July 4, 1852 speech
David Walker's *Appeal*
Black National Anthem
Kwanzaa
The Mystery

Law/Legal Issues

Plessy v. Ferguson
Dred Scott Decision
Brown v. Board of Education
Emancipation Proclamation
Affirmative Action
Jim Crow
Amistad Case
Fugitive Slave Acts
Integration vs. Desegregation

Locales/Countries

Songhai
Ancient Ghana
Palmares
Mali
Black Wall Street

People

Emmitt Till
Harlem Renaissance
Olmecs
Talented Tenth
Maroons
Moors

Kemetic Eighteenth Dynasty
Kemetic Twenty-fifth Dynasty
Little Rock Nine

*****

Questions to Ponder

1. What do I owe people who did not know me but who sacrificed, suffered and, sometimes, died to give me a better life?
2. What is freedom really?
3. Do I really want freedom or do I want a more comfortable enslavement?
4. How do I get my freedom?
5. If we are not free, what are we doing to get freedom?
6. What is war?
7. If we are not free, are we at war to get our freedom? Why? Why not?
8. If we are at war,
   a. Who knows?
   b. Who are we fighting and what are we fighting for?
   c. What philosophy of war are we using?
   d. What philosophical precepts are we using?
   e. What value system are we using and living by?
9. Do we know our native philosophy, culture and value system?
10. If we are not using our native philosophy, culture and value system, are we using our enemies' philosophy, culture and values?
11. If we are using our enemies' philosophy, culture and values, can we be successful?
12. What does freedom look like?
13. If we are truly free, how do we protect our children?
14. Who am I? What is my identity, my purpose and my direction?

15. Am I really who I think I am?
16. Am I all that I can be?
17. If I am not my true self, am I willing to be transformed into my true self?
18. Can economic and political movements be successful without a true cultural foundation?
19. Is freedom truly free or just is it just "running loose"?

AFTERWORD

The Last Word?

This speech was given by Burnett Kwadwo Gallman at Allen University, July, 2017 at the Pan-Afrikan Festival sponsored by the Organization of Afrikam Unity of South Carolina

I AM AN AUSA!! I am an Afrikan from the United States of America, an Afrikan American. I share this space with my brothers and sisters from the mother continent, Afrika, and from the Diaspora of the Caribbean, Europe, Asia and the Americas.

We Ausa have a unique and singular claim to the title Afrikan. My Ancestors were kidnapped and stolen from Afrika long before most of the artificial geopolitical entities (or countries) were created at the Berlin Conference in 1884-85 in the scramble for Afrika. In other words, we were Afrikans before there was a Nigeria, before there was a Ghana, before there was a Senegal or Kenya or Tanzania, and so forth. We also contain the mixture of blood from many of the ethnic groups. On my father's side, I am unmixed Umbuntu from Angola. On my mother's side, I am Mende and Temle from Sierra Leone, Kru from Liberia and Fula from Guinea-Bisseau. I have been welcomed to the continent by Asante and Fante and Ga people in Ghana and by Nubians in the south of Egypt (Upper Egypt). My Ausa brothers and sisters and I are Afrika!

First, it should be noted that Afrika ruled the world politically and culturally for most of the history of the world, but the development of Afrika was rudely and savagely interrupted at three junctures in history: the invasions of Kemet, chattel slavery and the colonial expansion of Europe into Afrika.

Many lectures and essays on the history of Afrika focus on the advanced civilizations, the creative occurrences, and the "firsts" that have occurred there, especially those that have been written out of the respectful commentary of world history, as Dr. John Henrik Clarke has told us many times. Frequently, focus is on the Kemetic origins of astronomy, government, trigonometry, medicine, architecture, mathematics, agriculture astrology, writing, geography, geology, philosophy, theology, mineralogy shipbuilding, the calender and symbolic thought. In fact, many East Afrikan and West Afrikan peoples trace their origins to the nations, empires and kingdoms of the Nile Valley.

The histories, culture and achievements of great early Afrikan civilizations such as Nubia, Axum, Meroe, Kush, Great Zimbabwe, Ancient Ghana, Mali, Songhai, Carthage, Punt, Nok, Benin, Kanem-Bornu, Wolof, Songhai, Oyo, Mossi, the Hausa States, Kongo, Ndongo and Ethiopia are frequently discussed. And the culture, science and theology of the Dogon are studied extensively also.

When we talk about education, frequently we discuss the University of Sankore at Timbuktu. It is fascinating and ironic that many of the Afrikans who were kidnapped in the fifteenth and sixteenth centuries were more educated, cosmopolitan and often more intelligent than the people who kidnapped and enslaved them.

The Islamic world also benefitted from the genius of these ancient Afrikans. We only started hearing about the inventions and innovations of the Moors and other Islamic accomplishments after 642 A.D., when the Muslims conquered Kemet.

We talk about the resistance and genius of the Afrikans who were separated from their homeland. In Brazil, the escaped Afrikans formed *quilombos* in their attempt to re-create home. We discuss the Zanj Rebellion in Iraq. We discuss the Maroons in Jamaica who escaped into the mountains, and the Maroons in America who lived in the swamps of South Carolina and the Great Dismal Swamp of Virginia. And, we cannot forget the glorious Haitian Revolution!

Formerly enslaved Afrikans in America walked off the plantations after the American Civil War and within a generation had started to innovate, create and invent things that we take for granted now. These accomplishments were achieved despite rampant, virulent, brutal and violent racism. Accomplishments such as the stoplight, gas mask, golf tee, refrigerated trucks, the carbon filament (a vital component of the light bulb), and the early air conditioner; medications like physostigmine and steroids; the folding bed, seed planter, ironing board, home security systems, and letter-drop mailbox; and the touch tone phone, caller ID, call waiting, blood banking and many more.

So…the question is, *why are we still in the shape that we are in?*

First, I would say that, as Afrikan people, our greatest strengths are also our greatest weaknesses: our xenophilia, spirituality and trusting nature. We welcomed the wrong visitors and trusted that they meant what they said and meant us well. That led to chattel slavery, which has been discussed earlier. In truth, Europe would have never been able to conquer Afrika if it had not been for the 700-plus years of Arab/Islamic slavery and encroachment in North and East Afrika, the Sahel and in the Sudan from 711 A.D. to 1492 A.D. We accepted foreign deities that did not look like us and never referenced us in their teachings except as slaves and pitiful people. I feel Afrika is in the shape it is in for two reasons: colonialism and tribalism.

Colonialism

Colonialism is the policy or practice of acquiring political control over another country and exploiting it economically. In Afrika, it began with the Berlin Conference of 1884-5 when the major European powers met to divide Afrika up among themselves with no regard to ethnic boundaries because Europe had few mineral or natural resources. European countries are the wealthiest in the world, but their wealth is based on the wealth they have stolen from and the human resources that they have exploited in their colonies.

Colonialism was and is extremely insidious and multi-faceted. The early European visitors hit us with what I call, the twin whammy! They brought missionaries to take the Afrikans away from their own grounded, tried and true spirituality. They taught Afrikans that the

European way of worshipping the Creator was superior to the way Afrikans had done for generations.

The Europeans convinced Afrikans not only to worship a deity that didn't look Afrikan but also taught the Afrikan to venerate the ancestors of the Europeans rather than their own. As Dr. Clarke has said, the Europeans also colonized the image of God.

Europeans then sent in teachers to teach the Afrikan how to be European. They taught European history, European styles of government, and the superiority of European culture. They taught us that they were beautiful and god-like and we were not. We have adapted their standards of beauty even today (hair straighteners, skin bleaching creams). The worst part was when they taught the Afrikan European political and economic systems and gave favored status to one ethnic group in their artificially created nations that imposed European political and economic systems alien to Afrikans. This set up rivalries that were based in capitalistic greed and political jealousy. Ethnic conflicts resulted and puppet leaders were raised. Even today, all over Afrika, the leadership is too often greedy and corrupt. As my Ghanaian friend and colleague, Dr. Arthur Kennedy, has stated in the past, there are many types of democracy and the European styles are not superior to what our Ancestors created. The noted Nigerian intellect, Chinweizu, has expounded on this in his books, *Decolonizing the African Mind* and *The West and the Rest of Us.*

The colonizers used different methods of colonization. In my opinion, there were three basic methods. The first was blatant savage brutality as used by King Leopold of Belgium. The British method was what is called *indirect rule* where native rulers were used to govern the colonized people which worked well for small ethnic groups without a strong central rulership but was not as effective with large ethnic groups with well-established rulers who frequently ruled from "underground." The French used direct rule where Frenchmen occupied all the important positions. Afrikans were allowed to fill subordinate positions and were encouraged to consider themselves as Frenchmen.

Tribalism

Finally, tribalism! First, let us examine the word "tribe." Frequently, the word conjures up a vision of a stereotype and cultural assumptions of primitive people. Tribe refers to an outdated social theory of inferiority and was used extensively during colonial rule in Afrika. On the other hand, *ethnic group* has been used to describe European tribes like Angles, Saxons, Picts, Finns, Kurds, Celts, Albanians, Croats, Armenians, and so on. When you think about it in this light, the "world wars" were European tribal conflicts. Their colonial teachers have taught Afrikans to think of themselves in terms of tribalism, as if no one else but Afrikans and Native Americans comprise tribes.

Although historically Afrikan ethnic groups have had rivalries, they did not become as vicious and deadly until contact with the colonizers. While most Afrikan countries are said to be independent, frequently they are still culturally, financially, politically and economically dependent on their former colonizers. Tribalism is a negative concept that has stunted Afrika's growth. Even today, blind loyalty to the worst in your tribe simply because they are members of your tribe does tremendous harm to the tribe as a whole.

*****

I have outlined the problems, and many may be asking, "Well then, what is the solution?"

Perhaps I am naïve, but I fervently believe that true Pan Afrikanism is the answer. I am not naïve enough to believe that the achievement of a Pan Afrikan reality will be easy to attain. There are too many people who are prospering materially and who have achieved an emotional comfort in blind tribalism or thoughtless allegiance to European systems. This ever-present tribalism is a cancer that keeps Afrikan people struggling at the mercy of our former slave masters and colonial masters. I believe in the possibility of Dr. Cheikh Anta Diop's dream of a United States of Afrika. The Afrikan Union is a beginning but we must never be lulled to sleep by our traditional enemies just because they sing a more pleasant song and throw money at us.

My grandmother would have never believed that Ausa would have attained the freedoms that now we take for granted. But she continued to struggle and persevered. Those of us who want to see Afrika reach her potential must likewise continue to strive for what is best for us all. My Ausa sisters and brothers, we will never be respected until there is an economically, politically and yes, militarily strong Afrika. My continental sisters and brothers, you need us and we need you. We Ausa have been conceived, born and reared in "the belly of the beast" and can see things that you may not be able to see.

PAN-AFRIKANISM OR PERISH!!

A LUTA CONTINUA!!

ADDENDUM

PLEDGE TO SUPPORT

BLACK BUYING DAYS

FROM INDIGENOUS PEOPLES' DAY TO IMANI

AND

FROM THE KING HOLIDAY TO FEBRUARY 28TH

AND

ALL YEAR LONG

Spend money
at least once daily with
a deserving Black-owned business and
maintain an account in a Black-owned bank.
Economic Strength in the Black Community
Means Political Strength for the Black
Community!

THEN, YOU *MUST* HOLD YOUR POLITICIANS ACCOUNTABLE!!

INDEX

ABOUT THE AUTHOR

Burnett Kwadwo Gallman is an eternal student with many interests. As a physician, he is focused on the health and welfare of all humanity and especially eradicating racial health disparities. As an amateur historian, he has studied, taught, lectured, and written on topics as varied as ancient Kemetic (Egyptian) history and culture, medieval West Afrikan history, and Ausa (Afrikans from the United States of America) history and culture.

As a science fiction buff, he has enjoyed reading the works of Walter Mosley, Isaac Asimov, Michael Harriot and Harlan Ellison. As a former musician, he has amassed a large collection of vinyl albums, cassette tapes, and CD's of jazz, R & B, gospel, Afrikan music and drumming, and European classical music. As an amateur genealogist, he has researched his family history, tracing his paternal line to 18th century Angola.

As a race man, he has studied, lectured, and written on such varied topics as Agnotology, Epigenetics, and Afrikan-centered Rites of Passage. This work is an attempt to marry some of his interests.